TIDES OF WAR

TIDES OF WAR

MICHAEL McKINNON PETER VINE

B⊞XTREE

First published in the UK in 1991 by

Boxtree Limited
36 Tavistock Street
London WC2E 7PB

Text © Dr Peter Vine 1991

Designed by The Image

Maps by Thames Cartographic Services Limited

Colour reproduction in Hong Kong by Fotographics

Photoset by Rowland Phototypesetting Limited
Bury St Edmunds, Suffolk

Printed and bound in Italy by
New Interlitho spa, Milan

A CIP catalogue entry for this book is available from
the British Library

ISBN 1-85283-158-8

CONTENTS

ACKNOWLEDGEMENTS

WILDLIFE conservation is a relatively recent priority for the countries of the Arabian peninsula. However, during the last twenty years a fundamental understanding has emerged of Arabian wildlife and ecology as a result of the work of organizations such as Saudi Arabia's Meteorological and Environmental Protection Agency (MEPA) and National Commission for Wildlife Conservation and Development (NCWCD); the Royal Commission for Jubail and Yanbu (RCJY); Saudi Aramco (ARAMCO) and national universities in Saudi Arabia; the Kuwait Institute for Scientific Research (KISR); Kuwait University; the Kuwait Foundation for the Advancement of Science (KFAS); Gulf organizations including the Regional Organization for the Protection of the Marine Environment (ROPME); and studies carried out by several international institutions including the International Union for the Conservation of Nature (IUCN) and the Food and Agricultural Organization (FAO) of the United Nations. Without such fundamental information it would not have been possible to assess the environmental impact of the Gulf War.

The magnitude of the oil-slicks was without precedent, demanding local and international co-operation in the fields of wildlife rescue and conservation, and the pooling of knowledge and experience together with a pragmatic approach to problem-solving. Despite the inevitable pressure on time and resources which the situation dictated, we were not only hospitably received by the above mentioned institutions but also personally assisted by HRH Prince Abdullah bin Faisal bin Turki Al-Saud, Chairman of the Royal Commission for Jubail and Yanbu; Dr Abdul Aziz Abuzinada, Secretary General of the NCWCD; Faisal Al-Bassam and Ismael Nawwab, Directors of Public Affairs for Saudi Aramco; Abdullah Bishara, Secretary General of the Cooperation Council for the Arab Gulf States and by H. E. Tariq Al-Moayed, Minister of Information in Bahrain.

Arrangements were coordinated at extremely short notice by Mohammed Al-Edrisi of Faisal & Faisal Associates in Riyadh and Bader Al-Sayegh in Kuwait, who spared no effort to assist us. For helicopter flights along the oil-impacted shores of Saudi Arabia, kindly coordinated by the Royal Commission for Jubail and Yanbu, we are grateful to the United States Coastguard Service. In Kuwait we flew with the Kuwait Airforce, and were able to extensively survey damage wrought by the Iraqi occupation.

In Bahrain logistical support was given by the Ministry of Information (through the office of Ahmed Al-Sherooqi, director of public relations and media); by the Bahrain Petroleum Company (BAPCO); the Environmental Protection Secretariat through the offices of Khalid Fakhroo and Walter Vreeland; and the University of Bahrain, where Dr Mohammed Saeed and Professor Philip Basson were most helpful. Our special interest in observing bird life in and around Bahrain was aided by the advice and assistance of Dr Mike Hill.

Dr Badria Al-Awadhi from the Kuwait-based

ROPME actively supported our work from the temporary headquarters of ROPME, before her return to Kuwait. Professor Charles Pilcher provided us with an important insight into key Kuwaiti habitats.

We were also briefed on a regular basis by MEPA in Saudi Arabia and should like to thank the head of that organization, Dr Abdulbar Al-Gain, together with the author of MEPA's daily oil-spill briefing reports, Dr Nizar I. Tawfiq. A major source of our scientific and field data on the natural history of Arabia, as well as on the impact of the oil and smoke pollution, was the National Commission for Wildlife Conservation and Development (NCWCD) in Saudi Arabia which also coordinated the activities of the Al Jubail Wildlife Rescue Centre. Dr John Grainger, Peter Symens, Dr Hani Tatwani, Dr Khushal Habibi, Mohammed Shobrak, Mohammed Sulayem and Nicholas Pilcher were fully engaged in wildlife rescue work and provided valuable insights into the impact of the oil-slick. At the National Wildlife Research Centre in Taif, Abdel Rahman Khoja, Holger Schulz and Jean François Asmode coordinated our activities and Jean François Asmode also guided us on questions of desert ecology. Philippe Gaucher and Patrick Paillat advised on ornithological questions. All parties generously assisted our filming activities.

Further information on environmental impacts and extent of pollution was provided by Saudi Aramco (ARAMCO); the Royal Society for the Prevention of Cruelty to Animals (RSPCA); the Scottish Society for the Prevention of Cruelty to Animals (SSPCA); Greenpeace; the International Council for Bird Protection (ICBP); the Royal Society for the Protection of Birds (RSPB); the Worldwide Fund for Nature (WWF); the International Union for the Conservation of Nature (IUCN); the World Conservation Monitoring Centre (WCMC); the Marine Conservation Society (MCS); the Meteorological Office of the United Kingdom (Met. Office); the International Maritime Organization (IMO); the Bahrain Biological Society (BBS); the Natural Environment Research Council (NERC); the Kuwait Petroleum Companies (KPCs); The Association for Free Kuwait (TAFK); and the World Society for the Protection of Animals (WSPA).

We wish to acknowledge the cooperation and assistance of the following people in the above organizations: Joseph Kenny (ARAMCO); Tim Thomas and Ian Robinson (RSPCA); Darroch Donald (SSPCA); Paul Horseman (Greenpeace); Dr Mike Rands (ICBP); Richard Porter (RSPB); Aban Marker Kabraji (Pakistan Country Representative for IUCN); Jo Taylor (WCMC); Dr Bob Earl (MCS); Barry Parker (Met. Office); Cdr. David Pascoe (IMO); Nader Al-Sultan, Muna Al-Mousa and Ralph Brown at Kuwait Petroleum Company (KPC) for valuable comments; Dr Fawzia Al-Sayegh McKinnon (TAFK); John Walsh and Jonathon Pearce (WSPA). We should also like to thank the following additional scientists who have provided valuable advice: Dr Abdel Rasheed Nawwab; Anthony Preen; Dr Jeffrey Jenkins of the Atmospheric Survey Unit attached to the UK Meteorological Office; Professor J. N. B. Bell of Imperial College, London; Dr David Clayton.

Tides of War was filmed by McKinnon Films and supported by National Geographic Television and Survival Anglia. We are grateful to Tim Kelly, Julia Maer, Tom Simon and Michael Rosenfeld at National Geographic and Graham Creelman and Malcolm Penny at Survival Anglia for their enthusiastic response to this project which enabled us to be filming within days of the emergence of the first oil-slick from the war zone.

The legal appendix was written by Paula Casey-Vine to whom we are most grateful. She in turn wishes to acknowledge the support and advice of the Law Department at University College, Galway, especially of Professor Dennis O'Driscoll, of the same department, and Mr Michael A. Meyer, Head of the Legal and Committee Services at the British Red Cross, both of whom kindly commented on the first draft. She wishes to stress that any errors or omissions are her own.

Our insight into the Gulf's history and the development of its oil industry was greatly aided by discussions with Angela Clarke whose book on the subject, *Bahrain Oil and Development* (Immel Publishing, London), proved to be a valuable source of inspiration and information. We should also like to thank Don Hepburn, Chief Executive of BAPCO, who extended his hospitality to us and gave much more valuable advice.

We are happy to acknowledge the efforts of the various newspapers, journals and magazines which brought such excellent reporting of the Gulf War and its environmental consequences. In this regard we wish to mention in particular Richard Small, Peter Aldhous and Samir Radwan who wrote for *Nature*; Ken Wells of the *Wall Street Journal*; the Insight team of the *Sunday Times*; Christopher Bellamy of the *Independent*; Rosamund Kidman-Cox (editor of the BBC's *Wildlife* magazine); Drs Andrew Price and Charles Sheppard, who have carried out considerable ecological research in the Gulf and who wrote for *New Scientist*; environment correspondent Fred Pearce, who wrote well-balanced articles for *New Scientist* and the *Guardian*; John Vidal, Frank Barnaby, Matthew Engel and Kathy Evans writing in the *Guardian*; Brian Ford, who wrote for *The Times*; John Horgan, who wrote for *Scientific American*; Philip Elmer-Dewitt, who wrote for *Time*; and John Schwartz and colleagues, who covered the story for *Newsweek*.

For help and assistance with travel arrangements we are grateful to Gulf Air and Abdullah Abdel Karim, the airline's Director of Public Relations.

Had we not been making films, we could not have had the first-hand experience necessary for writing this book. John Bulmer brought his great photographic talents to our task and once again produced wonderful images of Arabian wildlife. In this regard we should also like to thank Alastair Kenneil, Anthony Bomford and Peter Scoones. David South and Samantha Musgrave provided valuable support from McKinnon Films' office in London.

For their early vision and enthusiasm in this publishing project we thank Sarah Mahaffy, managing director of Boxtree, together with Elaine Collins and Penelope Cream. We are also pleased to acknowledge with thanks the support of Immel Publishing Ltd, which is publishing this book for sale within Gulf Cooperation Council countries and Egypt; and the German-based VGS, who are doing the same for the German market.

We thank especially our respective wives, Dr Fawzia Al-Sayegh McKinnon and Paula Casey-Vine, for their personal involvement, assistance and encouragement throughout the project. Finally we wish to acknowledge the patience and understanding of our children: Rakan, Sarah and Faris McKinnon; and Catriona, Sinead and Megan Vine, for putting up with our long absences from home. We hope that they will grow into a more environmentally conscious world, where wildlife has been replenished and the Gulf region has recovered from the wounds of war.

PREFACE

MANKIND *differs from all other animal species on this planet in a multitude of ways. One of the unique features of our species is the tendency to exploit the biosphere and its species so that we may flourish. We consider that our use of the biosphere is a 'right'—a resource available for man's well-being. Over the many thousands of years in which we have evolved, our ability to use the biosphere has come to know few bounds. We hunt animals, we clear vegetation to make way for agriculture, we build our cities and our lines of communications, we pour out our pollutants into the biosphere, all with little or no thought of the effects our actions may have on the way in which the biosphere functions. (Gareth Jones,* The Conservation of Ecosystems and Species, *1987)*

This is the worst oil disaster I have ever seen. As I walked the beaches I came across a dead bird every two or three paces. They were just blobs of oil. I saw birds diving into the black water and never coming up again. It was horrific. (Tim Thomas, RSPCA)

Saddam Hussein is waging a war on the region's wildlife. (Dr Abdulbar Al-Gain, President of MEPA, Saudi Arabia)

A spill of oil of this size in tropical waters has never been tackled before—let alone in war. The odds against even limited success are daunting. (John Vidal, Guardian, *February 1, 1991)*

It was clear right from the start this would be seen as a legitimate war effort on Saddam Hussein's part and the environmental damage is obviously going to be very severe indeed. (Jonathon Porritt, formerly director of Friends of the Earth)

*Saddam had warned the World that he would destroy Kuwait and its oilfields in the face of a ground assault. He was making good on his word a little early . . . (*Newsweek, *March 4, 1991)*

The environment itself has become both a weapon and a victim.

In his quixotic madness, the Iraqi strongman seems intent on waging what he calls 'the mother of all battles' against the mother of us all—the earth itself. (both Richard Lacayo, Time, *February 4, 1991)*

INTRODUCTION

WAR in the Gulf has focused international attention on a region where the natural environment has hitherto received relatively little media coverage. Our own interest in Arabian wildlife results from over twenty years of studying, filming and writing about the Gulf countries and their natural heritage. Before the Gulf War, our collective works in this field included film productions of *Arabia: Sand, Sea, Sky, Treasures of the Gulf* and *The Arabs* broadcast by the BBC, Discovery Channel, National Geographic Television, WNET Nature on PBS and others, together with a number of books on Arabian natural history and the Gulf countries. Conservation authorities throughout the region had recently made impressive commitments in the field of wildlife management. Successful projects such as Operation Oryx proved that threatened species could be rescued from the very jaws of extinction; and more recent programmes, such as the protection in Saudi Arabia of more than one hundred key wildlife habitats, provided a basis for some optimism when assessing the future of Arabian wildlife. Few people, however, had forecast the devastating impact of a major war.

Oil-covered cormorants struggling from the slick would become a symbol of the manner in which the Iraqi invasion of Kuwait was savaging the lives of innocent victims. However, it had been clear from the start that the occupying force would disregard animal life: birds and mammals at Kuwait Zoo were butchered and eaten; elephants and giraffes were reported to be staggering about in the

First signs of the Al Khafji spill in January 1991

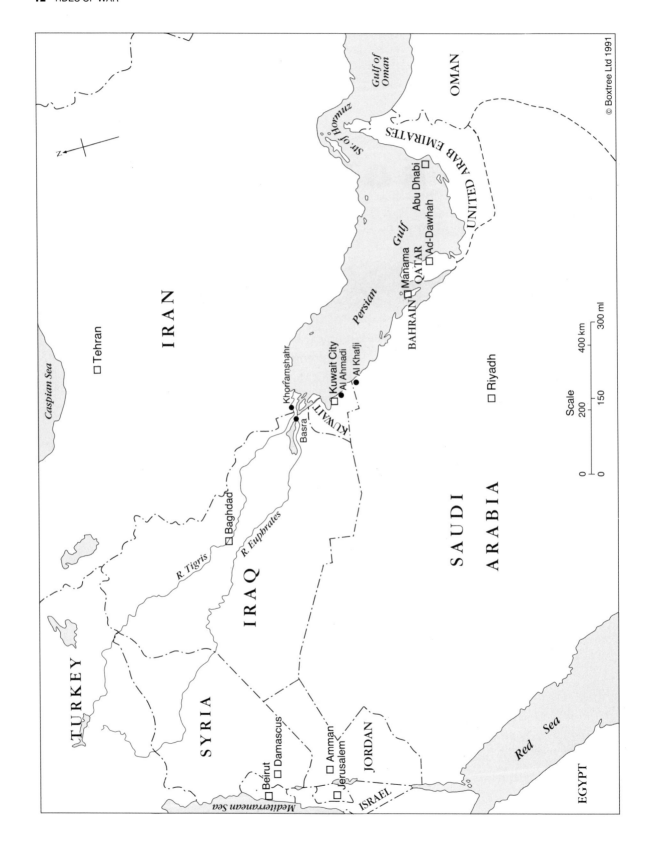

© Boxtree Ltd 1991

August heat, unable to reach their shaded compounds; the finest racehorses in Kuwait were stolen and others were left to starve; torture and shooting of family pets became a routine method of instilling fear in the local populace.

The surface of the desert was bulldozed apart and planted with mines, and long trenches were filled with oil. Delicate desert plants, recently germinated after winter rain, were silent victims in a natural environment previously renowned for its austere beauty but now compared to 'hell on earth'. The shallow, semi-enclosed Gulf, whose marine life is already stressed by temperature and salinity extremes, had inflicted on it, in the course of a single week, a world-record in oil spills. Smoke from raging oil fires cast a dark shadow over the northern Gulf, dramatically reducing daytime temperatures and spreading black rain like 'hell blest tears' to the distant heights of the Himalayas and the wheat fields of Pakistani farmers.

As the magnitude of both marine and air pollution were without precedent, when we came to write this story we were unaware of many of its ramifications. It was, however, clear that there were many different interest groups involved and that getting to the truth of the matter might be as difficult as finding one's way in an Arabian sandstorm. Throughout the conflict, and up to the time of publication, military sources provided very limited information to scientists and other interested parties trying to assess or report on the environmental impact of the war. Information given to the media during the height of the conflict has become highly suspect and debates continue to rage as to whether inaccurate assessments were deliberately issued or were the result of genuine mistakes.

It had not occurred to us that the efforts of conservationists could possibly be construed as anti-Gulf War or as exonerating Iraq's vicious aggression against Kuwait. We entirely supported the allied coalition's use of force to liberate Kuwait from the evils of occupation and the re-establishment of Kuwait's legitimate government. The environment suffered as a direct consequence of the military actions of both sides. It is clear that tactical considerations led allied military spokesmen to place virtually all the blame for environmental damage at Iraq's door. While it is true that Iraq played by far the major role in creating this ecological nightmare, and one could legitimately argue that it carries indirect responsibility for the entire consequences of the war, it was inevitable that some of the damage would be inadvertently created by the coalition forces.

Given that this war was arguably the most ecologically devastating military conflict in history, there is clearly a case to be made for examining its environmental impact. While we strongly support the coalition's firm stance against Iraq, we believe that the Gulf War has vividly demonstrated humankind's awesome ability and readiness to attack both our own species and the wide range of life-forms with which we share this planet. It is vital that we now focus on this facet of our development and seek ways to prevent such widespread devastation in future.

Some areas of Kuwait and the northern Gulf may never fully recover from the ecological impact of the invasion. It would be quite wrong, however, to characterize what has happened as the end for Arabian wildlife. The challenge in Arabia today is the same as that which faces our entire world community. We must strive not just to slow down the accelerating pace of environmental destruction but to push back the hands of the clock. Oil and smoke have damaged many key habitats of the northern Gulf and future development programmes for the region must include appropriate environmental conservation and rehabilitation measures. We must learn from tragedies such as that which has befallen Kuwait to acquire a greater respect for all forms of life and recognize that our own survival depends on improving the health of the natural world.

ONE

THE SEA OF CHANGING WINDS

HUMAN association with Arabia goes back to the early Stone Age, around three-quarters of a million years ago. At that time the earth's climate fluctuated between ice ages and warmer interglacial periods. During cooler epochs vast quantities of water were trapped in polar ice-caps and the oceans' volume contracted, lowering sea levels. As temperatures increased ice-caps melted, oceans expanded and sea levels rose again. The most recent of these ice ages came to an end around ten thousand years ago. At that time the main floor level of the Gulf formed an extended delta for the Tigris and Euphrates rivers, which meandered through the depression until their waters eventually entered the Indian Ocean close to the Strait of Hormuz. Humans were thus able to roam, not just over the Arabian peninsula as we know it, but also across what today constitutes the shallow seabed of the Gulf.

Following the most recent ice age, as the climate warmed and seas rose, the Gulf gradually flooded with water from the Indian Ocean and Arabia's southern land-bridge to Iran was once again broken. A few areas of higher ground within the basin remained above sea level, forming islands or peninsulae joined to the mainland. Evidence from archaeological excavations in the region indicates that humans relied heavily on the sea for food and generally settled close to its edge. These early inhabitants of the Gulf formed a link between the developing river-delta civilizations of Mesopotamia and the Indus valley.

Hadra **traps, used to fish the Gulf's intertidal waters**

The Sumerians, who built their villages on the Mesopotamian plain south of present-day Baghdad, not only traded throughout the Gulf and beyond, but were also the first people on earth to develop a system of writing, known as cuneiform script. Early cuneiform inscriptions deciphered from clay tablets excavated from the ruins of five-thousand-year-old dwellings in this region of Mesopotamia provide the first written descriptions of the people who occupied the shores of Saudi Arabia and the islands of Bahrain. Pearl-diving and pearl-fishing were already well-established pursuits of local inhabitants and we read of Uperi, the King of Dilmun, who 'lives like a fish 30 beru away in the midst of the sea of the rising sun'. Other tablets refer to the bustling entrepôt nature of Dilmun, which was famed for, among other things, its sweet dates. The precise boundaries of this ancient kingdom remain the subject of debate among historians but the predominant view is that it was centred on the island of Bahrain, with areas of the eastern province of Saudi Arabia and the Kuwaiti island of Failaka on its peripheries.

The ancient and exotic maritime province of Dilmun fired the imagination of Mesopotamia's inhabitants, spawning many legends. It is clear that those who ventured south down the Gulf to Bahrain later returned to speak in lyrical terms of the island and its people. Clay tablets refer to it as 'clean', 'bright' and holy or sacred. According to Sumerian mythology the source of Bahrain's (Dilmun's) great natural wealth can be traced to the persistent entreaties of the goddess Ninsikilla to her father and husband, the god Enki, to provide Dilmun with the bounties of life. Enki is reported to have ordered the sun god Utu to fill Dilmun with sweet water brought up from underground. Visitors to Bahrain today are taken to visit the ancient Dilmunite temple of Barbar, where a neatly carved stone stairway leads down to a sacred underground well at which the ancients worshipped Enki. Much of the northern part of Bahrain is, like large tracts of eastern Saudi Ara-

bia, presently irrigated from the same vast underground aquifer which proved such a source of inspiration and mystery to these ancient inhabitants of the Gulf.

The Sumerians often referred to Dilmun as *Ni-Tukki*, 'the place of the bringing of oil'. The Dilmunites are believed to have used natural seepages of oil to caulk their wooden ships and to have exported oiled cordage to their various trading partners. Five thousand years later the same signs of underground oil were used to support a novel theory that the Arabian Gulf may have more than pearls and dates to offer the world's hungry economies.

From early times the Gulf's inhabitants were seafaring people who developed skills of navigation, fishing, diving, boat building and sail making. These traits have remained with them to the present time. We know from examination of artefacts that the Gulf's Dilmunites lived well, hunting sea cows, turtles and fish as well as diving for pearl-oysters, depending on the sea for sustenance and prosperity.

Above all, the western Arabian Gulf, the islands of Bahrain and the coastal regions of eastern Arabia were famed for their pearls. Around four thousand years ago a citizen of Ur, in Mesopotamia, wrote on a clay tablet about 'a parcel of fish-eyes' from Dilmun. It is clear from repeated mention of 'fish-eyes' in subsequent inscriptions that this was a description of pearls. A separate cuneiform text recovered from a tablet found at Nineveh comments 'In the sea of changeable winds [the Arabian Gulf] his merchants fished for pearls.' During recent excavations of some of the 160,000 or so ancient grave mounds on Bahrain several examples of pearls have been discovered, including an exquisite five-thousand-year-old gold-and-pearl ear pendant.

Much later Alexander the Great sent three vessels on a reconnaissance mission to the Arabian Gulf between October 325 BC and the following March, with a second voyage through the Gulf in the winter of 324–323. Alexander's admiral,

Today camels are seldom used as traditional desert transport but are bred for racing and for their produce.

Androsthenes, recorded his observations in a journal entitled *Voyage along the Indian Coast*. Although the original text has not survived it was used extensively in the writings of later Greek historians. One of the few surviving quotations from Androsthenes' manuscript concerns his observations on pearl-fishing around the islands of Bahrain. He mentioned that Bahraini pearls, which he said the 'natives' called 'berberi', were highly prized throughout the region. It seems likely that the Roman name for this coastline, 'Barbary', derives from the local word for pearls.

Strabo, writing at the end of the first century BC, also drew on Alexander's admiral as a source of information. He wrote: 'Androsthenes, who travelled through the Gulf with his fleet, states that the navigator who comes from Teredon and who afterwards keeps the continent to his right sees the island of Ikaros where a sanctuary dedicated to

Apollo as well as an oracle of Tauropolos can be found.' The island known to the Greeks as Ikaros is the Kuwaiti island of Failaka, the site of recent intensive archaeological excavations and of one of the last surrenders by Iraqi occupying forces during the Gulf War. The Greeks were probably unaware that the shrines to which they referred comprised remnants of a much older civilization, established by the Dilmunites more than a thousand years before Alexander's sailors arrived on the scene.

By the time the Portuguese arrived in the Gulf in the fifteenth century, it was clear that great fortunes had been made from the pearling trade.

A pair of onagers illustrated in the *Manifa Al Hayawan* ('Usefulness of Animals') manuscript by Ibn Bakhtishu (Iran, early fourteenth century). Kuwait National Museum

Opposite The richly productive Arabian Gulf hosts a wide range of marinelife, including 15 recorded species of the grouper family.

Duarte Barbosa, writing in 1485, observed of Bahrain: 'Around it grows much seed pearl, also large pearls of good quality. The merchants of the island itself fish for these pearls and have therefrom great profits.' Pearls and pearling were by no means confined to Bahrain, although this was the centre of the trade. A British sailor, Ralph Fitch, who visited Hormuz, at the Gulf's entrance, in the late sixteenth century described 'great stores of pearls which came from Bahrain . . . the best pearls of all others'.

A British report on Bahrain written by J. Calcott Gaskin and published in 1901 emphasized just how important pearling had become to the local economy:

The prosperity of the Bahrein Islands primarily depends upon the pearl fishery, in which about one half of the male population is occupied. The fishery in the year under report opened on the 12th May . . . and closed on the 17th September. One of the principal pearl banks situated to the north of the islands, where the oysters

were found to be diseased and producing no pearls, was abandoned in the early part of the season . . . the chief cause in the falling off in the quality of pearls obtained.

Such were the vicissitudes of the pearling business. One year the boats went out to the pearling banks and found rich pickings, another year their efforts were thwarted by natural events such as weather or disease. Commercial pearl-diving has all but ended in the Gulf. Its demise was not caused by any shortage of good pearl shells but by changing conditions in both the world market for natural pearls, primarily stimulated by the advent of the Japanese cultured pearl, and in the rising fortunes of Gulf countries following the discovery of oil.

In the early years of this century at least twenty thousand men and boys left Bahrain each summer to join the pearling dhows. An inventory of pearling ships and their crews working out of Qatar in 1907 shows that 817 pearling vessels were manned by 12,890 men. By the First World War Kuwaitis worked as many as seven hundred boats, which would have required crew and divers totalling ten to fifteen thousand men. Elsewhere in the Gulf elegant dhows and sambuks set sail from Saudi Arabia and the emirates of Abu Dhabi, Sharjah, Dubai, Ras al Khaimah, Umm al Quain and Fujeirah. They were joined at the pearling banks by dhows from Oman and even further afield. It must have been a truly magnificent sight to watch the proud craft preparing for the annual mission; to see them raise their sails in unison as they set off for the pearling banks. In today's mechanized world it is a scene which can never be repeated. Recognizing that he was witnessing the end of an era, the late Sir Charles Belgrave did his best to set down in writing many such cameos of life in the Gulf as he carried out his political duties there on behalf of the British Government:

I shall never forget the first time I saw the pearling fleet set sail out from Muharraq. It was evening and the tide was full. The graceful ships, like Roman galleys, with huge lateen sails, moved smoothly through the iridescent water, silhouetted against the sunset sky. The sound of sailors singing and the throbbing of their drums was borne across the water to where I stood with the people who were watching the departure.

Belgrave paid a visit to the pearling fleet as they worked the offshore banks in 1926. He described his impressions of this trip in his book *Personal Column*:

I clambered up the slippery side of the dhow on a loose rope and was received by the captain, who invited me to join him on a sort of shelf in the poop where he slept and kept his carved wooden sea-chest, which contained his own belongings and the pearls. The crew, who numbered about sixty men, were squatting in the middle of the deck around a huge heap of shells which had been caught the previous day. With their short knives they prised open every shell, searching each one carefully, prodding about in the flesh of the oyster. When a man found a pearl he placed it between his toes and when two or three were collected he handed them over to the captain who watched the men from his eyrie with an eagle eye . . .

Pearl-divers were full of stories about the sea and the dangers they faced while diving. They had their own folkloric explanation for how pearls are formed. According to tradition, during rain-storms pearl-oysters swam to the surface and opened their shells to receive a drop of rain water. Supposedly these droplets were eventually transformed into pearls. It is perhaps a more fitting explanation for the shape and exquisite lustre of natural pearls than the prosaic scientific one which states that pearls are the result of sand grains lodging in the oyster's fleshy mantle and becoming coated by nacreous secretions similar to those deposited on the inner surface of the shell itself.

Pearl-diving was carried out only by traditional means in the Gulf. Even towards the end of the pearling era, when diving helmets and air pumps became available, divers clung to traditional methods which had remained unchanged for hundreds and possibly thousands of years. Despite the demise of the Gulf's pearl-based economy, pearl-oyster beds continued to flourish in the Gulf, and recent studies indicate a very high percentage of natural pearls.

The Gulf is a shallow, landlocked sea with a mean depth of 31 m (102 ft). It has a total area of approximately 239,000 sq. km (92,280 sq. miles) and a volume of 8630 cubic km (1268 cubic miles). Water loss due to evaporation is ten times the input from rivers and rainfall, causing unusually high salinities of 40 parts per thousand (ppt) in open water and much higher levels in shallow lagoons (compared with normal sea water, which has a salinity of around 36 ppt). In winter sea temperatures can fall below 10°C (50°F) while in summer they can exceed 36°C (97°F). Average sea-surface temperatures off Kuwait are 14–15°C (57–59°F) during the coldest months of January and February, rising to 28–30°C (82–86°F) in July and August. Therefore the Gulf has higher salinity levels and a much greater annual temperature fluctuation than do most other seas. Conditions for resident species are at times stressful but it is also clear that unique circumstances combine to promote rapid development and growth of many types of marine life.

In all, 244 fish species have been recorded in the Gulf, including twenty-three different types of sharks and rays. Seven fish are found nowhere else: a pseudochromid or dottyback (*Pseudochromis persicus*); a cardinalfish (*Cheilodipterus bipunctatus*); a bream (*Petrus belayewi*); a goatfish (*Upeneus oligospilus*); a blenny (*Blennius persicus*); a goby (*Istigobius dayi*); and *Callionymus persicus*. Major fish migrations occur within the Gulf, especially by pelagic species such as many large scomberids like gill-raker, or Indian, mackerel (*Rastrelliger kanurgata*), narrow-barred Spanish mackerel (*Scomberomorus commerson*) and albacore (*Thunnus albacares*). The milkfish (*Chanos chanos*), which is as at home in brackish water as in sea water, probably spawns outside the Gulf, then enters via the Strait of Hormuz), swims through it and penetrates 100 km (60 miles) up the Shatt al-Arab waterway, the main permanent source of fresh water flowing into the Gulf. Milkfish are regularly sold at Basra fish-market in southern Iraq.

Ever since humans have lived along the Gulf's shoreline they have depended on the sea for food. A six-thousand-year-old shell-midden along the ancient coastline of Bahrain marks a dumping ground used by fishermen who trapped and speared fish in local waters. As time passed their methods improved and they became adept at catching a wide variety of marine life, including large sea cows or dugongs. Fishing is one human activity in which traditional methods are passed from generation to generation, often changing little over thousands of years. This is particularly evident in the Gulf, where methods employed to trap fish at least two thousand years ago are still practised by today's fishermen.

The shores of Kuwait, Saudi Arabia and Bahrain are patterned along much of their length by intertidal nets or fish traps woven from branches bound together with string. Both materials are derived from locally grown date-palms. Seen from the air, these *hadra* traps form long barriers extending across the shore and leading into circular or triangular enclosures close to the low-water mark. They provide an ingenious and highly efficient means of harvesting a wide variety of commercially valuable fish which swim over the rich, tide-covered beaches in search of food. As the tide falls, or when they encounter these fenced barriers, fish turn back towards deep water, making their way along the impenetrable face of the barrier. In so doing they are led into the trap, where they remain until low tide, when the *hadra*'s owner returns to harvest them by spear and hand-net. *Hadra* fishing has been a way of life in the Gulf for almost as long as humans have been there. Despite the simplicity of this method, around a fifth of the total artisanal harvest is caught in this way. *Hadra* traps support thousands of people.

Traps are fished at least once and sometimes twice a day all year round. Before the Gulf War, during recent years, only one event has put *hadra* fishermen out of business: the 'black tide' of oil pollution which clogged traps and poisoned Gulf beaches following the Nowruz oil spill of 1983. As date-palm plantations diminish (because of pressures on land use as well as a lowering of the water-table) materials for traditional construction of the traps have fallen into short supply. Increasingly, imported bamboo or galvanized chicken-wire have supplanted natural materials. The use of such commercial products has forced up the cost of constructing *hadra* traps and many have fallen into disrepair. The Gulf War not only polluted the intertidal, killing marine life, but also destroyed many *hadra* fish traps, causing the suspension of a traditional way of fishing which has continued unchanged for thousands of years.

Below tide level other forms of fish trap are employed. *Gargoors*, skilfully woven from fine wire, come in a variety of sizes. They consist of a more or less hemispherical cage with a single opening through which fish swim to reach the bait. In shallow water small traps of this kind, about 1–1.5 m (3–5 ft) in diameter, baited with seaweeds such as *Ulva latuca* and *Enteromorpha intestinalis*, are especially employed to catch the fish most favoured by Gulf Arabs: a small rabbit-fish known locally as *saffee* (*Siganus canaliculatus*). The importance of this fishery is such that bait gatherers may be seen working the intertidal areas, energetically shovelling, raking or scraping up algae with their hands. Once collected, the weed is crushed so that it will give off more 'juice'. Mixed with a sticky fine mud the algae form a nutritious paste which is placed in the traps as bait. Greatly valued for its delicate sweet flavour, the *saffee* supports a multi-million pound artisanal fishery with annual catches around Bahrain alone exceeding 1000 tonnes (984 tons).

Rabbitfish or *saffee* are herbivores which graze sea grasses and algae in shallow water. They are among the first fish to follow the tide as it floods in over extensive algae-covered sand-flats, to graze on richly productive intertidal pastures. Since the *saffee* is a locally spawning fish which has been caught for thousands of years, it is not surprising that a great deal of folkloric knowledge has passed from generation to generation regarding its life cycle. Many traditional fishermen also have their own date-palm trees and are equally familiar with

Previous page Kuwait dhow harbour, May 1991, where traditional Gulf trade was quick to re-establish itself following the liberation.

Right The same harbour photographed a month earlier with the skeletal remains of the dhow fleet, burnt by retreating Iraqi troops

the life cycle of this economically important species. Professor Philip Basson, in a brief paper on the use of algae as bait around Bahrain, commented that fishermen had told him that they knew when to switch from using traps to nets by the ripening of dates. When the dates change from green to yellow—the point at which they become edible—the fishermen abandon algae-baited *saffee* traps in favour of mesh nets designed to catch spawning and schooling *saffee*.

Nobody enjoys sea fish more than Gulf Arabs, and none is relished more by them than *saffee*. Sustainable production of the Gulf's *saffee* fishery depends on healthy shallow and intertidal environments. Previous oil-slicks have brought about a virtual cessation of *saffee* fishing, causing virtual panic buying at local markets. As oil once more spread over coastal waters, Gulf fishermen again faced the potential collapse of this important fishery.

In deeper water small-boat fishermen use larger *gargoor* traps and gill-nets to catch other fish such

as grouper (*hamoor*), snappers (*sharee*), jacks such as *zobaidy* (*Carangoides malabaricus*) and Spanish mackerel. Throughout the Gulf over a thousand small motorized fishing boats are actively engaged in harvesting fish and shellfish from these rich waters. The Gulf's shrimp-fishing industry reached a peak in 1973–4 when Kuwait landed 2075 tonnes (2042 tons), while the combined landings by Saudi Arabia, Bahrain and Qatar were over 12,000 tonnes (11,810 tons). Overfishing, pollution and destruction of crucial shallow-water habitats have taken their toll since then but shrimp fleets are still active with catches from single trawlers sometimes reaching six or seven tonnes per day. Recent figures for annual landings from Gulf waters are around 14,000 tonnes (13,780 tons) of shrimps and 335,000 tonnes (330,000 tons) of other shellfish and finfish. The finfish catch from the United Arab Emirates is particularly significant, reaching around 73,000 tonnes (71,850 tons) per year, the vast bulk of which is sardines. At times the sardine catches off

Ras al Khaimah and parts of the Omani coast, near the Strait of Hormuz, are so large that the fish is spread out to dry in the sun in order to make fertilizer. The UAE alone used over 28,000 tonnes (27,560 tons) of sardines for this purpose in 1986.

Among the Gulf's most valuable marine species are its crustaceans: shrimp, slipper lobsters, crayfish and crabs. Around twelve species of shrimp make up the commercial catch but by far the most important is the green tiger prawn (*rubian* in Arabic), *Penaeus semisulcatus*. Other commonly caught species include the Indian brown shrimp (*Metapenaeus affinis*); the killi shrimp (*Parapenaeopsis stylifera*) and *Metapenaeus stebbingi*. Shrimp populations are sensitive to depletion resulting from overfishing, pollution and destruction of nursery or feeding areas. Like many animals, they occupy a range of habitats at various stages of their lives and damage to just one of these can affect the entire life cycle of the species, causing a population collapse.

Green tiger prawns begin spawning in northern waters during late November or early December, reaching a peak between January and March. Male shrimps mate with females immediately after they have moulted and the females may carry the male spermatophore for days or weeks before spawning. When they are finally ready to do so, large females release several hundred thousand eggs, fertilizing them from the conveniently carried sperm packages as the eggs are set free in the water column. Synchronized spawning generally takes place under protection of darkness, above the nursery grounds in Kuwait Bay, Tarut Bay or other areas such as off Umm al Maradim, Kubba or Al-Khafji. The eggs drift in midwater for about a day before hatching into pear-shaped, actively swimming, nauplii larvae. These planktonic larvae develop, by a series of moults, into protozoan larvae which feed on plant plankton. A further series of moults produces the carnivorous mysis larva which eats larger animal plankton. Three more moults bring the developing shrimp to the

'post-mysis' stage, which sinks down to the seabed and develops into the familiar form of a juvenile shrimp. It is a delicately balanced, finely tuned life cycle which can be easily upset at any stage along the difficult path to adulthood and maturity. The most sensitive stage of the entire juvenile phase is when the nauplii larvae are dependent on finding abundant phytoplankton (drifting plant cells) on which to feed.

Early commentators on the Gulf War oil-slick drew attention to the vulnerable nature of the area's shrimp stocks. The slick drifted across the northern Gulf's most concentrated shrimp spawning grounds precisely at the peak of the spring spawning season, when trillions of fertilized eggs were being released into the water column. Seagrass meadows off Safaniya, Saudi Arabia, are known to support large numbers of spawning shrimp and their young each spring. The rapidly spreading slick cast a dark shadow over the water, cutting out light, slowing down or totally stopping photosynthesis and causing massive mortality of drifting plant life on which shrimp larvae depend for food. Later, as the slick mixed with the water column, it killed huge numbers of shrimp larvae and recently settled juveniles. The acrid tide, whose blackened waves slopped against the shores of the northern Gulf during February and March, each day deposited a fresh batch of dead shrimps on the oily tide mark. For each such stranded carcass there must have been many, many more which fell to the dead carpet of the sea.

The timing of the Al-Ahmadi spill could hardly have been worse for shrimp production. In addition to killing large numbers of larvae, the oil destroyed shallow-water nursery grounds in the northern Gulf, killing sea grasses and algae where juveniles usually settle. Potential recovery of the northern shrimp fishery is influenced by the characteristically discrete nature of shrimp stocks, which lessens the likelihood that southern populations will migrate northwards or that their larvae will replenish the oil-impacted northern population.

TWO

OIL AND WATER

THE ancient Dilmunites were the first to benefit from Arabia's natural oil resources. See pages of oil to the surface created deposits of tar which were melted down and used for filling the cracks between planks on wooden boats. The Dilmunites even exported the caulking materials to neighbouring countries. Despite these encouraging early indications of hydrocarbon deposits, the full extent and potential of Arabia's great store of underground wealth has been recognized only in the past half century.

In 1904 a British political agent based at Bahrain, J. Calcott Gaskin, listened with great interest to some stories recounted by local fishermen. Commenting on these in a letter to the Political Resident in Bushehr, he wrote:

At the end of March, when some of the headmen of the Dawasir Arabs came to me to pay me a friendly visit, amongst other things in their conversation they mentioned that on the conclusion of the pearling season in September 1902, a diving boat owned by a friend of theirs was beating up the Gulf from one of the southern pearl beds. At about ten to fifteen miles north of Ha'lul island, the attention of the people aboard was attracted by an agitation at the surface confined within a circle of some yards in diameter. As the locality was known to have deep water, they sailed up to the spot to satisfy their curiosity and were surprised to find on reaching it, that liquid bitumen was being thrown upwards to the surface which smeared the sides of the boat as they passed through it. If these statements are true it would appear that a natural spring of bitumen or crude petroleum, which is occasionally found in eruption, exists

Recuperating cormorants at the NCWCD Centre in Jubail

somewhere in the locality indicated and may be worth exploiting. (Calcott Gaskin, April 23, 1903; quoted by Angela Clarke in Bahrain Oil and Development, *1991)*

Considering that this news did indeed merit further study, the authorities responded by despatching the Deputy Superintendent of the Geological Survey of India, Guy Pilgrim, to investigate on board the British naval vessel HMS *Lapwing*. His failure to locate traces of floating oil, however, led him in 1905 to a pessimistic view of the chances that oil might be found in the region: 'I cannot recommend that any serious thought be given to possible mining operations in the sea North of Halul. . . .'

The discovery of oil in Persia (Iran) in 1908 caused the British to once again sit up and take notice. The find was exploited by the newly formed Anglo-Persian Oil Company. An international oil rush was already under way, led in the United States by John D. Rockefeller, who formed the Standard Oil Trust; in the Dutch East Indies by Henri Deterding, one of Rockefeller's main competitors in the international arena; and elsewhere by various other interests from Britain and Europe. At each new prospect for oil drilling rival companies competed for valuable concessions. During all this frantic activity Arabia's leaders remained blissfully unaware that they were sitting on the greatest prize of all.

Pilgrim's geological study had gone far beyond searching for oil seepages north of Ha'lul and, following discovery of the Iranian fields, his complete report was examined with renewed interest. Within Bahrain's central depression he had investigated rock strata around Jebel Dukhan, the 'hill of smoke'. He did not discount the possibility that the weathered and eroded anticline may have created an underground oil reservoir but was far from optimistic. In the absence of more convincing evidence geologists and oil drillers were directed towards other areas. Scepticism continued to mount as to whether Arabia merited test dril-

ling for oil, despite a number of promising geological reports, including one by S. Lister James, Chief Geologist of the Anglo-Persian Oil Company, who wrote in 1914: 'In view of the definite occurrence of asphalt and the ideal nature of the structure [on Bahrain], it appears inadvisable to ignore the area before testing with a fairly deep well'.

After the First World War a serving officer who had explored eastern Arabia during that conflict arrived at the personal conviction that the area was sitting on a huge reservoir of oil. In 1918 Major Frank Holmes, subsequently named by the Arabs *Abu Al-Neft* (Father of Oil), wrote to his wife in New Zealand: 'I personally believe that there will be developed an immense oilfield running from Kuwait right down the mainland coast' (Angela Clarke, 1991, quoting from the BAPCO archive).

Following demobilization from the army, Holmes continued to vigorously pursue the prospects for Arabian oil, becoming Middle Eastern representative for a new British consortium, the Eastern and General Syndicate Limited, which was established in August 1920. Over the next four years he obtained concessions for oil exploration at Al Hasa in Saudi Arabia as well as in Kuwait and Bahrain. Not wishing to draw too much attention to his activities he travelled without ostentation, by foot, donkey or camel, accompanied by an interpreter and a Somali servant. He would often tell people he encountered along his route that he was travelling for the good of his health.

It was one thing to gain a concession but quite another to raise the finance to explore and exploit its potential. The Eastern and General Syndicate did not have sufficient resources to go it alone and so they needed to convince one of the larger oil companies that oil indeed lay hidden beneath Arabian sand. Despite Holmes's certainty, decision makers within the oil companies remained far from sure that there was anything worth pursuing in Arabia. Rivalries remained intense, however, and the central objectives often became clouded by peripheral issues. The Anglo-Persian Oil Company, already meeting with success in Iran, was particularly keen to remain the dominant player in the region. This entailed fending off all competitors, and such a policy was clearly enunciated by Charles Greenway when he stated to a management committee:

Although the geological information we possess at present does not indicate that there is much hope of finding oil in Bahrain or Kuwait, we are, I take it, all agreed that even if the chance be 100 to 1 we should pursue it, rather than let others come into the Persian Gulf and cause difficulties of one kind or another for us.

Despite such expressions of interest, British and Dutch oil companies had more than enough to do to develop more certain prospects in Iraq, Persia, Venezuela and the East Indies for which concessions had already been issued. Holmes kept up his effort to 'sell' his concessions but it was five years before he found a buyer. Meanwhile, having failed to drum up early financial support for drilling oil wells, he succeeded in gaining a contract to drill on Bahrain for water. In the summer of 1925 sixteen wells were bored on the island, all of which produced useful quantities of fresh water, a commodity of more immediate value to local people than oil. Holmes was rewarded for his efforts with an exclusive exploration licence to drill for oil on Bahrain.

The story of how Holmes tried desperately but unsuccessfully to convince British financiers that oil would be discovered in Bahrain has been told elsewhere (see *Bahrain Oil and Development*, Angela Clark, 1991). Suffice it to say here that the British buried their heads in the sand, ignoring much good evidence of oil, and were subsequently out-manoeuvred by American interests. Just a short time before oil was finally discovered in Bahrain there were still senior oil company personnel who remained totally dismissive of the idea that Bahrain, or indeed anywhere else in Arabia,

had oil. At the forefront of these pessimists was Dr George Lees, chief geologist for the Anglo-Persian Oil Company, who announced that he would 'drink any commercial oil found in Bahrain'.

On June 1, 1932 Arabia's first commercial oil well began to flow. American engineer and head of the drilling crew, Edward Skinner, described the historic event: 'the drill pierced a layer of the shale. The men smelled oil and heard an ominous rumbling. Very cautiously they drilled another eight feet. . . . The well came in like a lamb. It was a driller's dream' (Angela Clarke, 1991, quoting from the BAPCO archive). Arabia's first oil well had begun flowing from 612 m (2008 ft) at a potential rate of two thousand barrels per day. In the calendar of Arabian history it marked a turning-point. From now on people would talk of Arabia's pre-oil and post-oil eras. There was to be no turning back. As Angela Clarke comments in her recent book, 'Little did Dr George Lees know that he had just ordered the longest drink of his life.'

On the same day in 1932, when Bahrain's Well Number One finally laid to rest any doubts that Arabia was to become an oil producer, dwindling remnants of the Gulf's pearling fleet were gathered over the pearling banks, divers desperately straining aching lungs to collect more pearls than ever before. Despite rising harvests, incomes were plummeting because of a catastrophic price collapse on international markets. The arrival of the Japanese cultured pearl exacted a cruel toll on this traditional way of life in the Gulf. The discovery of oil could hardly have occurred at a more opportune moment since pearling, long the mainstay of the Gulf's economy, was all but dead.

Anyone present at that time on Karan island would probably have seen, soon after sunset and almost within sight of the pearling fleet, a large green turtle emerge over the island's shallow reef and lumber up its steep, sandy beach before hauling its way towards the centre of the cay.

Over the next three hours it would have hollowed out a depression in the sand, deposited over eighty soft, white eggs within it and buried the precious clutch. Two months later a group of young turtle hatchlings, having emerged from the sand, must have made their own way down the coralline beach to the turquoise shallows. They were the Gulf's first oil-era turtles, destined to experience almost as many great changes to their maritime world as humankind would see in its own realm. Perhaps some of these hatchlings of the 1930s were among the adults which returned to nest on

the recently oiled beach of Karan in the summer of 1991.

Bahrain was the first oil producer in Arabia but it could not for long claim to be the only source of Arabian oil or even its major source. Despite the fact that Holmes obtained the first concession for oil prospecting in Saudi Arabia, his concentration on Bahrain resulted in a failure to take up the concession on mainland Arabia and, much to the annoyance of King Abdul Aziz Al Saud, the contract lapsed without a single well being drilled. It has to be said that the king had little faith that his

Wild bees and praying mantids are among the desert fauna of Arabia which are particularly adapted to arid conditions. Heavy smoke pollution has affected many insects, both through direct contact and through disruption of their food chain.

country's desert sands covered any oil reserves, but he would have welcomed the 'rental' payments which went with the contract. From that point on he refused to deal with Holmes and it was an American businessman, Charles R. Crane, who was to hold the key to Saudi Arabia's massive mineral wealth. The Depression which had gripped the world's major economies since 1929 had caused a dramatic reduction in the numbers of pilgrims visiting Mecca, and this had a serious effect on the nation's finances. Something had to be done, and quickly. Crane arranged for a

mineral survey to be carried out under the direction of an engineer by the name of Karl Twitchell.

By the time Twitchell arrived in the eastern province of Saudi Arabia he was aware that prospecting by Socal was already well under way in Bahrain. Socal had been seeking permission from King Abdul Aziz to investigate the Dammam dome, which seemed to offer excellent prospects for oil, but since the approaches had involved the discredited Holmes, the king would have none of it. Realizing the cause of the impasse, the Americans selected Harry St John Philby as their go-between. Socal's principal negotiator was Francis Loomis, who dined with Philby at Simpson's restaurant in London six weeks after his company had struck oil in Bahrain. Philby informed Loomis that the way to obtain a similar concession in Saudi Arabia was to offer a significant amount of cash as part of a royalty advance. When the negotiations finally took place in Saudi Arabia Socal found themselves up against the British in the form of the Iraq Petroleum Company (formerly the Anglo-Persian Oil Company). Philby's prognosis was correct: the concession was duly awarded to the highest bidder, Socal, which paid £35,000 down, £20,000 after eighteen months, £5000 rental per year, £50,000 on discovery of oil, followed by a further £50,000 a year later, with all these payments to be set against a royalty of four shillings' worth of gold per ton of oil.

Finding oil in Saudi Arabia proved more difficult than in Bahrain, where oil was struck at the first drill site. Socal's prospectors on the mainland spent five years searching, drilling seven wells into the Dammam dome before striking 'black gold' on March 16, 1938. Oil gushed from the well at a rate of 2130 barrels in the first day and showed no tendency to diminish. Four days after the strike Princess Alice, cousin of King George VI, following an official itinerary across Arabia, arrived at the oil company's headquarters in Dhahran. Although somewhat shaky on her facts, she conveyed the essence of Britain's lack of foresight about Arabian oil when she wrote: 'We British were awful juggins's as we were offered the concession for this remarkably rich oilfield and turned it down as being no good; the Americans came along, used the same drills and found the oil—and we can't even have any of the share.'

Bahrain's reserves were soon dwarfed by discoveries in Saudi Arabia, Kuwait and the United Arab Emirates. Kuwait's first oil flowed at Burgan in February 1938. However, full-scale commercialization of the field was set back by the Second World War, and it was not until 1946 that the country exported its first cargo of crude oil. Kuwait's first marine terminal, refinery and desalination plant were constructed at Mina al-Ahmadi between 1946 and 1949. From then on development of the nation's petroleum industry never faltered.

By 1990 Kuwait's crude-oil production and refining capacity had reached staggering proportions for such a small area. Almost a thousand producing oil wells were distributed throughout the country, concentrated in seven major fields (Burgan, Raudhatain, Sabriyah, Magwa, Ahmadi, Minagish and Umm Gudair) together with five other oilfields in the Neutral Zone, where production is shared with Saudi Arabia. The four major refinery complexes, at Mina al-Ahmadi, Mina Abdulla, Mina Shuaiba and

TABLE 1: PRODUCTION CAPACITY OF MAJOR OIL FIELDS AND REFINERIES

Kuwaiti Fields	Capacity (in 1000 bpd)
Burgan	1500
Raudhatain	300
Sabriyah	200
Magwa	50
Ahmadi	50
Minagish	50
Umm Gudair	50
Others	100
Neutral Zone Fields*	
Wafra	300
South Fawaris	5
South Umm Gudair	40
al-Hout	35
Khafji	200
Refineries	
Mina al-Ahmadi	270
Mina Abdulla	200
Mina Shuaiba	200
Mina Saud	72

* Production shared with Saudi Arabia.

Mina Saud (in the Neutral Zone), had a combined capacity of 742,000 barrels per day (bpd). The bulk of Kuwait's crude-oil production comes from the Burgan oilfield, which has four hundred wells with an average daily output of around 1.5 million bpd.

Oil was at the very heart of Iraq's invasion of Kuwait. Following years of an expensive armed conflict with Iran, Iraq's foreign debt had reached staggering proportions and the only means of financing this crippling burden was oil exports. Physical constraints on Iraq's ability to extract

The peregrine falcon is a winter visitor to Arabia, preferring wild, open country, marshes and coastal regions.

Overleaf **Modernisation has created many new water sources in central Arabia, such as the Al Hair wildlife reserve which provides a habitat for birds like the heron.**

and pump oil to marine terminals meant that the country's earnings were highly sensitive to the per-barrel price. In July 1990, shortly before Iraq invaded Kuwait, a report in the *Middle East Economic Digest* highlighted this dilemma by stating that if prices held at their July 3 levels (Brent crude $16.03; Dubai crude $13.75) Iraq's current-account deficit for 1990 would be three and a half billion US dollars. If, however, the OPEC reference price of $18 per barrel were achieved the deficit would be halved. This point had been emphasized earlier by the Iraqi Deputy Prime Minister, Sa'adoun Hammadi, when he pressed for other OPEC or Gulf Cooperation Council countries to cut back on production so that the consequent price rise would benefit Iraq's financial situation. According to Hammadi every one-dollar fall in price cost Iraq a billion dollars in annual receipts.

At the time of Iraq's invasion of Kuwait in August 1990, it was calculated that 65 percent of the world's oil reserves were in the Middle East. Saudi Arabia alone possesses 25 percent, not counting the possibility of billions more barrels from promising but so far unexplored areas of the kingdom. Other major producers are Iraq, Kuwait, Abu Dhabi and Iran, each of which has around 10 percent. These figures were uppermost in Saddam Hussein's mind when he invaded his neighbour. Had he succeeded in his conquest of Kuwait he would have controlled 20 percent of the world's oil resources. Had he gained control over Saudi Arabia as well he would have had almost half the world's oil resources in his grasp.

If Iraq's only interest had been an increase in the price of oil its invasion of Kuwait might have been considered successful. By August 22, owing to UN and other sanctions, four million barrels per day of normal production from both Iraq and Kuwait had been lost to world markets and the price per barrel had risen above $30. A week later agreement was reached at a meeting in Vienna of eleven OPEC member-states for Saudi Arabia, the UAE and Venezuela to raise their oil output by about three million barrels per day to compensate for this loss; this stabilized world markets. Meanwhile Iraq and occupied Kuwait remained cut off by an increasingly effective economic blockade imposed under the mandate of various UN Security Council resolutions. On September 23 Saddam Hussein threatened to destroy Israel and all Middle East oilfields rather than allow the trade embargo to strangle Iraq. Within a month his forces were reported to have mined at least half of Kuwait's one thousand oil wells. If Saddam Hussein's lust for Kuwait's riches was to be thwarted he was determined to do his utmost to destroy the source of those riches: Kuwaiti oil.

The aerial phase of Operation Desert Storm, to liberate Kuwait, was launched just before midnight GMT on January 16, 1991. The following day the price of oil fell from $30 to $18 per barrel. In the face of overwhelming coalition air attacks the Iraqi airforce remained concealed underground or fled to Iran, and ground troops hid in their bunkers, while Saddam Hussein resorted to the use of oil as a weapon. On January 22 massive quantities of oil began pouring into the Gulf and three days later the US government accused Iraq of deliberately pumping oil from storage tanks at Al-Ahmadi via the Sea Island loading terminal and from five fully loaded Iraqi tankers anchored at Kuwaiti oil harbours. Simultaneously Kuwaiti oil wells and storage tanks were set on fire in an apparent attempt to obstruct the allied air campaign. And finally, on successive days just before the allies launched their ground attack, almost all of the 645 wells in one of the world's largest oilfields, the Greater Burgan, were blown up by demolition charges and most of them set alight. Subsequently most of the other wells in Kuwait were also blown up. Flames shot hundreds of metres into the air with such ferocity that inhabitants believed they were hearing waves of jet fighters immediately overhead. The sky darkened with billowing acrid black smoke that blocked out the sun. Saddam Hussein's war, rooted in economic necessity and the political fantasies of his vast ego, had found an even more defenceless victim than Kuwait: the world of nature.

Arabia is widely perceived as a land of great deserts where rain never falls and where few plants or animals survive. This is, however, only part of the truth, as the allied forces discovered to their cost during January and early February of 1991. The heavy rains which hampered the allies' advance were part of a cyclonic system from the eastern Mediterranean. In the south-west of Saudi Arabia, the highlands of the Asir mountains may receive up to 600 mm (24 in) of rain a year, while there are parts of the Rub al Khali desert which do not receive a single drop of rain for ten years or more. The Riyadh area of central Saudi Arabia has a mean annual rainfall of 100 mm (4 in), while that in Dhahran, on the Arabian Gulf coast, is around 90 mm (3½ in). Arabia's desert plants and animals are as adapted to take advantage of ephemeral rain squalls as they are to survive long periods of drought.

The climate of the Middle East has not always been as hot and arid as it is today. Arabia's landscape still bears the scars of wetter phases in its past. Indeed, in the driest of all deserts, the great Rub al Khali of central Arabia, deep within the heart of an immense sandy wasteland, there are clearly defined ancient lake beds where fossil hunters have unearthed all kinds of skeletal remains, including skull bones from that most water-dependent of large mammals, the hippopotamus, which survived in Arabia until eight or nine thousand years ago.

TABLE 2: RAINFALL FLUCTUATIONS IN NORTHERN ARABIA OVER THE PAST 2000 YEARS

Period	Rainfall	Period	Rainfall
1–180	Very moist	1428–1460	Very moist
180–390	Dry	1460–1540	Dry
390–415	Moist	1540–1680	Very moist
415–670	Very dry	1680–1708	Dry
670–925	Very moist	1708–1838	Moist
925–1100	Very dry	1838–1875	Dry
1100–1310	Very moist	1875–1900	Moist
1310–1428	Very dry	1901–	Very dry

Source: Butzer, K. W. 1955. 'Some Aspects of the Postglacial Climatic Variations in the Near East Considered in Relation to Movements of Population'. PhD thesis, McGill University, Toronto.

The nature of climatic change over the past million or so years has been referred to already in our discussion of rising and falling sea levels associated with ice ages and the warmer intervening periods. While these descriptions are relevant on a global scale they tend to somewhat distort our perception of Arabia's ancient weather patterns since the ice ages did not mean that Arabia was covered by ice. Instead its climate went through associated and equally dramatic fluctuations in rainfall, so that we speak of Arabia's pluvial and interpluvial periods. During pluvial periods rain fell with such persistence and intensity that it shaped the landscape. During the interpluvials Arabia experienced long periods of low rainfall similar to those of the present time.

The pattern of fluctuating rainfall did not totally reflect the temperature shifts of glacial and interglacial periods. During the last ice age, or Wurm glacial period, rain fell over much of Arabia, rendering areas which are now desert more like the savannah grasslands of East Africa than the parched sands of today. Towards the end of this most recent ice age, as the climate warmed, Arabia suffered an intensely dry and hot period, more hostile even than that which it is experiencing at present. This drought of the Middle Stone Age ended around 8800 BC and was followed by a period of relatively abundant rainfall which brought renewed growth to the Arabian deserts and encouraged the great blossoming of Middle Eastern civilizations such as those of Mesopotamia and Dilmun. This moister climate continued throughout the New Stone Age but suffered a sharp reversal between 4700 BC and 4200 BC. The wetter weather returned, however, and remained until around 2500 BC, when the climate began to deteriorate and vast areas which had hitherto supported grazing herds of wild and domesticated animals became desiccated. The fortunes of Arabian and Middle Eastern civilizations were severely affected by these climatic shifts.

Fluctuations in rainfall have still not ended in Arabia. Indeed, as shown in table 2, there have been dramatic shifts in the pattern of rainfall over the last two thousand years.

Until recently humankind has been entirely at the mercy of these climatic shifts. Dramatic changes have, however, taken place in Arabia and the Gulf countries during the last few decades, since the discovery of oil. As we have seen already, the Sheikhs of Arabia were initially more interested in finding water than oil. When Holmes was unable to raise money for oil drilling in Bahrain he

The Rub Al-Khali is the largest continuous sand desert on earth and is linked to the great Nafud desert by a vast dune system extending along much of eastern Arabia.

Right **Desert plants beneath heavy smoke clouds. The sky is black with smoke, even in the daylight hours.**

applied his geological skills to finding water. He drilled sixteen wells and every one of them delivered fresh water in substantial quantities. Whether or not Bahrain was sitting on oil reserves it was apparently floating on fresh water. The ancient Dilmunites were well aware of this: there was an ocean of fresh water underground ruled over by the god Enki.

The Dilmunites were not far off the mark. The real source of Bahrain's underground water is a vast aquifer, covering an area of oceanic proportions, stretching right across Arabia. This capacious reservoir has been filled, not by the intermittent rains of the present era but by rains which fell on Arabia thousands of years ago, during its pluvial periods. The most recent of these truly wet climatic phases was during the last ice age, at least ten thousand years ago. True, there have been moister periods since then but these hardly qualify as pluvials during which the quantity of rainfall was sufficient to leave a firm imprint on the landscape.

Even before humankind started tapping into Arabia's huge underground water store, signs of its existence were scattered across the region, particularly on the eastern side of the peninsula.

The luxuriant oases of Hofuf, Qatif, Al Kharj and Al Hassa in eastern Saudi Arabia blossomed as the result of geological movement of the underground rock strata bringing the hidden aquifer within reach of ground level. Their fertile stands of date-palms and other plants depended, not on the vicissitudes of present-day climate but on the ability of the vegetation's roots to tap into this source of fossil water wherever it was brought close to the surface. At a few sites the land has opened up to reveal the water itself in freshwater lakes such as those at Al Flaj or in open springs such as the wells of Al Kharj or at the virgin's pool (Ain Adhari) on Bahrain, a popular venue for bathers. There are also places within the Gulf itself where freshwater springs open on the sea-bed, creating shimmering currents in the ocean as the sweet water mixes with salt water.

Once oil was discovered in Saudi Arabia and its neighbouring countries exploration of the peninsula's geology took on a new impetus and meaning. As a result, in addition to exploring and mapping oilfields, geologists recorded the extent and distribution of underground water. By the early 1970s it was becoming apparent that Saudi Arabia was almost as rich in fresh water as it was in oil. This was a novel concept for people who in the past were used to fighting over fresh water and spent much of their lives searching for sufficient vegetation to feed their camels.

Beneath the arid desert sands, provided one dug deep enough, one eventually found fresh water. Saudi Arabia and her neighbours used their rapidly accumulating oil wealth to exploit this newly discovered resource, transforming vast areas of desert into wheat fields or farms producing fast-growing alfalfa to feed cattle. The size of these enormous agricultural projects can be fully appreciated only by flying over the desert, taking a bird's-eye view of the velvet-green pivot-irrigation circles surrounded by stark, arid desert. Between 1973 and 1979 the area of land used for wheat production more than doubled from 250,000 ha (965,590 sq. miles) to 580,000 ha (2240 sq. miles). In less than a decade Saudi Arabia has become a net exporter of wheat and has established a large output of dairy products. All of this has depended on the non-renewable fossil resources of oil and water. Before the Gulf War there were already signs that Arabia's agricultural bubble was in danger of bursting. The conflict increased this possibility in a way which few people had foreseen.

Traditionally in Arabia underground water was used in relatively small quantities for drinking, domestic purposes and agriculture. Throughout modern Arabia there has been a drift to the cities which has placed great pressure on water supplies. As table 3 indicates, this trend is continuing. Almost every household in Saudi Arabia, Kuwait and the other Gulf countries is served, not by fresh water from underground but by sea water from which salt has been extracted at gigantic desalination plants situated along the shores of the Arabian Gulf and the Red Sea. The world's largest desalination plant is at Jubail, along the oil-threatened Gulf coastline. In addition to providing water for local and industrial consumption it also feeds into a 450-km (280 miles) pipeline which runs into the centre of the peninsula, delivering up to 830,000 cu. m (1.09 million cu. yards) of water per day to Saudi Arabia's capital, Riyadh.

There are parts of Arabia where rainfall is sufficient to create seasonal rivers and a major dam-building programme has been aimed at conserving and managing run-off water: around eighty such dams are to be found in Saudi Arabia alone.

During the early stages of development Ara-

TABLE 3: PREDICTED WATER DEMAND FOR SELECTED POPULATION CENTRES IN SAUDI ARABIA		
	Demand per year (in million cu. m/yards)	
	1990	2000
Riyadh	225/294	362/473
Jeddah	207/271	329/430
Mecca	115/150	182/238
Dammam	74/97	125/163
Abha-Khamis		
Mushait	22/29	34/44
Tabuk	14/18	23/30
Hofuf	44/58	70/92
Jubail	26/34	41/31
Yanbu	13/17	22/29

Source: Ministry of Agriculture and Water, Saudi Arabia. Report dated 1986.

bia's artesian water was considered to be virtually limitless. Between 1970 and 1975 over a thousand wells were brought into action in Saudi Arabia and 760 more were added in the next five years. During this ten-year period water was even used to extract oil. It was pumped under pressure into deep reservoirs of oil to improve production from the wells. In a single year, 1980, 360 million cu. m (471 million cu. yards) of groundwater were used in this way—enough to fulfil all the needs of the city of Riyadh for over a year. In addition to groundwater, treated sea water was also used for this purpose. As the water-table fell it became obvious that groundwater was not inexhaustible and that its use would have to be carefully controlled.

So much water has been extracted from Arabia's reservoir of ancient rainwater that the water-table has been falling at an alarming rate. The water level in a well at Buraydah fell 9 m (30 ft) in just

Vast subterranean reservoirs of ancient freshwater lie beneath Arabian deserts. These supply modern central-pivot irrigation systems, creating a boom in agriculture.

two years and similar, if not as dramatic, falls were noticed at almost every well from which groundwater was drawn. Not only is groundwater becoming scarcer but its quality is also deteriorating. Whereas cities such as Riyadh traditionally drew their water from natural springs, urban growth has led to contamination of many of these by sewage effluent. Coastal communities which survived for hundreds of years on groundwater from quite shallow wells have seen these spoilt by salt water. In rural areas groundwater pumped from a falling water-table for agricultural use is showing increased concentrations of sulphur compounds and greater acidity. These factors pose a major dilemma since traditional water sources are no longer suitable or sufficient to replace the demands now served by desalination plants. Most Arabian countries have thus become totally dependent for their survival on replenishment of dammed reservoirs by unpredictable rainfall and on the continuous operation of desalination plants with virtually no practical fall-back position.

Polluting the Gulf with millions of barrels of crude oil posed a direct threat to desalination plants around its shores. It was imperative to prevent the oil-slick closing down these plants since Gulf countries had come to depend on them for the bulk of their fresh water. Burning the oil wells polluted the atmosphere, creating acid rain and depositing millions more tons of sulphurous particles over land and sea. Oil from leaking well-heads in Kuwait seeped back into the desert sands, contaminating natural groundwater reservoirs. Saddam Hussein had not only attacked the basis of Kuwait's economic wealth, he had also used the weapon of oil to attack the very basis for survival in Arabia: its water.

THREE

THREATENED HABITATS

RECENT evidence suggests that Stone Age people were less than environmentally friendly. The discovery of fire necessitated the burning of wood and there is little doubt that they and their flocks of goats were responsible for deforestation on a scale which would cause uproar among present-day conservationists. Arabian vegetation did not escape this early onslaught and the pressure has hardly let up for the past eight to ten thousand years. Given also the hot, dry conditions which have prevailed during most of the current millennium, it is a miracle that there are any trees left standing in Arabia. Around the shores of the Gulf one particular type of tree is threatened with local extinction.

It is remarkable how the passage of time conceals the scars which our ancestors inflicted on our planet. The visitor to the Gulf today might be excused for wondering what all the fuss is about, and might never even see the plant which once dominated these shores. Mangrove (*Avicennia marina*) stands which survived years of cutting and burning have more recently suffered a new onslaught from the great rush to create land by dumping millions of tons of rock and sand in the intertidal, blotting out old shores and pushing coastlines further and further seaward. Despite pleas from conservationists to preserve the last vestiges of the Gulf's mangroves, not much has survived except along the remotest sections of coastline.

Along the Arabian shores of the Gulf (except for Kuwait) there are

Al-Khafji oil slick near Safaniya, February 1991

isolated patches of mangroves, remnants of a much more impressive natural fringe long since destroyed by human hand. In Saudi Arabia the remaining stands are in Tarut Bay and between Ra's al Ghar and Abu Ali (north of Jubail). Tubli Bay in Bahrain was until quite recently thickly lined by mangroves and formed an important retreat for many birds, including the magnificent greater flamingo which settled there in large flocks each winter. Land reclamation has reduced the mangroves of Tubli dramatically and with them the numbers of resting waders. Towards the south of the Gulf mangroves tend to be more abundant, particularly in the Gulf of Hormuz. Iran has the largest area of surviving mangroves with an estimated 8900 ha (34½ sq. miles).

Decision makers throughout the region might be excused for wondering, as they often do, what is the harm in removing mangroves. The generally held view seems to be that they clutter up the shoreline. In fact they have a vital role to play and one which works, if it is allowed to do so, for our ultimate benefit. The Gulf's mangroves, or at least the stands which still survive, provide vital nursery and juvenile feeding grounds for many commercially important species of fish and shrimps. Elsewhere a close relationship has been demonstrated between coastal mangroves and commercial shrimp production. Mangroves trap and stabilize sediment, protecting shores from erosion and helping to build the coastline by natural means. They create sheltered, nutrient-rich habitats for a host of sea life and for birds, and even provide grazing for camels. They also act as vital seed-beds for possible future mangrove re-colonization. Once the mangroves are destroyed it is very difficult to re-establish them by artificial planting. At the eleventh hour and fifty-ninth minute the conservationists' message had finally sunk in and the few remaining mangrove areas were being designated for special protection.

Then the oil came. Sadly, the various spills have already taken a severe toll on the mangroves, which act like oil traps. Observed from the air,

the slick appeared to flow like an immense river of black glaze. It spread along the coastline, separating the turquoise sea from the bleached desert with a brown stain at high-water mark where it had drenched the sand. With a viscosity varying from that of milk to that of thick cream, the oil was carried by the tides deep into the mangrove areas. Plant life was left dripping and glistening as though freshly sprayed with black gloss paint.

Mangroves are typically found growing in fine, silty, anaerobic (lacking in oxygen) mud and their root systems receive air via pneumatophores, aerial roots which project vertically from the mud around the base of each tree. These 'breathe' through small pores or lenticels. If the lenticels become clogged by oil the mangroves' roots are starved of oxygen and the trees lose their leaves and die. Once that happens the protective barrier of mangroves ceases to shield the shore against wave action and erosion sets in, removing the essential fine silt which their roots require for growth. In many cases the whole microhabitat is altered to such an extent that the mangroves disappear completely. If natural recovery does occur slow growth rates and delayed maturation mean that it can take twenty to fifty or even more years before the system is returned to its previous state.

Mud-flats
When media attention focused on the ecological devastation likely to be caused by the Gulf War oil-slick, journalists wrote volumes about the Gulf's mangroves, coral reefs and sea-grass beds, but generally avoided mention of the predominant and most biologically productive habitat of the entire region: mud. It is understandably hard to generate much public interest in, or support for conservation of, muddy areas and yet they are without doubt among the most vital links in the food-chain for many species of marine life and for countless birds. The vital role played by intertidal mud-flats was vividly illustrated by marine scientist David Vousden, who reported that a single

The oil slick from Al-Khafji drenched the sand at highwater mark and could be transported by tides deep into the mangroves and saltbush areas.

haul of a 20-m (66 ft) long beach seine net across 80 m (260 ft) of intertidal mud-flat yielded twelve hundred fish and six hundred juvenile shrimps.

Over 50 percent of the Gulf's seabed is covered by mud and in the northern Gulf this figure rises to almost 100 percent. The Iranian Gulf coastline is much steeper than the Arabian shoreline and the intertidal zone is therefore less extensive and more rocky. The main areas of mud-flat along this eastern shore are near Bushehr, Lingeh and Bandar Abbas. Elsewhere, however, intertidal mud-flats are a predominant feature of many shores. Tarut Bay in Saudi Arabia, Tubli Bay in Bahrain, Al Khor in Qatar and Dubai creek are all prime examples of productive mud-flats. But among the Gulf's biologically fascinating mud-flats there are few areas that compare with Sulaibikhat Bay, which forms part of Kuwait City's sea front. To most residents of Kuwait, as they drove in air-conditioned comfort along the corniche, the mud-flats were, at best, a source of mild curiosity. At low tide, especially in winter, large numbers of wading birds congregated here, including flocks of elegant flamingos. Sulaibikhat mud-flats were heavily mined by Iraqi occupying forces, who also cordoned off the area with barbed wire. The large mud-flats are rich in food but in order to appreciate just how rich, one needed to abandon one's car, leave the road and venture across the muddy beach, finally coming face to face with a fascinating array of inhabitants. On many of our visits to Kuwait we would do this, either to film the intertidal life or simply to watch the fascinating antics of mud skippers.

Walking out towards the sea, one first encounters an area of 'algal mats' formed by intertwined filaments of blue-green algae mixed together with cyanobacteria, diatoms (simple algae), green algae and even anaerobic bacteria. These algal mats, resembling dirty grey or brown crusts covering the surface of the mud, are more akin to bacteria than to common seaweeds. A key to their exceptional productivity is that in addition to photosynthetic algae, they also contain nitrogen-fixing bacteria. At low tide the mud-flats where these algal mats occur are often baked by the sun with air temperatures of up to, or even more than, 50°C (122°F), while the salinity of the water over the mud can reach 200 ppt—more than enough to kill almost all forms of marine life. These desiccated, brittle mats survive harsh extremes in a dormant condition, bursting into life again when inundated by water. One secret of this remarkable resistance to drying out is that they secrete a material which encapsulates cells, preventing them from dying from water loss. The important role of algal mats in the productive tropical ecosystem of the Gulf has only recently received full recognition.

In some areas of the upper shore neat holes in the mud, each surrounded by radiating trails of tiny mud balls, are formed by deposit-feeding crabs such as *Scopimera scabricauda*. Just beyond, around the level of high water, are dense colonies of claw-waving fiddler crabs (*Austruca lactea annulipes*, *A. inversa* and the endemic fiddler, *Cleistostoma kuwaitense*). It is a wonder how these crabs manage to survive the crippling heat and exaggerated salinities of Kuwait's upper shores in mid-summer. Although the fiddler-crab burrows were gathered close to high-water mark they penetrated 70 cm (28 in) or more below the surface. Salinities inside their confined homes can reach 130 ppt, or three and a half times that of normal sea water, while temperatures of over

40°C (104°F) have been recorded.

Immediately below the fiddler-crab zone, slightly further out across the mud-flats, was the unique world of mud skippers—air-breathing gobies as at home on land as are other fish under water. Three species occurred here, each adapted to its particular niche. The one seemingly most comfortable in air was *Periophthalmus koelreuteri*, a

Each autumn large flocks of greater flamingos arrive in the Gulf from southern Russia and northern Iran. Many were probably weakened by carrying oil on their feet and in their feathers.

meat-eating goby feeding on tiny crabs, shrimps and other invertebrates. Overlapping with this species was a larger herbivorous goby, *Boleophthalmus boddarti*, which builds polygonal mud-walled enclaves, each one a miniature 'farm'. The shallow pools thus created promote the growth of diatoms and algae on which the mud skipper feeds. Finally, in wetter areas of the mud-flat, lived an omnivorous mud skipper, *Scartelaos viridis*. The mud skippers' world is a truly fascinating one which has been beautifully revealed in several films. For nature-lovers, however, there can be nothing to replace the thrill of actually visiting such mud-flats, sitting quietly among the mud skippers, watching them meticulously construct their walled territories, aggressively fight off intruders, or calmly skate across the glistening mud with an air of apparent nonchalance suggesting that there was nothing more natural than a fish out of water.

Towards the seaward side of the mud-skipper zone one approached an area where burrows of the crab *Macrophthalmus pectinipes* were marked by light-coloured pools with adjacent mounds of excavated mud. Several other crabs also lived here, as did a small goby (*Apocryptodon madurensis*) sharing its burrow with a pistol shrimp in an unusual commensal arrangement.

The mud-flats, then, are rich in bacteria, diatoms and algae, providing food to a host of invertebrates and to fish such as the mud skipper. These pastures are also important for the greater flamingo, which gathers here in considerable numbers. Algae, fish and buried animals within the mud form an important food source for a variety of other wading birds including avocet, shelduck, crab plover, herons, egrets, sandpipers, dunlin, curlew, turnstone and snipe. As the tide rises the mud-flats are invaded by abundant sea life, including mullet, anchovies and prawns.

What makes the northern Gulf's mud-flats so biologically rich? The fine muds of areas such as Sulaibikhat Bay have enormous concentrations of organic matter within their sediments. The source of these nutrients is primarily silt washed down from the Tigris and Euphrates river. Bacteria help to break down the organic silts to form an energy rich 'soup' nourishing algae and invertebrates. Fish and birds feed on these, creating a food chain which in many instances ends with humans.

Many mud-flats of the northern Gulf, including the highly productive Khawr al Mufatteh (close to the Saudi/Kuwaiti border), suffered the effects of the Gulf War oil-slick. Such key areas had already been earmarked as nature reserves since they are key sites for migratory birds and their finely tuned communities depend on maintenance of an intricate balance between all the organisms which inhabit the flats. Each has a part to play in maintaining a healthy environment. The fiddler crabs, for example, completely turn over and thus aerate the top ½ cm (¼ in) of their mud zone each year and play a vital role in keeping the top 15 cm (6 in) or more of sediment in healthy condition. Rich algal growth helps to bind sediments together, while many of the burrowing organisms, such as the fiddler-crabs, rework the sediment in the same way that earthworms do on land.

If the Gulf's highly productive mud-flats were to be destroyed there will be more at stake than the organisms described above. The northern Gulf's rich shrimp fishery was also at risk, along with important fin-fish stocks.

Sandy beaches

The Gulf's sandy beaches, among the habitats most threatened by oil pollution, are also one of the most productive. A recent Saudi Aramco sponsored study of sandy beaches in the area of Manifa and Safaniya, heavily affected by oil, showed that sandy shores there had almost half a million organisms greater than 0.5 mm ($\frac{1}{100}$ in) in size, belonging to 147 different species, per sq. m (11 sq. ft) of sand. The study was conducted as part of an investigation to assess the likely biological impact of the Tanajib marine facility, part of the oilfield development in this section of the Gulf. Although the survey revealed remarkably high species diversity (over two hundred recorded species) in the intertidal sands, particularly on beaches with a shallow incline, it also found that diversity was dramatically lowered by the presence of localized oil pollution.

Sandy nearshore seabed

As part of the Saudi Aramco programme a separate study was carried out on the nearshore soft-bottom benthic community within the same region of northern Saudi Arabia's Gulf coastline. This corresponds with the area most directly affected by the 1991 oil-slick. Abundance of organisms collected there ranged from 840 to 9670 per sq. m (11 sq. ft). Unexpectedly, the number of species and their abundance increased with increased salinity. Also somewhat unexpectedly, diversity of organisms living in the sand decreased with increasing depth. This apparently anomalous situation was explained by the author of the study, Dr J. C. McCain, as follows:

. . . the major factors controlling the distribution of organisms in the subtidal benthos were not accounted for by the environmental parameters measured at the time of sampling at each station. Based upon the importance of oil-grease and zinc in the water column . . . it is not unreasonable to assume that oil-grease and heavy metals in the sediment may be this important, unexplained factor. (Fauna of Saudi Arabia, 6, 1984, p.96)

The study highlighted the fact that coastal communities along the Saudi Arabian shoreline were already living under chronic conditions of oil and heavy-metal pollution. Given this fact the degree of species diversity and abundance is even more impressive.

Sea-grass beds

Shallow waters below the mud-flats are prime sites for another vital link in the Gulf's food-chain: sea grasses. Three common species of these marine angiosperms (*Halodule uninervis*, *Halophila stipulacea* and *Halophila ovalis*), more closely related to pondweeds than to true grasses, form extensive undersea meadows throughout shallow areas of the Gulf. Sea grasses, unlike algae, have roots, stems and leaves containing vascular tissues, together with inconspicuous flowers producing spiny seeds. Like their terrestrial equivalents, they create highly productive ecosystems, marine plants utilizing their chloroplasts in photosynthesis to convert dissolved carbon dioxide and water into the building blocks of life, carbohydrates. Abundance of organisms (larger than 1 mm/$\frac{1}{50}$ in) living in sea-grass beds along Saudi Arabia's northern Gulf coastline have been shown to range from 450 to 36,200 per sq. m (11 sq. ft). They included 369 different species. As with the shallow-sand communities, diversity and abundance of organisms increased with increase of salinity: an apparently anomalous situation most probably explained by levels of pollutants in the sediment.

The shallow Gulf, whose floor is dominated by sand and mud, forms an ideal habitat for sea-grass meadows. Some of the Gulf's largest examples are situated in the Gulf of Bahrain, including Saudi Arabian coastal areas such as Tarut Bay and the inner bay of Salwah, enclosed by the shores of Saudi Arabia, Qatar and Bahrain. A satellite image of Bahrain's marine habitats shows roughly two-thirds of its shallow seabed covered by sea grasses. To the south-east of Bahrain and around Qatar, as well as along the shores of the UAE, there are huge areas where the seabed for many kilometres in every direction is densely carpeted by the waving dark-green blades of sea grasses.

As primary producers sea grasses play a key role in the lives of many marine creatures and are directly responsible for the creation of several major fisheries in the Gulf. They provide shelter and food for a host of species from commercially important shrimp to large sawfish or endangered marine mammals. Over five hundred species have been identified from Saudi Arabian sea-grass beds. The grasses also help to keep Gulf waters clear and free from too much suspended silt since their blades absorb wave energy, trap silt and organic detritus, and stabilize these with criss-crossing networks of buried stems (rhizomes) and with their roots. Sea grasses capture the energy of sunlight in photosynthesis and, like those in temperate lands, the Gulf's sea grasses grow mainly in spring and summer, dying back in autumn before a relatively dormant winter.

This seasonality in the sea-grass meadows moulds life cycles of other species dependent on the grasses for settlement surfaces, shelter or food. Pearl-oysters (*Pinctada margaritifera* and *P. radiata*) spawn in early spring and their larvae must first find food among the plankton. After three or four weeks the larvae are ready to settle as 'spat' on suitable clean surfaces. This spatfall coincides with the early spring growth of sea grasses and huge numbers of larvae cling on to fresh blades, often more than a hundred to a single blade. As the sea-grass growth continues throughout the summer the translucent green shells, almost invisible to the naked eye, remain cemented to blades, conveniently suspended in the current, where they feed and grow. When grasses start to die back in October the young oysters lose their attachment from upper blades and reattach themselves to the remnants of stems, forming dense clumps of by now conspicuous dark pearl shells. As die-back continues even these clumps may lose their grip and reattach themselves again and again until, clinging to drifting fragments of grass, they drift in the current. There is enormous loss at this stage, many well-developed spat being cast ashore rather than carried to suitable areas for future growth. Those which are transported down the slopes towards deeper water may eventually be washed through areas of good currents, where old shells or dead coral rocks are exposed on the

seabed. The drifting young pearl shells once more attach themselves to these more stable surfaces and grow into adult oysters.

The life cycles of Gulf prawns may also be tied closely to the sea grasses. While the earliest stages of bottom-dwelling juveniles attach themselves to algae such as *Hormophysa* and *Sargassum*, they soon shift to adjacent sea-grass beds, which form essential nursery grounds. Green tiger prawns (*Penaeus semisculcatus*), the most commercially important of the Gulf's ten or so shrimp or prawn species, spawn in winter and spring, their larval settlement coinciding with the most prolific growth of brown algae. Their shift from algae to sea grass corresponds with exactly the time when winter-growing algae have reached their zenith and spring-growing sea grasses are entering their most productive phase. Within the sea-grass beds prawn grow rapidly, increasing in body weight by about two thousand times over two or three months. Eventually the immature prawns migrate into deeper water, where they continue their

growth and may eventually be caught by commercial trawlers. During 1988 alone over 16,000 tonnes (15,750 tons) of shrimp and prawn were harvested in Gulf waters. It is clear that the health of sea-grass beds is an essential ingredient in the Gulf's economically important prawn fishery.

Sea-grass beds are also important habitats for a host of invertebrates including crabs, seashells, starfish, sea cucumbers and many burrowing organisms; and provide vital food sources for many fish. In addition, as we shall see in Chapter 4, they are key elements in the survival of several endangered species such as green turtles and sea cows. Productivity of the Gulf's sea-grass meadows has been estimated by collecting, drying and weighing all the grass from measured quadrats. The area used for this study was Tarut Bay on the Saudi coastline south of Jubail. A total of 175 sq. km (68 sq. miles) of the bay's seabed is covered by sea-grass beds. On the basis of an average dry weight of 128 g (4½ oz) per sq. m (11 sq. ft) this suggests a total dry weight of 22,400 tonnes (22,050 tons)

The constant mist of smoke and tiny oil particles killed off most grasses and shrubs within the oil fields.

Opposite **Black-winged stilts are attracted to shallow ponds and were among those birds to mistake oil lakes for desert pools during their winter visits to the Arabian Gulf.**

of sea grasses within this bay alone. During the growing season the entire leaf biomass is replaced in three months, suggesting annual leaf production of *at least* twice the standing crop, or 256 g (9 oz) dry weight per sq. m—that is, around 45,000 tonnes (44,100 tons) per year. In reviewing these impressive statistics in their book *Biotopes of the Western Arabian Gulf*, Professor Basson and colleagues comment:

In terms more familiar to the non-biologist, the energy yield of the Tarut Bay grassbeds can be compared to that of another familiar Gulf product—crude oil. If the energy obtained by burning crude oil is estimated at 140,000 BTU per gallon, the grassbed annual production . . . is equivalent to the energy from about 95,000 barrels of oil. . . .

This production would have a market value of almost two million US dollars at present prices. If it were converted to fish via a two-step food-chain, Basson and colleagues pointed out, the value would be much higher, around eight million dollars, or up to twelve million if it went into shrimp production. Such calculations, admit-

tedly hypothetical, give some meaning to the statement that the Gulf's sea-grass beds are its energy powerhouse.

The effects of oil spills on the sea grasses have been investigated by several scientists. Heavy spills may cause enormous physical damage by smothering leaves and stems or by destabilizing the sediments in which the grasses are rooted. As the oil sticks to grass blades, forming balls and glutinous conglomerations, it may increase leaf buoyancy, rendering the grasses more susceptible to wave action, and leading to uprooting during storms. The plants are also prone to the physiological effects of oil and the dispersants used to break up spills.

Coral reefs

Much attention has centred on the Gulf's coral reefs. Reef-building corals generally depend on a well-defined set of environmental conditions for their successful growth and survival. Some, but not all, of these conditions are met within the Gulf. The most obvious factor militating against coral colonization is that of winter temperatures. Coral reefs are normally found in areas where sea

Griffon vultures are important to desert ecology since they feed only on carrion, thus reducing the breeding ground for flies and helping to control the spread of disease.

temperatures do not drop below 20°C (68°F): the Gulf's waters fall to as low as 10°C (50°F). Not only are winter temperatures well below the optimum for reef-building corals, but summer temperatures can exceed normal survival limits for these species. Not surprisingly, the Gulf's coral reefs are formed by relatively few species (only fifty-seven species from thirty-one genera are recorded from the entire Gulf). An additional factor affecting distribution of reef-building corals in the Gulf is high salinity. Normal sea water is around 36 ppt while Gulf waters are generally above 40 ppt. Most reef corals die at salinities of 45 ppt although three (*Porites nodifera*, *Cyphastrea micropthalma* and *Siderastrea saviguyana*) can survive at up to 50 ppt. In some ways this makes the Gulf's coral reefs of particular interest since they are living in conditions which are far from optimum for the species concerned. It also renders them exceptionally sensitive to any environmental disturbance such as oil pollution.

Despite its northerly location even Kuwait possesses some coral reefs but they are very limited in extent with a combined area of less than 4 sq. km (1½ sq. miles). The largest reef is also the most southerly in territorial waters, at Umm al Maradim the biggest of Kuwait's coral cays.

The small island of Qaruh is completely surrounded by coral reef. Kuwaiti reefs are confined to shallow water less than 15 m (49 ft) deep, with the most prolific coral growth at around 10 m (33 ft). Three coral species contribute to the great bulk of these northerly reefs: *Porites (Porites) lutea*; *Acropora eurystoma* and *Acropora valida*. The first of these is a sturdy coral whose tiny polyps create rounded colonies in sheltered water. At some sites the polyps build huge pillars of coral rising 8 m (26 ft) or so from the shallow seabed to just below the surface. The Getty Reef at Ra's az Zaur is almost completely formed by this single species. In all, only twenty-six reef-building coral species have been recorded in Kuwaiti waters.

In a recent assessment of the current status of Kuwaiti coral reefs (*Coral Reefs of the World*, edited by Susan Wells, IUCN, 1988) the threat posed by oil pollution was summarized as follows: 'Even a minor spill of crude, such as that discharged with ballast, could prove catastrophic if it reached a reef at very low tide . . .' The Gulf War spills of early 1991 reached somewhat larger proportions!

Further south, along the western shores of the Gulf, Saudi Arabia possesses a much more impressive coral-reef system, forming hundreds of patch reefs. Nearly all of these are some distance offshore, away from high sedimentation in the shallows. A large cluster of such reefs occurs between Ra's al Mish'ab Safaniya and the island of Abu Ali (now joined by a causeway to the mainland) and south of Abu Ali, between it and Ra's Tanura. About six of these reef systems support permanent islands of coral sand and rock, while others form coral banks. Once again, *Porites* and *Acropora* are dominant but several other genera, such as *Platygyra*, *Favia*, *Favites* and *Stylophora* are also reasonably well represented. An exceptionally hardy stand of reef corals in Tarut Bay, where salinities may reach 55 ppt, is formed by a large colony of *Stylophora* accompanied by patches of *Acropora* and *Platygyra*.

Off the Saudi coastline between Safaniya and Al Jubail, the islands of Karan, Jana and Al Jurayd have the most developed coral-reef systems of the entire Saudi Arabian Gulf region. Apart from containing a wider assemblage of corals, their underwater habitats are rich in other forms of marine life. Spawning conch shells (*Strombus decorus persicus*) are very common around Jana and Karan in summer and cone shells are also abundant there in shallow water, among the sea grasses and corals. The islands act like a magnet for fish life, including many large forms such as tuna, sailfish, black marlin and sharks.

These offshore coral islands are also vital breeding sites for marine turtles, with around 1500 adult green turtles depending on them for nesting. Jana and Karan between them probably account for 80 percent of turtle breeding in the Gulf. Free from rats or other mammals, they are also key sites for terns. Up to twenty thousand pairs of lesser crested terns (*Sterna bengalensis*) nest each summer on Kurayn island, together with smaller numbers of swift tern (*Sterna bergii*) and bridled tern (*Sterna anaethetus*). The nearby islands of Jana, Al Jurayd and Karan are also very significant as nesting sites for these sea birds. Socotra cormorants (*Phalacrocorax nigrogularis*) nest on Kurayn.

Sadly, many Saudi Arabian coral reefs and islands were hit by the Gulf War oil-slick. We shall examine its impact in Chapter 8.

Bahrain comprises a group of thirty-three islands, many of which are interconnected by man-made causeways. Thirty-one corals belonging to nineteen genera have been recorded from Bahrain. The main areas where reef-building corals occur are a number of large offshore platforms and patch reefs. Coral growth is quite limited at these sites, however, and on some reefs coral cover is less than 2 percent. The largest of these reefs are Fasht Adhm to the north-east of the main island and Fasht al Jarim, lying directly north of Bahrain. Coral growth on Fasht Adhm is more luxuriant than at other Bahraini sites. The saline-tolerant coral, *Porites nodifera*, has colonized some shallow, sheltered areas to the south.

Qatar, a large peninsula 200 km (124 miles) in length, projects into the Gulf. Corals are restricted to its north and east coasts. Reefs to the north of Qatar are in fact a continuation of the reef system running down the east coast of Bahrain and extending to waters of the UAE. Ras Rakan in the north, Ras al Matbakh in the east and Fasht al'Udayd in the south-east support relatively rich corals and associated marine life. Hawksbill turtles nest on the coral island of Shara'iwah. During the production of the *Treasures of the Gulf* film series in 1983 we observed large areas of staghorn *Acropora* coral at a depth of 5–10 m (16–33 ft) that had died over an extensive area both at Ras Rakan and on reefs east of Doha. Despite the protection offered by intact coral skeletons, the scene was totally devoid of fish life. The seabed reminded us of the dead monochrome forest beneath Mount St Helens after its recent volcanic eruption.

Despite being shallow and sandy, the UAE's Gulf coastline has a number of patch reefs and submerged coral banks, mainly consisting of *Acropora* corals and *Porites*. The islands of Quarnayn and Zarka are important breeding sites for Socotra cormorants, while hawksbill turtles nest on Dayyinah.

SAUDI ARABIA

Species	Common name	World category	Country status
Birds			
Marmaronetta angustirostris	Marbled teal	V	Va
Haliaeetus leucoryphus	Pallas's fish eagle	R	Va
Reptiles			
Chelonia mydas	Green turtle	E	
Eretmochelys imbricata	Hawksbill turtle	E	
Molluscs			
Pinctada margaritifera	Black-lipped pearl oyster	CT	
Pinctada maxima	Gold-lipped pearl oyster	CT	
Tridacna maxima	Small giant clam	K	
Tridacna squamosa	Fluted clam	I	
Mammals			
Dugong dugon	Dugong or sea-cow	V	
Sousa chinensis	Indo-Pacific humpbacked dolphin	nt*	
Neophocaena phocaenoides	Finless porpoise	nt*	

KEY:

*   = not internationally threatened but due special concern because of oil-pollution threat

E   = Endangered, likely to become extinct

V   = Vulnerable, likely to move into the endangered category in near future

R   = Rare, at risk through small numbers

K   = Insufficiently known, suspected to be at risk

CT = Commercially threatened, extinction not likely but sustainable resource level of population at risk

I   = Indeterminate status but considered to be endangered, vulnerable or rare

nt* = not threatened with extinction but local populations may disappear

Res = Resident   P = Passage migrant   W = Winter visitor   Va = Vagrant

Source: World Conservation Monitoring Centre

of extinction is reached only when its population has dwindled to a mere handful of individuals and it has become almost impossible to reverse the decline. In a few cases, such as that of the Arabian oryx, eleventh-hour intervention has rescued a species from complete annihilation, but such examples are the exception.

The major factor contributing to the final dis-appearance of species is destruction of natural habitats. It is for this reason that international conservation groups have been calling, not so much for species-rescue programmes as for the creation of larger protected reserves of land and water where the requirements of wildlife will take precedence over human needs. It is a concept which has been slow to take hold for it is difficult

When oil drenched turtle-nesting beaches on offshore islands there seemed little hope for the Gulf's green turtles. But, thanks to last-minute clean-up efforts, over a thousand greens successfully nested in the summer of 1991.

to convince politicians or businessmen that there are priorities even greater than those of wealth creation and the immediate demands of social or economic development.

Each year the International Union for the Conservation of Nature, IUCN, issues a list of species which it believes are threatened with extinction. The Red List of Threatened Animals, commonly known as the 'Red Book', aims to focus the attention of conservationists, scientists and policy makers on the plight of endangered wildlife. Each year species are dropped from the list: the ones which failed to survive and which have indeed finally disappeared from our world. Before human evolution species came and went in response to natural causes such as climatic change, competition or evolution of more successful mutants. Today, almost all species which become extinct have us to blame for their disappearance for we have taken over from nature in controlling the fate of wildlife.

Iraq, Kuwait and Saudi Arabia provide habitats for fifty species contained in the current Red Book (see table 4). These include twenty species of bird, twenty mammals, three reptiles, two fish, four

molluscs and one insect. The Gulf War, and the intense disturbance to nature created by it, have added considerably to the existing threats to the survival of these endangered species.

There is only one herbivorous and entirely marine mammal in the whole world. Huge herds of this unique creature once inhabited the Arabian Gulf. In a region surrounded by desert the docile sea cow or dugong provided a valuable source of red meat for early settlers. An ancient village of stone-built houses excavated at Umm al Nar, an island adjacent, and now linked by causeway to Abu Dhabi, contained remains of a fishing community which lived there at least 4600 years ago. Eighty percent of the animal bones found at the site were those of dugongs.

Gulf Arabs know the dugong by two names. In Saudi Arabia and Bahrain it is 'bride of the sea' (*arus al bahr*), while in the UAE it is better known by its more prosaic title 'cow of the sea' (*baghr al bahr*). The latter title may reflect a more utilitarian relationship between these southern Gulf Arabs and the sea cow. It is certainly true that the largest remaining concentrations of dugongs occur in this region; particularly between Jabal

Dhannah and Abu Dhabi, and offshore as far as the Bu Tinah shoal. For thousands of years these marine mammals have provided food for local people. As recently as the pre-oil era of this century fishermen made good use of any captured sea cows. Wilfred Thesiger, commenting on his twenty-day stay in the then small town of Abu Dhabi, wrote of an incident which captured his interest: 'Once they brought in a young dugong or sea-cow which they had caught in their nets. It was about four feet long, a pathetically helpless-looking creature, hideously ugly. They said its meat was good eating, and that its skin made sandals' (*Arabian Sands*, 1959). Clearly, dugongs have been a valuable source of meat for the Gulf's inhabitants since humans first settled here and deliberate hunting of them has only ceased in the past twenty or thirty years.

Dugongs are large creatures, weighing up to 350 kg (770 lb) and growing to 3 m (10 ft) in length. Together with manatees, they belong to the mammalian order of Sirenia which derives its name from ancient mariners' tales of sea serpents and mermaids. According to the ancient Greeks sirens were perceived as fabulous sea monsters, part woman, part bird, which lured sailors to destruction by their enchanting singing. Down through the ages sailors have remained fascinated by dugongs. Fifteenth and sixteenth-century seamen embellished sightings of dugongs into sensual descriptions of mermaids. The sea cow's mammalian nature is most obvious in the manner in which females suckle their young.

Stories of dugong singing undoubtedly derived from imaginative tales by sailors returned home from long sea journeys, but they are capable of making a sound very close to that of humans. Following the accidental netting of a dugong in the Red Sea the unfortunate animal's mate was clearly heard to let out a plaintive wail. At first it seemed as if someone was drowning but after a few minutes it became clear that the only source of the strange and evocative sound was the lonely dugong left swimming in the remote sheltered bay.

(This moving encounter is described in more detail in *Red Sea Explorers* by Peter Vine and Hagen Schmid, published by Immel, London).

Dugongs live entirely on sea grass. They are relatively slow-moving sea mammals and have been extensively hunted across their entire range, which extends from East Africa to eastern Australia and the Pacific islands. The Arabian Gulf contains the largest viable population of dugongs known to exist at the western end of their range. Recent estimates have placed the population found in this semi-enclosed shallow sea at around seven thousand individuals. Almost everywhere dugongs are found today they are being inadvertently killed by gill-netting. Since they are air-breathing mammals and must return to the surface every two or three minutes, they soon drown after becoming entangled in nets. The introduction of virtually invisible monofilament gill-nets has posed an even greater threat to their survival.

Until quite recently it was considered that large herds of dugongs were a thing of the past. Before 1986 the most recent account of major aggregations was that of William Travis in his book *Voice of the Turtle*. He was working at the time along the coast of Somalia.

So I decided to 'herd' these great aquatic browsers, to turn them south to our area, and for the next ten days two boats were deployed on this task. During this time I learnt much concerning their lives, most of which was at complete variance from what I had read. Many authorities regard the Dugong as an inhabitant of swamp and estuary, shunning the open sea and existing only in backwaters and in small family groups. Yet here, off the open coast, with the swamp 300 miles to the south, I found huge herds, sometimes as many as 500 strong, swimming freely within and without the reef. They were neither elusive nor shy; being great dumb sea-oxen that only responded when you whacked their backs with a paddle, blew conch-shell horns, or clapped the water with oar-blades. During the afternoon the young calves of up to 4 feet long would leave the herd and form a nursery close to the sandy beaches. Here they would play like slow, clumsy puppies. Wading amongst them, they would dive between my legs, brush against my side and generally use me as a pivot point and scratching post.

By the end of ten days I had succeeded in moving the 'flocks' of Dugong some fifteen miles to the south and this we reckoned was far enough for the time being.

The dugong, however, is a species whose name is prominently listed in the Red Book as being threatened with extinction. Marine scientists had more or less given up hope of ever seeing such dramatic herds again. Strangely enough it was an oil spill in the Gulf which changed all that and brought renewed hope for the dugong's survival. The Nowruz spill in 1983, a consequence of the Iran–Iraq War, took its own toll on the Gulf's marine life and was responsible for the death of at least thirty-eight dugongs. Concern for their survival, triggered by devastation in the wake of the oil spill, led to an aerial survey and methodical count of the western Gulf's sea cows. During the course of that survey a herd, even larger than those encountered by Travis, was located in Bahraini waters. Tony Preen, the biologist who made this exciting new find, later reported:

Counts from photographs reveal that the herd, which was remarkably dense, was made up of at least 674 dugongs, about 12 percent of which were calves. This makes the herd larger than any aggregations of dugongs to have been recorded in the scientific literature. What this herd was doing I'm still not sure, but it is becoming apparent that the Gulf waters in which the herd was sighted are a critical habitat of dugongs, especially in winter. In summer months, with warmer temperatures, they appear to disperse into neighbouring areas although the sighted location probably remains the core area of their distribution. When we've satellite tracked some dugongs we'll have a better handle on what is happening to them.

The Gulf's importance as a vital refuge for some of the world's last remaining sea cows can hardly be overemphasized. As we have seen already, they are highly vulnerable to modern gill-nets and the effects of oil pollution. A female dugong may be ten to fifteen years old before reaching sexual maturity. While she is actively breeding she can produce only one calf every three to six years. These are born in very shallow water during the spring and summer months, when sea-grass meadows are most luxuriant. The calves stay with their mothers, suckling milk from nipples under their fore flippers, for about a year and a half. Despite the fact that they may live for seventy years, their potential to replenish depleted populations is thus restricted by their own reproductive physiology.

The Gulf's dugongs were in 1991 once again threatened by a major oil spill. If the oil-slick trapped dugongs they would be likely to be asphyxiated or poisoned. If they breathed in oil they would suffer lung damage and probably die from pneumonia. If the sea-grass beds on which they feed were oiled they would suffer from starvation or poisoning from eating oil together with sea grass. Sadly, prospects for the continued survival of a viable population of dugongs in the Arabian Gulf took a further turn for the worse with the Gulf War.

The humpbacked dolphin (*Sousa chinensis*) is particularly threatened by the oil spill since it likes to stay close to the shore, often near the entrance of channels through coastal reefs. When mangroves were more widespread it was often found in channels between them and has adapted to changing environmental conditions by inhabiting dredged boat channels and canal entrances for large sea-water intakes. There are other ways in which its behaviour differs markedly from the larger and more familiar bottlenose dolphin, which tends to remain further offshore in the Gulf. Unlike the bottlenose, it is not strongly attracted to the pressure wave at the bows of motor vessels, although it will often swim for a short while with boats as they enter or leave channels. The humpbacked dolphin lives in small family groups, often in distinct areas of inshore waters. There is, for example, a group which can regularly be seen at the channel entrance near the bauxite-loading terminal of Bahrain.

As we have seen in Chapter 3, both green and hawksbill turtles nest on Gulf islands. Indeed, the Gulf is such an enclosed sea, and sea-grass beds on which green turtles feed are so extensive, that it seems likely many turtles spend their entire lives in local waters. This is of particular interest since there is very little information about what happens to turtle hatchlings in their first few years. If green turtle hatchlings are remaining within the Gulf, presumably fishermen should encounter them. Commercial shrimp fishermen do indeed often catch all sizes of young turtles in their trawl nets. Many of these are already dead when the nets are raised, having been trapped too long underwater. For those returned to the sea, still alive, their chances of escaping the unwelcome attentions of large grouper or shark are poor. Partly because of the financial interests at stake in the shrimp fishery it has been difficult to establish a clear picture of the turtle death toll caused by Gulf trawlers.

Despite this threat to their survival it is heartening to see how many turtles do arrive at offshore Gulf islands each summer in order to lay eggs in the sand. The islands of Karan, Kurayn, Jana, Harqus and Jurayd are all regular nesting sites for green turtles. Around five hundred to a thousand females nest on these islands between May and September each year. The total number of green turtles living in the area is several times this figure. Of the twelve hundred or so hawksbill nests which are built each year, around a thousand are on Iranian islands.

The Jubail Wildlife Rescue Centre has collected and cleaned a number of green and hawksbill turtles brought in from beaches totally smothered in sticky black crude oil. They are returned to the sea with beautifully cleaned carapaces but we have no way of knowing whether they survive for long after their traumatic encounter with the oil-slick. Unlike some other marine creatures, there is no evidence that turtles swimming in the open sea avoid oil-slicks. Since they are air-breathing animals they must break surface at regular intervals in order to inhale. Once trapped within a slick, to breathe they must emerge through the oil, becoming rapidly coated by it. If they breathe in fresh oil or creamy 'mousse' they are likely to damage lungs, digestive tract, central nervous system and other body organs. If their lungs are unable to function efficiently the turtles may not be able to remain underwater long enough to feed and may consequently die of starvation. Organ damage can lead to the onset of diseases such as pneumonia.

There is also the strong possibility that turtles will eat oil mixed up with sea grasses or, in the case of young turtles, brown algae. Indeed autopsies on many turtles killed by oil have found tar balls in their stomachs. Ingested oil irritates or blocks the digestive tract, often disrupts the functioning of the salt glands and with them the turtle's ionic balance, and may even prevent production of red blood cells or cause other problems for the body chemistry. Many of these effects are difficult to treat and when oiled turtles are brought in to the rescue centres they are generally given a thorough external clean which concentrates on eyes, nostrils, mouth and soft skin tissues of the neck and inner legs; and released in the hope that internal damage is not too severe.

A particular problem of oil-pollution damage to turtles, particularly hatchlings and the young, is that they remain susceptible for a very long time; long after an oil-slick has had its initial morbid effect. It seems that they are particularly prone to eating weathered tar balls which may have originated from oil spills of months or even years before. Beached oil congeals to form tar mats along the intertidal areas. These mats weather and gradually break up to form tar balls which drift around in the shallows or are taken by currents further offshore. This growing problem of immense proportions can be effectively tackled only by removal of tar mats from oiled shorelines.

**The sand viper
(*Cerastes cerastes
gasperetti*) is an
endemic species,
found only on the
Arabian peninsula. It is
often hunted by birds
of prey such as the owl
(*below*).**

Green turtles reach sexual maturity at between sixteen and twenty years. From then on they may mate close to the nesting beaches every three or four years. Only those females which have mated in a particular season emerge from the sea to bury their eggs above the high-water mark at traditional nesting sites. Once deposited in the warm sand the eggs take between fifty-six and sixty-eight days to hatch. The sex of each hatchling is determined by the temperature at which it was incubated, those in the centre of the clutch generally becoming females while the slightly cooler eggs around the periphery may become males. Once they have hatched, the young turtles have to scramble out of their buried nests and make their way to the sea. This is a particularly stressful time, for many are taken by birds and crabs or by groupers, snappers and sharks in the shallows. Some research on this delicate phase of their life cycle suggests that migration to the sea is a group effort in which the more hatchlings that take part, the better the chances for each one to survive. Once out in the open sea the hatchlings do not make straight for sea-grass beds but favour drifting rafts of brown algae, where they hide from predators and eat almost anything of suitable size, from algae to small fish. While adult turtles depend on sea grasses, they may still eat algae if grasses are in short supply.

In addition to the Saudi Arabian Gulf nesting sites, important green turtle sites occur off the Iranian coastline at, for example, Queshm, Hor-

muz, and Larak in the Strait of Hormuz; and on Lavan and Shetvar off the central coast of Iran. The fate of turtle nesting beaches was of particular concern in the Gulf War crisis. One mitigating factor was that the oil drifted down from the north creating the greatest impact on northerly or exposed sides of traditional nesting islands. The turtles generally approach nesting areas from the sheltered southern sides, so they may have found some beaches which were not heavily affected by

On the exposed plains of the Arabian desert this stone curlew is the potential prey of large raptors such as eagles.

the spill. Nevertheless, oil cast ashore on turtle nesting beaches threatened to cause massive mortalities of eggs and hatchlings. However, it was thanks to a special clean-up operation of key sites that such a disaster was avoided.

Whilst it will take some time to assess the full impact on the Gulf's green and hawksbill turtle populations caused by the present oil spill there are already some indications of how they have been affected. Although Karan island, a major nesting site, was heavily polluted a massive clean-up operation there removed oil together with huge amounts of flotsam which had accumulated over recent years. Thus turtles, arriving in June and July, not only found relatively clean beaches, but they were also able to climb up them without having their passage blocked by debris. Remarkably, very few green turtles on Karan were heavily oiled and they were generally considered to be in good condition. Hawksbills were, as usual, fewer in number but they also appeared to be much less healthy than the greens. Some workers believed that this was because the carnivorous hawksbills were accumulating toxins whilst the herbivorous greens, feeding at a lower level in the food-chain,

were not so seriously affected by the oil, at least in their adult phase.

The Gulf is renowned for its large population of sea snakes belonging to nine or ten different species. Like turtles, these are air-breathing reptiles which are particularly prone to surface pollution. The prospect of large mortalities of these highly venomous creatures may not be of great concern to many local people and yet the truth is that we have very little understanding of their role in the total ecosystem of the Gulf. They are likely to be just as important in the overall picture as turtles and dugongs, which evoke such intense public concern.

Among the various forms of wildlife placed at risk by the Gulf War, one species has received more widespread news coverage than any other. The Socotra cormorant (*Phalacrocorax nigrogularis*), named after the Indian Ocean island south of the entrance to the Red Sea, is locally abundant in the Gulf, where it breeds in massive colonies at a few remote, rat-free islands. Huge flights of these agile birds, usually in extended undulating formations, skim up and down the Gulf's surface,

TABLE 5: PRINCIPAL SHORE BIRDS IN THE ARABIAN GULF

Species	Common name	Status	Numbers
Ardea cinerea	Grey heron	Winter visitor	1000s
Egretta gularis	Western reef heron	Resident	1000s
Phoenicopterus ruber	Flamingo	Winter visitor	1000s
Dromas ardeola	Crab plover	Resident and summer visitor	1000s
Haematopus ostralegus	Oystercatcher	Winter visitor	10,000+
Charadrius leschenaultii	Greater sandplover	Winter visitor	5000+
Tringa totanus	Redshank	Winter visitor	10,000+
Xenus cinerus	Terek sandpiper	Winter visitor	2000+
Calidris alpina	Dunlin	Winter visitor	50,000+
Limicola falcinellus	Broad-billed sandpiper	Winter visitor	1000+
Limosa limosa	Black-tailed godwit	Winter visitor	15,000+
Limosa lapponica	Bar-tailed godwit	Winter visitor	20,000+
Himantopus himantopus	Black-winged stilt	Resident and winter visitor	2000+
Recurvirostra avosetta	Avocet	Winter visitor	1000+
Phalaropus lobatus	Red-necked phalarope	Winter visitor	10,000s
Podiceps nigricollis	Black-necked grebe	Winter visitor and occasional breeder	not known

Source: report issued by Natural Environment Research Council, UK, Feb 1991

journeying between their breeding colonies or roosting and feeding areas. During the winter they share the Gulf with their northern cousin, the great cormorant (*Phalacrocorax carbo*), but the latter is a winter visitor which departs from the Gulf during March and April to breed in Eastern Europe and Russia. The Socotra cormorant is present all year, using the cooler winter months for raising its young, while it disperses over a wider area of the Gulf and Indian Ocean during the summer. The Gulf War oil-slick occurred when both species of cormorant were present.

One of the largest breeding colonies of Socotra cormorants is on South Sawad island, part of the Hawar islands close to the west coast of Qatar. Each morning during February 1991 great flights of Socotra cormorants left their fledgling young standing in densely packed soldier-like ranks on the low, sandy island while they flew off to fish for food. Almost three hours would pass before the first parents returned to a crescendo of croaks from their hungry chicks. They invariably approached the colony from the north, flying low across the treeless island, rising at the last moment as they wheeled in over the colony. Once the adults had landed in the midst of the crèche the problem of identifying their own progeny among thousands of squawking and begging young birds was all too obvious. The parents flapped noisily through the seething mass, pursued by several hopeful youngsters, until recognition dawned. With identification completed the parent opened its mouth wide while the chick reached far inside to retrieve a stored anchovy or other fish. As soon as the young bird's head was extricated from its mother or father's gullet the parent once more took flight.

For many of this colony's young birds the long wait for parents to return extended into a nightmare of starvation and eventual death. The well-trodden ground was littered with thousands of skeletons and hunger-weakened stragglers wandered aimlessly across the island or sat quietly until they could no longer hold up their heads. The natural mortality rate is normally high at Socotra cormorant breeding sites, but here it appeared to be higher than might have been expected. It seemed clear that we were observing an unusual situation. Could it be that some of the parents were reaching the slick and were thus prevented from returning to feed their young? Or had the slick already affected the cormorants' food supplies? It was difficult to be sure but there was no doubt that large numbers of young birds, almost ready to fly, would die.

Meanwhile workers at the Jubail Wildlife Rescue Centre in Saudi Arabia were busily collecting oiled Socotra cormorants from the beaches between Abu Ali and Al-Khafji. We had no way of knowing for sure whether any of these were parents whose young were left abandoned at the Hawar breeding colony. It was quite obvious, however, that these heavily oiled Socotra cormorants were not going anywhere for a few weeks and then only if they were among the fortunate ones to survive the cleaning and captive feeding regime at the centre.

Socotra cormorants were by no means the only birds affected by the oil spill (see tables 5 and 6). Over seventy species of coastal and marine birds spend their winters in the Gulf. They include at least thirty wading birds, and the gulls and terns. Other important species include grebes, the Dalmatian pelican and the western reef egret, white spoonbill and the greater flamingo.

TABLE 6: SEA BIRDS BREEDING IN ARABIAN GULF AND GULF OF OMAN

Species	Common name	Breeding season	Breeding area
Phaethon aethereus indicus	Red-billed tropic bird	All year	Southern Gulf Gulf of Oman
Phalacrocorax nigrogularis	Socotra cormorant	Mainly winter	Arabian Gulf Gulf of Oman
Larus hemprichii	Sooty gull	Late summer	Southern Gulf Gulf of Oman
Sterna caspia	Caspian tern	Spring/summer	Arabian Gulf
Sterna bergii velox	Greater-crested, or Swift, tern	Summer	Gulf of Oman Arabian Gulf
Sterna bengalensis	Lesser crested tern	Summer	Arabian Gulf
Sterna dougallii	Roseate tern	Summer	Gulf of Oman
Sterna hirundo hirundo	Common tern	Summer	Arabian Gulf
Sterna repressa	White-cheeked tern	Summer	Arabian Gulf Gulf of Oman
Sterna anaethetus	Bridled tern	Summer	Arabian Gulf Gulf of Oman
Sterna saundersi	Saunders little tern	Summer	Arabian Gulf

Source: see table 5

FIVE

THE OIL AGE

ARABIA'S natural environment has been under pressure since
the first human settlement there but the growth of that pressure has
accelerated during the present 'Oil Age'. It was inevitable that the
oil-fuelled economies of the Gulf countries would finance major
infrastructural developments, guaranteeing that life for both humans
and nature would undergo dramatic change. One fascinating aspect
of this process is that change has been so rapid that many people alive
today can recall how things were in Arabia before the upheaval. There
are also animals which have lived through the entire period, such as
the sixty-year-old, tar-caked green turtle rescued and rehabilitated
by volunteers at the Jubail Wildlife Rescue Centre. As we assess the
ecological impact of the Gulf War it is necessary to understand how
this devastation, massive and horrific as it is, also forms part of a
continuing process of environmental attrition rather than a single,
isolated assault on nature. Unless we appreciate this fact 'conservation' ceases to have much meaning, for it will be impossible to agree
on what we are trying to conserve. Are we, for example, seeking to
maintain the status quo of July 1990, or are we trying to turn back
the clock much further to regain some of the natural beauty, diversity
and abundant wildlife of the Gulf and its surrounding lands before
the advent of the Oil Age?

*A cloud gathers, the rain falls, men live; the cloud disperses without rain,
and men and animals die. In the deserts of southern Arabia there is no rhythm
of the seasons, no rise and fall of sap, but empty wastes where only the*

Oil polluted sand ripples in the intertidal zone

changing temperature marks the passage of the year. It is a bitter, desiccated land which knows nothing of gentleness or ease. Yet men have lived there since earliest times. Passing generations have left fire-blackened stones at camping sites, a few faint tracks polished on the gravel plains. Elsewhere the winds wipe out their footprints. Men live there because it is the world into which they were born; the life they lead is the life their fathers led before them; they accept hardships and privations; they know no other way. Lawrence wrote in Seven Pillars of Wisdom, *'Bedouin ways were hard, even for those brought up in them and for strangers terrible: a death in life.' No man can live this life and emerge unchanged. He will carry, however faint, the imprint of the desert, the brand which marks the nomad; and he will have within him the yearning to return, weak or insistent according to his nature. For this cruel land can cast a spell which no temperate clime can match.*

So wrote Wilfred Thesiger in his prologue to *Arabian Sands*, a classic account of his travels through Arabia between 1945 and 1950. He is one of the few Westerners to have experienced the real life of Arabia before oil wealth and modernization took their inevitable toll.

But the Arabian landscape was not always so bleak. A great historic richness was alluded to in an account written in the second century BC by a Greek author, Agatharchides of Cnidus:

there is a great well-watered plain which, because of the streams that flow through it everywhere, grows dog's tooth grass, lucerne and also lotus the height of a man. Because of the abundance and excellence of the pasturage it not only supports flocks and herds of all sorts of unspeakably great numbers but also wild camels and, in addition antelope and gazelles. In response to the abundance of animals which breed there, crowds of lions, wolves and leopards gather from the desert. Against these the herdsmen are compelled to fight day and night in defence of their flocks. (Translation of Greek text in On the Erythraean Sea, *Haklyut Society, 1990.)*

Oil money has changed the face of the peninsula. Towards the end of his Arabian journeys, in the spring of 1949, following a month's stay with Shaikh Zayid bin Sultan at his fort in the Buraimi oasis, Thesiger rode the ruler's best camel, known as 'the gazelle', together with his two *bedu* companions, to the coast:

*We arrived at Sharja on 10 May. We skirted the aerodrome, passing piles of empty tins, broken bottles, coils of rusting wire, and fluttering bits of paper. A generator thumped in the distance, and a jeep roared down a track, leaving a stink of petrol fumes behind it. We approached a small Arab town on an open beach; it was as drab and tumble-down as Abu Dhabi, but infinitely more squalid, for it was littered with discarded rubbish which had been mass-produced elsewhere. To me the sun-blistered skeleton of a car seemed infinitely more horrible than the carcass of a camel which we passed a little further on. (*Arabian Sands, *1959)*

Thesiger realized that Arabia was changing so rapidly that he would never again be able to feel so much a part of the land and its people as he had in the immediate post-war years of his travels. At the same time it was hard to criticize the Gulf Arabs for striving to improve their harsh living conditions. Whereas in the past they had been at the mercy of nature, now they reversed roles, taking control of their own lives and interfering with nature only if it hindered progress or if it gave them pleasure to do so.

In a few short years the exploitation of oil brought such wealth that Arabia and its people were transformed. Journeys which only a few decades ago were accomplished by camel over days, weeks or months are now measured in hours on immaculate tarmacadam roads which slice straight across vast deserts or snake through rugged mountains. Villages have become towns and towns cities. Electricity, water and the telephone are universal. Air travel is the norm rather than the exception and the region's airports are among the world's most modern. Islands have been linked to each other, and to mainland Arabia, by causeways. The once dusty streets of cities such as Abu Dhabi, Dubai, Riyadh, Manama and Doha are lined by verdant green verges, blossoming with flowers and shaded by flourishing trees. Modern, air-conditioned buildings have replaced traditional ones in which summer heat was modified by wind towers. Tall office buildings and high-rise residential blocks dominate city skylines. Natural creeks and small fishing harbours have become major ports. Schools, colleges, universities, clinics, hospitals, research centres and many other socially important structures have been established. Oil money has made living in Arabia much less arduous than before. But more than Arabia's traditions have suffered. The rapid development and expansion of the region's modern infrastructure has been at the cost of wildlife and its natural environment.

The first to notice a decline in wildlife were the local people. Many of the larger species which were once numerous, such as cheetah, leopard, gazelles, ibex, dugong and sea turtles have suf-fered dramatic reductions in their populations. Despite an increasingly modern existence, living in towns and cities and driving fast cars or four-wheel-drive vehicles instead of riding camels, the ' Bedouin Arabs remained in touch with nature through a deep affinity with the desert and a passion for traditional hunting techniques. Most important of all was their use of trained falcons to catch houbara bustard.

The hubara *appears on the eastern and north-eastern seaboard of the Arabian Gulf in about October of each year, and birds continue to come till about April, when they gradually disappear again to cooler climes. . . . On first reaching Arabia the* hubara *makes for the small new green shoots of grass that come up with the early rain or* wasm *season (October). As the rainy season develops and grass comes up everywhere, the birds scatter and proceed deeper and deeper into the interior, until they are found as far inland in the north as the Syrian desert, and in the south around Riyadh and the oasis of Jabrin. Except in small numbers the birds do not penetrate much west of this line.*

Round about Zubair, Kuwait and further south as

TABLE 7: DESERTIFICATION OF THE GULF STATES

Country	Area sq. km/miles	Wind Erosion m*%	s%	Water Erosion m%	s%	Soil Structure m%	s%	Soil Salinity m%	s%	Total** m+s%
Bahrain	620/239						97			97
Kuwait	17,820/6880					21	33		11	65
Oman	212,460/82,030	2	0.5	15		16	60		1.4	95
Qatar	11,000/4250		16	12			62		10	100
Saudi Arabia	2,149,690/830,000	9	19	21		10	13		3	75
UAE	83,600/32,280	1	22	4		5	11		13	56
Total	2,475,190/955,679	8	17	19		11	18		3	76

Key: *m = moderate   s = severe   ** = total for moderate to severe conditions of desertification
(slight to moderate values not included)

far as Qatar, the birds are plentiful throughout the winter, and many thousands of birds are each season killed for food by local Arabs. In Kuwait the Shaikh generally bags about two thousand birds every cold weather, and the combined members of the Al Sa'ud get about the same number in the Najd proper, as also do the Shaiks of Bahrain, both on their own islands and on the mainland where they regularly hunt. (H. R. P. Dickson, The Arab of the Desert, 1949)

A skilled Arabian falconer may now count on one hand the number of houbara his best bird takes in a season. They still breed in and visit Arabia, but in greatly reduced numbers. While the impact of traditional hunting may have taken its toll, the introduction of all-terrain vehicles to Arabian game hunts proved devastating:

Suddenly it became possible to travel line-abreast across hundreds of miles of desert plain, flushing wildlife from every dune and wadi—bustards and hares fell to the falcons and gazelle and oryx to the guns. Within 15 years, oryx became extinct in the wild; hares so rare they have to be augmented by imports from North Africa, and bustards confined to Oman, where such hunting did not occur, or to certain royal preserves. (Paul Goriup, ICBP)

An additional and vitally important reason for the houbara bustard's decline is destruction of natural habitat caused by goats and sheep grazing in areas which were its traditional resting and feeding grounds. The houbara favours areas of sparse seasonal growth in arid desert or semi-desert plains. These areas simply cannot sustain grazing by flocks of sheep and goat transported

Most desert plants have extensive root systems and grow far apart from each other. There is little evaporation as moisture from condensation collects and is stored between dampened sand grains. Some plants such as these Orobanchs are parasitic and feed on the roots of other vegetation.

and watered by trucks. This problem of over-grazing by domestic herds is central to many of Arabia's wildlife problems.

Since rainfall is scattered and insufficient to sustain livestock in enclosed areas, grazing by wandering animals tended by nomadic herdsmen, has been the pattern of Arabian life ever since humans settled there. As population increased, more and more trees were cut down and greater numbers of animals were raised. Studies have indicated that large areas of desert in Arabia are man-made: mainly through allowing livestock to overgraze semi-arid lands. The soaring numbers of livestock raised in Arabia are the result of increased irrigation through pumping of under-ground water; the ease with which animals may be transported by vehicles; improvements in vete-rinary services; and subsidies on importations of animal feeds. The overall effects are increased rates of destruction of rangelands and accelerated desertification. A Saudi Arabian study in the 1970s indicated that up to 85 percent of the rangelands in some areas were in a severely de-graded condition. The figure today is likely to be significantly higher. The effects of this policy on sustainable production and on natural plant and animal life can hardly be overemphasized.

Desertification is now increasingly evident throughout the Gulf States. It is sometimes hard to appreciate that it is largely the result of human mismanagement of the land. Prolonged over-exploitation and hence disappearance of natural vegetation has led to abnormally high soil erosion by wind and water; higher salt content in topsoil and groundwater; and a general deterioration in the structure of soil. Wind erosion removes the thin layer of topsoil from previously stable areas and allows underlying sand to be blown into agricultural land, often blocking irrigation sys-tems and thus interfering with production. Water erosion washes away alluvial soils and destroys terraces in mountainous areas. Seventy-six per-cent of the Arabian peninsula exhibits signs of desertification (see table 7).

TABLE 8: STATUS OF THREATENED PLANTS IN SAUDI ARABIA

Extinct species:
approximately four species including the rose *Cratequs sinaica*.

Endangered species:
approximately fifty-four species in imminent danger of extinction including the milkweed *Ceropaeqia mansouriana*; myrrh *Commiphora erythraea*, a second myrrh plant *Commiphora* sp. nov.; the tree-like succulent *Euphorbia* sp. nov. aff. *parci-ramulosa*; the iris *Iris alpicans* and *Iris postii*; *Pancratium tenuifolium* and the mimusops tree of which only ten remain in Arabia, *Mimusops laurifolia*.

Rare species:
around a hundred species are left with small but stable populations which are vulnerable to disturbance. They include *Ochna inermis*, *Scadoxus multifloris* and *Gladiolius dalenii*.

As we have seen in Chapter 2, a series of surveys carried out in Saudi Arabia during the 1970s led to the discovery of large groundwater resources and to the identification of 900,000 ha (3475 sq. miles) of potentially agricultural land overlying these aquifers. Much of this land has been de-veloped for food production, generally with pivot systems, each of which covers an area of 50 ha (⅕ sq. miles) and uses 5000 litres (1100 imperial gall.; 1320 US gall.) of fertilizer-laced water per minute. Production of wheat was increased from 3000 tonnes (2950 tons) in 1975 to 1.25 million tonnes (1,230,250 tons) in 1984. Much of this impressive development is in the Al Kharg region where underground water lies at least 1000 m (3280 ft) beneath ground level. Although the permanent arable land in Saudi Arabia is around 500,000 ha (1930 sq. miles), at least three times

In order to mate, a male rheem gazelle must take temporary control of all females in the herd. This ascendancy lasts only a few days as constant battles to defend his position, frequent mating and the rounding up of females soon take their toll.

this area is cultivated for crop production.

In Saudi Arabia the preeminent crops are sorghum and wheat, but in recent years efforts to diversify have been made. Vegetable production has been increasingly important in recent years and the most modern methods have been applied to their cultivation. Arabia's great progress in agriculture, already under threat from a falling water-table, is now threatened by the effects of smoke from Kuwait's burning oil wells, a topic we examine in more detail in Chapter 11.

The combined impact of overgrazing and intensive agriculture has had a marked influence on Arabia's natural vegetation. Plants which are able to survive in arid zones, despite their apparent hardiness, are in fact very sensitive to any disturbance of their natural environment. Table 8 illustrates how these recent disturbances have brought several plants to the verge of extinction and have led to the complete extinction of others.

Around the shores of the Gulf, land reclamation, another facet of the Oil Age, has taken its toll on wildlife. Intertidal communities have been wiped out by the dumping of dredged material over the shore, building the level above the high-water

mark. In almost every coastal city along the Arabian side of the Gulf, if one walks along sea-front roads or visits buildings overlooking the sea, it is most likely that one is standing over a reclaimed beach. According to a series of studies commissioned by Saudi Arabia and undertaken by the World Conservation Union and the United Nations Environment Programme, landfill and dredging pose a greater problem for the Gulf's marine life than oil pollution. It indicated that approximately 40 percent of Saudi Arabia's Gulf coast has been subjected to landfill and/or dredging. Given that many commercially important species, particularly shrimps, inhabit shallow areas during their nursery stages, it is not surprising that this intense pressure on coastal habitats has been accompanied by dramatic fall-offs in shrimp harvests.

As Thesiger so depressingly predicted, the Oil Age would create numerous problems for both humans and wildlife in Arabia. Not least of these would be how to handle the huge quantities of garbage generated from imported produce. The Saudi Arabian Meteorological and Environmental Protection Agency (MEPA) estimates that 4 tonnes (3.9 tons) of solid waste are created in

Saudi Arabia for each head of population, each year. This equates to around 15 million tonnes (14,763,000 tons) per year, or five times the average per capita waste generation in other developed countries. However, modernization in Arabia has not always been to the detriment of wildlife. One unforeseen consequence of urbanization and desalination is that large quantities of fresh water have been created which, after use, must be disposed of. The city of Riyadh uses this water for irrigation of municipal parks, of which there are over sixty, and of tree-lined boulevards and cultivated roundabouts. Given also the large number of well-watered private gardens and swimming pools, the city has become a magnet for migrating birds. Many birds have actually ceased travelling further afield and have remained to breed there.

Today in Riyadh there are numerous ring-necked parakeets, collared doves and other urban-adapted species. A really dramatic increase in local bird life, brought about through Oil Age development, is to be seen at the Al Hair reserve, south of the city, where disposal of treated sewage has created a new wetland and wildlife reserve. Over a period of ten years the list of migrating bird species found here has increased from 90 to 278. In the midst of the desert, the dense reed beds and tamarisk clumps provide a secure habitat for water-associated birds such as moorhens, mallard, black-winged stilt and avocet.

Although wildlife was given little thought in the rush to develop the infrastructure of the Oil Age, there is now a growing awareness of the need to take more care of the environment. This is rooted in a firm adherence to the Islamic faith and its teachings about humankind's attitude towards nature. The Koran makes frequent mention of how God has created a diverse and balanced

An interdependence betwen camels and their owners forms the basis for a unique partnership enabling both to cross large deserts which are otherwise impassable.

natural system: 'We have produced therein all kinds of things in due balance' and 'We have not created the heavens and the earth and all that is between them carelessly' are but two examples. Islam teaches that humankind holds a special place and shoulders special responsibilities within this universe. This unique relationship is on three levels: firstly one of meditation on, and consideration and contemplation of, the universe; secondly a relationship whereby humankind makes use of nature for its own benefit; and thirdly a relationship of care and nurture. This latter state is repeatedly emphasized in the Koran, where it is stated 'there is a reward in doing good to every living thing'. This third relationship of care or stewardship of nature, *khilafah* in Arabic, considers that humankind does not own the earth but is a manager or trustee of it with the responsibility to ensure that it is truly respected as part of God's creation. Islam teaches that while God gives to all people the right to utilize nature, this right places a responsibility on users to also protect nature so that others may also enjoy similar rights. This also implies a responsibility to ensure that future generations may also enjoy these rights.

The fourth Caliph, Ali ibn Abi Talib, expressed to his followers the most desirable relationship between the farmer and the land when he said: 'Partake of it gladly, so long as you are a benefactor, not a despoiler; a cultivator, not a destroyer.' The Koran goes deeper still into how we should respect nature. It stresses, for example, the importance of water and how it should be preserved and used wisely: 'Say: Have you considered, if your water were one morning to have seeped away, who then could bring you clear flowing water?' Water also is held to be so pure that it plays a religious role in cleaning the body: 'and We send down pure water from the sky'. The sea too is considered to play a vital role in nature: 'It is He who has made the sea subject, that you may eat thereof flesh that is fresh and tender, and that you may extract therefrom ornaments to wear; and you see the ships therein that plough the

waves, that you may seek thus the bounty of God.'

A recent paper on Islamic law and conservation by Dr Abou Bakr Ahmed Ba Kader and colleagues, revised and expanded by Othman Abd-ar-Rahman Llewellyn, makes the point that since water is essential to life, and since pollution threatens the imperative function of water in sustaining life, 'What leads to the forbidden is itself forbidden', and that it is therefore strictly against the basic teachings of Islam to pollute either fresh water or the sea. The same arguments can be equally applied to the air and pollution of it. In Llewellyn's discussion of Islam and conservation he states:

Therefore the protection, conservation and development of the environment and natural resources is a mandatory religious duty to which every Muslim should be committed. This commitment emanates from the individual's responsibility before God to protect himself and his community. It is also a common social duty which rulers, administrative and municipal agencies and organisations must undertake in accordance with the responsibilities assigned to them.

Given such a well-founded basis for conservation among Arab nations, it is not surprising that some of the first conservation practices originated in Arabia. Under Islamic law 'no-go' areas are defined, where developments are either forbidden or restricted so that utilities or natural resources are not interfered with. The Holy City of Mecca is one such area; a sanctuary for humankind and nature: 'Its thorn trees shall not be cut down, and its game shall not be disturbed. . . .'. and its fresh herbage shall not be cut.' This rule was modified to exclude the sweet rush plant or *idhkhir* (*Cymbopogon schoenanthus*) which was vital to the city's smiths. Another protected area was established by the Prophet Muhammad around the holy city of al-Medinah. He stated: 'Verily Abraham declared Makkah a sanctuary and I declare al-Medinah, that which lies between its two lava flows, a sanctuary; its trees shall not be cut and its game shall not be hunted.' Under Islamic law other towns and villages are considered to be surrounded by common land (*harim*) which shall be managed for the good of the whole community rather than for individual profit.

Similarly, Islamic law protects many sources of fresh water and other essential facilities. A system still practised in parts of the peninsula today involves the careful management of large areas of open ground so that plants were protected from over-grazing and the soil remained in good condition. *Hima*, as such areas are known, are public reserves administered by local communities in the best interests of sustained production and preservation of nature. The *hema* (singular) system may be the world's first efficient method for management of rangelands. There are different types of *hema* depending on what is in need of protection. Some prevent animal grazing but permit the cutting of grass; others allow grazing and grass cutting but only at certain times of year; others permit grazing all year round but restrict the number of animals allowed to enter the area, thus controlling the grazing pressure; while others are protected for special uses such as bee-keeping or forestry.

One *hema*, situated in the Hijaz mountains of Saudi Arabia, has enjoyed protection for at least fifty years. Unlike in surrounding unprotected areas, the soil profile is good and cover of vegetation remarkably thick. Grass cutting is permitted during emergency periods or towards the end of the growing season. Syria has adopted the traditional *hema* system and incorporated it into a modern range-management programme, with the cooperation of the local Bedouin.

Wildlife reserves are merely an adaptation of the *hema* concept. Given the great pace of modern development and our increasing estrangement from our natural surroundings, it has become vital to set aside areas where wildlife takes precedence over the demands which we make on the environment. Arabia's first such reserves were established to protect the threatened Arabian oryx and as safe refuges for migrating bird life. As soon

as large areas of desert or semi-desert were fenced off and thus protected from grazing by camels, goats or sheep, grasses and shrubs revealed their true potential for growth in this arid region. Driving around the perimeter of such parks is an illuminating experience for, while one drives across sparsely vegetated sand or gravel around the outside, inside the fence the grass is often taller than a man and so thick that one cannot see through it.

In recent years a great deal of attention has been brought to bear on the problems of Arabia's threatened wildlife and how best to protect it. A variety of areas had been designated for protection or were in the process of receiving such a status when Iraq's invasion of Kuwait suddenly threatened all the progress which had been achieved. Under Kuwait's Master Action Plan key areas of special wildlife interest were to receive conservation status. The Jal az-Zoor National Park, formed from the sand and limestone hinterland of the conspicuous escarpment which runs for 60 km (37 miles) along the northern shores of Kuwait Bay, was to be among the first of Kuwait's wildlife parks. Forming one of Kuwait's major topographical features, reaching 145 m (475 ft) above sea level at its highest point, the steep sand and rock cliff face separates the Bahrah oilfield from the Gulf coast. During spring and autumn large numbers of steppe eagles (*Aquila rapax orientalis*) and booted eagles (*Hieraaetus pennatus*) congregate each morning at the crest of the escarpment, waiting for the sun's heat to create thermal currents on which they effortlessly soar upwards, renewing their migratory passage. They winter in Ethiopia, other parts of East Africa or South Africa, and breed in central Asia. The Gulf lies along their main north–south route and the Jal az-Zoor escarpment is an important resting point along their extended journey. This National Park area harbours at least twenty-two species of mammals, including at least one endangered species. Over 150 species of birds have been recorded and the area is of particular importance to wintering

species and passage migrants. The Iraqi invasion turned the park into a lethal minefield, a massive disposal area for the machinery of war, a no-go area for both people and wildlife.

Another important conservation area in Kuwait were the reed marshes of Jahra, where thousands of migrating birds rest each winter. It was a place we particularly enjoyed visiting and one of the greenest locations in the whole country, teeming with wildlife. Kuwait's implementation of effective conservation measures was just beginning to show results, with the Jahra pools receiving protected status. But Jahra is adjacent to the Mutlaa Gap, through which the main road ascends 60 m (200 ft) or so on to the plateau. It was here, and in the surrounding desert, that about fifteen thousand fleeing Iraqi soldiers were caught by American attack helicopters and a squadron of tanks. At the time of writing, what was pre-

Above During its elaborate mating display the male houbara bustard buries its head within its neck feathers and raises its legs in a high pronounced step as it dances in front of the crouching female.

Opposite The peregrine falcon is a winter visitor to Arabia. Much admired by Peninsula Arabs, it is sought after for falconry and was once widely used for catching the houbara bustard.

viously one of the most attractive sites in the country resembles a scrapyard. The whole area is peppered with live ammunition, bomb craters and fox-holes. The air is heavy with the stench of mass graves, burnt-out wreckage and drifting smoke from sabotaged oil wells.

A further site within Kuwait which has been earmarked for special protection has suffered greatly as a result of the most recent Gulf War. It

is the small offshore island of Qaruh which, before the impact of the recent oil-slick, had the best-developed section of coral reef in Kuwait. Corals here had been living at the very limits of their tolerance, surviving despite winter temperatures which were far below those normally tolerated by reef-building corals. The island's sandy beaches were also the only place in Kuwait where green turtles nested. It is unlikely that they will be doing so for several years to come and they may have been finally driven away from this most northerly breeding site.

Saudi Arabia has been very active in recent years in establishing protected areas for wildlife conservation. A list prepared by MEPA and IUCN of important marine and coastal sites includes several which have been devastated by the effects of pollution caused during the 1991 Gulf War. These include the sandy coastlines of Safa-

niya and Manifa Bay with its nearshore reefs and the offshore islands in the Karan/Kurayn complex. The Saudi Arabian Commission for Wildlife Protection and Development has played a key role in designating terrestrial and marine areas for protection and in management of reserves.

Iran has designated a 296,000-ha (1140 sq. miles) area along its border with Iraq as the Shadegan Wildlife Refuge, a key section of the lowland Iranian wetlands which in total cover 3.8 million ha (14,670 sq. miles). The area, which under the Ramsar Convention is listed as a Wetland of International Importance, comprises brackish sedge marshes, with salt marshes and mud- or sand-flats along its seaward side. Forming part of the frontier zone between Iran and Iraq, this area has already suffered from chemical pollution during the Iran–Iraq War.

The soggy marshes are difficult to cover by

vehicle and they remain a critical wintering and breeding area for over 125 species of waders and wildfowl. A high percentage of the total world population of marbled teal pass this way on their migrations and several thousand endangered Dalmatian pelicans live there. Another protected area in Iran which is likely to suffer from the most recent ecocide is the Hara Biosphere Reserve, which contains the Gulf's largest preserved stands of mangroves and is an important breeding and wintering site for many birds. It is also an important site for green turtles.

The most direct impact of the Oil Age has been in the Persian Gulf. The first underwater concession was granted by Saudi Arabia to ARAMCO in 1948 and since then all the countries surrounding the Gulf have developed oil and gas wells drilled into the seabed. Extensive development of oil-production facilities, both on land and in the sea, combined with increased use of shipping lanes and docking facilities by large oil-tankers, has resulted in chronic levels of oil pollution throughout these shallow waters. The Central Criminal Court of Kuwait considered forty-seven cases of oil pollution from tankers discharging oil into the sea, or leaking oil during loading or deballasting operations, in a six-month period during 1965. Ninety ships were fined for similar reasons in 1971 and cases are still regularly brought to court by authorities fighting a rearguard action against oil pollution in the Gulf. Oil pollution knows no political boundaries and Gulf States, equally threatened by the potential damage caused by oil spills, have signed the Kuwait Regional Convention for Cooperation on the Protection of the Marine Environment from Pollution. Signatories include Bahrain, Iran, Iraq, Kuwait, Oman, Qatar, Saudi Arabia and the United Arab Emirates.

The Convention gets straight to the heart of the matter:

REALIZING that pollution of the marine environment in the Region shared by Bahrain, Iran, Iraq, Kuwait, Oman, Qatar, Saudi Arabia and the United Arab Emirates, by oil and other harmful or noxious materials arising from human activities on land or at sea, especially through indiscriminate and uncontrolled discharge of these substances, presents a growing threat to marine life, fisheries, human health, recreational uses of beaches and other amenities,

MINDFUL of the special hydrographic and ecological characteristics of the marine environment of the Region and its particular vulnerability to pollution,

CONSCIOUS of the need to ensure that the process of urban and rural development and resultant land use should be carried out in such a manner as to preserve, as far as possible, marine resources and coastal amenities, and that such development should not lead to deterioration of the marine environment,

CONVINCED of the need to ensure that the processes of industrial development should not, in any way, cause damage to the marine environment of the Region, jeopardize its living resources or create hazards to human health,

RECOGNIZING the need to develop an integrated management approach to the use of the marine environment and the coastal areas which will allow the achievement of environmental and developmental goals in a harmonious manner,

RECOGNIZING Also the need for a carefully planned research, monitoring and assessment programme in view of the scarcity of scientific information on marine pollution in the Region . . . .

It was clear that all the governments of the region were determined to halt the process of environmental decay in the Gulf, but conventions do not clean beaches or prevent birds dying from oil pollution. They provide useful guidelines for cooperation and direct action and their success must be measured in the field: on the mud-flats, sea-grass beds, turtle beaches and coral reefs, rather than around the conference table. Nevertheless, the Convention marked a major step forward in regional cooperation to prevent oil pollution. It was followed in April 1978 by a Protocol, signed by signatories of the Kuwait

Regional Convention, to establish a Marine Emergency Mutual Aid Centre to play an active role in assisting states to combat oil pollution.

Before the invasion by Iraq, the Kuwait Institute for Scientific Research (KISR) was studying a wide variety of environment-related questions ranging from desert ecology to marine research and mariculture. Kuwait had been at the forefront of environmental research and pollution control. During the 1970s four meetings were held there to discuss these matters, leading to a major gathering in February 1982 at which scientists from a broad spectrum of disciplines contributed to the First Arabian Gulf Conference on Environment and Pollution. Their deliberations were in a sense timely for they came almost exactly a year before the Gulf was to experience its largest case of oil pollution (up to that time) which resulted from Iraq's attack on the Nowruz oil platform. The Conference adopted a series of strong resolutions calling for more research and effective action to halt pollution in the Gulf.

It has been estimated that the Gulf's sea water contains forty-seven times as much petroleum as the world average for water bodies of its size. Concern that oil pollution posed an increasing threat to both marine life and the livelihood of local people stimulated research into the Gulf's physical and biological environment. Some of the fruits of this scientific effort were presented at the 1982 meeting and subsequently published in a report of the proceedings entitled *Marine Environment and Pollution* (Riad Halwagy, David Clayton and Manaf Behbehani (eds.), Kuwait University, 1986). Among the papers presented is a lucid account of the characteristics and movements of water in the Gulf ('The physical oceanography of the Arabian Gulf: a review and theoretical interpretation of previous observations', J. R. Hunter, 1986). In an explanation of why the Gulf's waters move in an anti-clockwise gyre—entering via surface currents through the Strait of Hormuz, flowing up the Iranian coast, around past Iraq and Kuwait and down along the shores of Arabia to

eventually depart the Gulf as denser water in a deep current—the author discusses how long it takes for water within the Gulf to be replenished by new sea water from the Indian Ocean. He estimated that the 'turn-over time'—the time taken for all the water in the basin to come within the influence of the open sea boundary—is 2.4 years, while the 'flushing time'—the time for all the Gulf's water to be exchanged with water from the open sea—is 3–5.5 years. These figures underline the acute sensitivity of the Gulf's ecosystems to pollution. The Gulf's circulation pattern offers very little respite in terms of water exchange with the open ocean.

These oceanographic characteristics, together with data from weather records and bathymetry charts, were fed into a computer programme which was based on the Slickforcast package devised to predict movement of oil spills in the North Sea. The modified programme, known as Gulfslik, went through a series of stages: Gulfslik I, Gulfslik II etc. Its predictions were tested against actual drifts of oil spills and it was found to be remarkably accurate on the general course of drift but initial models took insufficient account of natural diminution of oil-slicks. Subsequent models improved on these early programmes and have enabled increasingly sophisticated analysis of oil-slick movements in the Gulf.

The Oil Age has spun a complex web of influences throughout the Gulf and its surrounding countries. On the one hand it has caused major environmental problems while on the other it has provided the wherewithal for education and scientific research to help combat these problems. As understanding and awareness about nature has increased, so people have become more interested in wildlife and its protection. The one thing which galvanizes public opinion and governmental action is a major environmental catastrophe. The Iran–Iraq War was to have exactly that effect on the Gulf Arabs who witnessed at first hand the horrific potential for pollution which the Oil Age had brought to them.

SIX

THE
IRAN–IRAQ WAR

SADDAM Hussein began planning his invasion of Iran in July 1979, shortly after assuming the presidency. In May 1980 he instructed his Chief of Staff, General Abdul Jabbar al-Shenshan, to prepare a military campaign. The general is reported to have based his strategy on a British plan, prepared in 1941, to capture the Iranian cities of Khorramshahr, Abadan, Ahwaz and Dezful in a rapidly fought campaign lasting ten days to two weeks. It had never proved necessary to activate the plan but the British documents found their way into the syllabus of the Baghdad War College and seemed to provide a framework suitable for Saddam Hussein's purposes.

When its military preparations were complete, hostilities were instigated by Iraq, which unilaterally abrogated a treaty which had been signed by both countries in Baghdad on June 13, 1975. This treaty, based on an earlier agreement signed in Algiers by Saddam Hussein himself, set out to create stable relations between the two countries by, among other things, mutual recognition of a dividing line along the deepest channel of the Shatt al-Arab waterway, Iraq's only outlet to the sea. The Thalweg line, as it is known, was readopted as the agreed border between the two countries, apparently settling a dispute which had been simmering for some time.

The first shells had been fired by Iraq against a border region of Iran on December 14, 1979, a claim denied by Iraq. In an atmosphere of heightened tension, in early April 1980 Iraq attacked

Sabotaged oil pipeline at Al Ahmadi, Kuwait

Iranian oil-storage facilities 160 km (100 miles) inside Iran and was presumed responsible for explosions which destroyed oil and gas pipelines serving the Abadan refinery. These acts of hostility against Iran eventually led to a call by Iranian leaders for the overthrow of Saddam Hussein and the Ba'ath Party. Matters finally came to a head on September 17, 1980, when Saddam Hussein announced to the Baghdad Parliament that the Government of Iraq had formally and unilaterally abrogated the 'reconciliation' treaty of June 13, 1975, and that it now claimed full sovereignty over the Shatt al-Arab waterway. Four days later Iraq mounted a full-scale offensive against Iran and the war began in earnest.

Regrettably, the eyes of the West were at times shamefully averted from the atrocities of the Iran–Iraq war. Fearful that the tide of Islamic fundamentalism, as represented by the teachings of Ayatollah Khomeini, would sweep through the entire Middle East, Western governments and Gulf countries played a significant role in helping Iraq to pursue its aggressive action, with little regard for the cost in human life and environmental destruction. Oil installations were prime targets from the beginning of the conflict, with Kharg Island oil terminal being set on fire by the Iraqis on September 24, 1980. The Iranians counter-attacked with a bombardment on Iraqi oil refineries and storage facilities near Basra and in the Shatt al-Arab area. Over 150 oil-storage tanks at the Iranian city of Abadan, set on fire by Iraqi shelling, were still burning so fiercely three weeks after they had been attacked that Iraqi forces were prevented from entering the city.

Unlike the allies' technologically sophisticated 'Desert Storm' operation against Iraq, the Iran–Iraq war did not turn out to be the blitzkrieg envisaged by its instigators. A relative stalemate was reached very early in the conflict, Iran eventually succeeding in making inroads into Iraqi territory, despite the latter's air superiority. Offensives and counter-offensives were launched in the border regions as intermittent battles fre-

quently caused horrendous casualties, especially among Iranian 'human waves' of massed infantry. Meanwhile life carried on more or less as normal in both capitals. Lulls in the war were repeatedly broken by attacks on oil facilities such as Iraq's numerous assaults on Iran's Abadan refinery and the Kharg Island oil terminal, and these were countered by Iranian attacks, particularly on Mina al-Bakr, Khor al-Amaya, Az Zubayr, Tikrit and Iraqi oil-storage tanks at the port of Fao. Apart from the immediate and highly significant economic damage caused to both sides—oil revenues provide the primary source of military funding—these attacks exacerbated already high levels of oil pollution in the Gulf. Oil spills were not solely linked to artillery or bombing assaults on fixed facilities, but also to leaks from oil-tankers damaged by mines or other means. One such victim was the 16,000-tonne (15,750 tons) tanker *Mokran*, owned by the National Iranian Tanker Company, which hit a mine on leaving Bandar Mahshahr in mid-February 1982.

From an early stage the war also seriously curtailed the freedom of passage for foreign ships in Gulf waters, the 'tanker war' in the sea-lanes intensifying as the conflict progressed. Between 1981 and March 1987 314 attacks on tankers took place, 70 percent carried out by Iraq. But not all the war's oil pollution resulted from military actions by Iraq and Iran. In October 1987 an oil well in the Rostam field was attacked by the US navy and another US attack on Gulf oil facilities took place in April 1988 when two Iranian platforms were damaged. 'Significant but unknown quantities of oil were discharged as a result of these incidents' (NCWCD Fact File, February 1991).

On March 2, 1983 an Iraqi air-and-sea attack on the Nowruz oilfield sank five Iranian ships and broke open two producing wells. A third oil well was damaged when it was accidentally struck by an Iranian vessel. As with the most recent crisis, the fact that a war was in progress and the surrounding waters were mined, made assessment

of the size of the spill difficult. Initial reports that the slick was the size of Belgium were later discounted but there was no escaping the fact that the Gulf States had never before experienced oil pollution on this scale. In addition to widespread concern over the fate of fisheries and wildlife, emergency measures were taken to defend desalination plants and other sea-water intakes in Saudi Arabia, Bahrain and Qatar. At one point it seemed as if these would be put to the crucial test but a strong offshore wind arrived just as the oil approached Arabian shores, averting disaster at the last moment. The major slick was blown away from the coast and dispersed.

While the general population of the Gulf States followed the reported progress of the slick with mounting apprehension, pollution-control experts from eight oil-producing Gulf countries came together under the aegis of ROPME (Regional Organization for the Protection of the Marine Environment) at a meeting in Bahrain on April 4, 1983. To many observers one fascinating aspect of this and other ROPME meetings was that representatives of the two warring countries were seated around the same table to discuss how to ameliorate the environmental consequences of the battle in which they were engaged. Their deliberations concerning the damaged Nowruz oil wells were further considered by ministerial meetings on April 7 and 13–15 which were attended by the Iraqi Health Minister, Sadiq Hamid Allush, and the Iranian ambassador to Kuwait, Ali Shams Ardakani. Red Adair and members of his Texan-based oil-fire-fighting company were standing by to undertake the dangerous task of sealing the wells. But despite agreement that the wells needed to be capped the two sides could not agree on the ceasefire indispensable to such an operation. Iran requested Iraq to consent to a limited truce covering shipping and oil installations in the northern Gulf but the Iraqi Government, faced by increasingly successful Iranian offensives on land, insisted that it wanted a more general ceasefire involving the United Nations

Truce Supervision Organization (UNTSO). These political delays were to prove critical for wildlife, with the spill exceeding a million barrels and oil continuing to leak at a rate of two to five thousand barrels per day as late as November 1983.

The widespread environmental damage created a renewed impetus for peace efforts and President Hussein, who now found himself militarily on the defensive, leapt to take advantage of this opportunity by writing an open letter (dated June 6, 1983) to the Iranian people calling for a ceasefire throughout the Gulf: 'including its waters, ports, coasts and skies'. He was well aware of the potential damage and suffering caused by oil pollution and showed little hesitation in using it as a weapon to bring pressure on his opponents. It was a strategy he was to pursue throughout the remainder of the Iran–Iraq war and one to which he returned following his attack on Kuwait. In case we give the impression here that Iran was the major obstacle to a settlement, we should explain that Iran had issued its own terms for a ceasefire, which hinged on an Iraqi withdrawal from Iranian territory, payment of reparations by Iraq and the 'punishment' of the Iraqi regime.

The Nowruz spill took a heavy toll on the Gulf's marine life. A shore survey of the Saudi Arabian coastline during March and April found many dead birds, together with fifty-six turtles, thirty-two dugongs, thirty-three porpoises and fifteen hundred seasnakes. A subsequent estimate put the death toll of turtles at round five hundred, a figure which the Gulf's already beleaguered population of these endangered reptiles could ill afford to lose. Although many of these fatalities could not be definitely linked to the oil spill, it was widely believed that a toxic red tide (formed by single-celled algae known as dinoflagellates) had been triggered by the oil and that this is what had caused the high mortalities.

The slick continued to threaten wildlife and coastal installations. Several Saudi Arabian desalination plants were temporarily closed and concern over contamination of fish by oil caused

Dubai to ban imports of seafoods from all neighbouring Gulf countries. As the oil continued to drift southwards, gradually weathering, environmentalists viewed the events with increasing dismay. A second ROPME meeting on June 25–30 formulated a plan for capping the wells and the Iranians announced on September 21 that one of the three leaking wells had been successfully capped without the assistance of foreign experts. The Iraqis confirmed that this was the case.

Other members of ROPME, together with the international conservation lobby, had been putting pressure on both governments to take action to halt the environmental damage to the Gulf. Among the most prominent of the external organizations was the World Wildlife Fund (now known as the Worldwide Fund for Nature). On July 11, 1983 the WWF published a report summarizing the environmental consequences of the massive oil spill. Among its conclusions was a claim that the slick had completely devastated the entire Gulf population of dugongs. As we have seen already, this report proved to be far from true. Of greater relevance, however, was their 'growing suspicion' that tankers and coastal industries were hiding their own polluting activities behind the slick: dumping oil and toxic chemicals into the Gulf.

Iraq's attacks on the environment were not restricted to creating oil spills or setting fire to oil-storage facilities. Its readiness to use chemical weapons was proven to the international community during 1984 when medical representatives of the International Red Cross examined wounded Iranian soldiers in Tehran. Their report, dated March 7, 1984, stated that the soldiers had been 'affected by substances prohibited under international law'. Other soldiers were flown to medical centres in Europe and Scandinavia for further treatment and examination. It was found that they were suffering from the effects of mustard gas and a mycotoxin commonly known as

The Iraqi occupying force dug thousands of trenches along the Kuwaiti coastline and borders. Many were filled with crude oil or unexploded ordnance and remain a danger for people and wildlife.

'yellow rain'. A subsequent study carried out by a UN delegation in Iran confirmed that these chemical weapons had been delivered in the form of 'aerial bombs' and a third substance was added to the list, a nerve gas known as tabun. All these chemicals were directed with devastating consequences at people, but they also killed wildlife and domestic animals. The Iraqi regime's belief that the end justified the means was enunciated by various politicians and military commanders throughout the war. Not denying that such weapons had been used, nor promising that they would be avoided in future, a commander is reported to have informed a journalist: 'We shall use any means and any destructive or deterrent weapons against anyone who tries to cross our borders or occupy our land.' Perhaps he should have added 'and against our own people inside Iraq if we find it necessary to quell unrest or to suppress popular uprisings against Saddam Hussein or the Ba'ath Party'.

The official Iraqi line, however, was that chemical weapons had not been used. This was clearly untrue and Iranian officials, increasingly frustrated by the West's unwillingness to believe their claims, had been complaining of their use since the very beginning of the war. Eventually however, in the face of incontrovertible evidence, Western governments who had been tacitly supporting Iraq were forced to express their condemnation of such weapons. The question of the origins of Iraq's chemical stockpile was addressed on numerous occasions and it became clear that Iraq was using numerous subterfuges to satisfy its demand for these lethal substances. West Germany, by no means the only supplier, was implicated on a number of occasions. The CIA in America claimed that a pesticides manufacturing plant sold to Iraq from Germany in December 1983 could be used for production of the nerve gas tabun. The West German government tightened its control on supplies of equipment which might be used in chemicals manufacture and their repeated requests to be allowed to send a team to investigate the pesticides plant were ignored by the Iraqi authorities.

Throughout 1985 and 1986 Iraq continued to use chemical weapons on the battlefield. In April 1985 the UN Secretary-General, Sr. Javier Pérez de Cuellar, appointed a doctor to examine Iranian patients in London. He reported that they were suffering from the effects of Yperite, a variety of mustard gas. A motion of the UN Security Council on April 26 condemned the use of such chemical weapons but fell short of accusing Iraq of their use. Almost a year later, in March 1986, following further UN-sponsored missions to examine Iraq's reported use of such weapons, the UN Security Council finally named Iraq as the guilty party. Despite Iraq's repeated use of such weapons since the early days of the war, this was the first explicit condemnation of Iraq for such actions by a UN body.

Iraq's southern frontier with Iran is characterized by extensive marshlands which hampered

movements of armour and artillery. This did not prevent the wildlife-rich region suffering spasmodic bombardment from shells, most of which seem to have missed their targets to land 'harmlessly' in the mud. Neither did it prevent the extensive use of chemical weapons in these areas, resulting in considerable suffering and loss of life to both humans and nature. Eventually, however, the marshes themselves came under attack when Iranian forces dug a series of drainage channels leading south-eastwards from the marshes around 'Fish Lake' north-east of Basra, to the Karun river, a tributary of the Shatt al-Arab. The intention was to drain the swampy land so that the Iranian army could mount a renewed infantry attack on Basra during the next dry season.

Across the border in Iran a similarly low-lying, swampy area has been granted protected status by the Iranian authorities in view of its importance as a breeding and overwintering site for large numbers of birds. The Shadegan Wildlife Refuge, comprising 296,000 ha (1140 sq. miles) of brackish sedge marshes, together with salt marshes, mud-flats and sand bars, is one of the truly wild places remaining in the Gulf. A remarkable total of 125 wildfowl species have been recorded there, either nesting or resting and feeding through the winter. Sadly the destructive tentacles of the Iran–Iraq war penetrated the deepest channels of the wetland, saturating its waters with deadly chemicals, killing untold numbers of birds and the freshwater life on which they feed.

Despite a ceasefire proposed in UN Resolution 598, passed by the Security Council in August 1987, the war dragged on, applying relentless pressure on the beleaguered waters of the Gulf. Throughout December 1987 and until February 1988 Iraqi aircraft continued to stage raids on tankers carrying Iranian oil and coastal oil installations, while Iranian speedboats carried out hit-and-run attacks on ships trading with Iraq or with its Gulf allies. Nor were civilian populations in Iran and Iraq immune from the effects of war.

Shelling and air attacks against population centres were particularly severe in January 1987, a three-week period dubbed the 'war of the cities' in which it was estimated that at least 1800 Iranians and 470 Iraqis had been killed in bombing raids and missile attacks. However, some of the worst incidents of civilian targeting occurred in Iraqi Kurdistan. Following capture of Halabja town by Kurdish freedom fighters backed by Iranian troops in an operation codenamed 'Val-fajr-10', on March 16–17, 1988 the Iraqi airforce bombed the town and nearby settlements with a lethal cocktail of chemical weapons including mustard gas and the nerve gases sarin and tabun. Approximately five thousand men, women and children, the vast majority of whom were civilians, died in the dreadful assault. This brought cries of protest from all over the world but did not elicit the international action against Iraq which Kurdish citizens demanded.

Halabja has been left ruined and deserted—an open grave. Bodies lie in the dirt streets or sprawled in rooms and courtyards of the deserted villas, preserved at the moment of death in a modern Middle East version of the disaster which struck Pompeii. (Daily Telegraph, March 22, 1988)

I propose March 18, 1988, that is the day Iraq launched its chemical attack on Halabja, be named the 'international day of campaign against chemical arms'. (Professor Businco, Italian histologist)

Halabja has been assured an eternal place in history. However, the world's mute silence vis-à-vis the inhuman crime is totally unacceptable. . . . the daylight massacre in Halabja was perpetrated without warning . . . and the Iraqi regime resorted to this 'insane crime' under the pretext that some of them (Iraqi Kurds) were cooperating with Iran. . . . no justification can be offered for such a crime. (Il Giorno, March 20, 1988)

A Resolution of the UN Security Council on May 9, 1988 vigorously condemned the con-

tinued use of chemical weapons but refrained from allotting blame for their use. Finally Tariq Aziz, Iraq's Foreign Minister, admitted during a press conference in Bonn on July 1 that Iraq had used chemical weapons but claimed they had not been the first to do so in the conflict. Several UN reports were compiled on the subject, most confirming Iraq's use of chemical weapons but failing to find any evidence that Iran had resorted to their use. A study dated August 1, carried out on behalf of the UN by two doctors who visited both countries, reiterated widespread evidence of Iraqi use of mustard gas, cyanide and phosphorus and claimed that Iran had also done so but to a much lesser extent.

The Halabja massacre did not mark the end of Iraq's use of chemical weapons against civilians. More gas attacks were reported in the Qara Dagh region between March 21 and 26 and an Iraqi spokesman warned on March 29 that Iraq reserved the right to use chemical weapons 'as a deterrent and punitive measure' against Iranian towns. Shortly before the ceasefire came into effect Iraq carried out this threat, killing or wounding 2400 people with a chemical attack on Oshnoviyeh in western Azerbaijan on August 2.

Iran's acceptance on August 20, 1988 of ceasefire terms laid down in UN Resolution 598 was accompanied by a claim that 'an international conspiracy [of] arrogance and reaction' had, 'with a flood of military, financial and political propaganda assistance', sustained the Iraqi war effort. The Iranian statement focused in particular on Iraq's 'extensive and unprecedented use of chemical weapons, which also coincided with the silence of international circles'. Iran's deep anguish at the lack of understanding it had received was further emphasized when it accused the world powers of attempting 'to put a deceptive peace-loving mask on the face of our aggressive enemy. . . . and to present as a warmonger to world opinion and even to Moslems, our innocent nation whose sole aim was the repulsion of aggression'. Believing that Saddam Hussein would now reveal his true

colours, the statement concluded that by accepting a ceasefire Iran hoped to 'remove the mask of deception from the aggressor's face and to take the initiative out of the hands of the enemies of Islam in international circles'. It was particularly hard for Ayatollah Khomeini to accept that his goal of removing Saddam Hussein was not to be achieved. On July 20 he said: 'taking this decision was more deadly than taking poison . . .'.

The final cost of the war, according to the Stockholm International Peace Research Institute, was US$112 billion to Iraq and $91.4 billion to Iran. This equated to approximately half of the total oil revenues earned by both countries up to that time. Estimates of casualties varied widely, from Iran's claim to have lost 123,220 soldiers to Iraq's estimate that it had killed 800,000. The truth probably lay somewhere between these two figures. It was impossible to measure the impact of the war in terms of human grief and suffering or to accurately assess the damage caused to wildlife and the natural environment. Everyone hoped that these terrible events could be put behind them and that the Gulf region could look forward to a long period of peace. But negotiations for a permanent peace settlement became bogged down and, despite the continuing ceasefire, a final settlement was not agreed until Iraq was involved in a new conflict. Two weeks after Iraq's invasion of Kuwait, Saddam Hussein finally announced on August 15, 1990 that he was prepared to accept Iranian terms for peace between Iran and Iraq. Having relinquished his demands over the Iranian section of the Shatt al-Arab, Saddam's eyes were focused on a much richer prize. Among the lessons Saddam learnt during the Iran–Iraq war was the tremendous pressure which could be applied by using oil as a weapon, for it could cause economic and environmental damage potentially more effective in achieving political objectives than conventional weapons. He wasted little time in adopting similar strategies following his invasion of Kuwait.

SEVEN

INVASION OF KUWAIT

TRUTH is not a major ingredient of Iraqi propaganda. If we are to believe its accounts of events surrounding the invasion of Kuwait, we would have to accept that large numbers of Kuwaiti 'revolutionaries' begged Iraq to enter Kuwait in order that the downtrodden citizens could be relieved of their great burden. Following Iraq's lightning strike, commencing at 2.00 a.m. (local time) on August 2, 1990, in which its troops gained military control of their small neighbour, the pro-Iraqi 'Provisional Free Kuwaiti Government' broadcast warnings against 'foreign intervention' in Iraq or Kuwait; and announced that the Revolutionary Command Council of Iraq would 'turn Kuwait into a graveyard' if any country was 'moved by the lust of invasion'! Two days after Iraq's invasion the newly imposed puppet government in Kuwait was revealed to comprise all Iraqi citizens, headed by Saddam Hussein's son-in-law. To the great credit of the legitimate opposition in Kuwait, not one of its members agreed to participate in this charade, despite being imprisoned and tortured by the Iraqi security forces.

Deception and dishonesty were nothing new to this Iraqi regime. Saddam Hussein had promised President Mubarak of Egypt in late July that Iraqi forces would not enter Kuwait. Now his troops occupied the entire country. His propaganda announcements continued to contradict what was actually happening in occupied Kuwait. Many of his own soldiers appear to have been deceived into

Sabotaged installations at Burghan oilfield

believing that they were invading Israel rather than Kuwait. On August 5 Saddam announced that his forces were commencing their withdrawal, having fulfilled their function of establishing an Iraqi-controlled government. International opinion was not quite as gullible as Saddam had been led to believe. On August 6 the UN Security Council passed Resolution 661, which roundly condemned Iraq for its unjustifiable aggression, called for its immediate withdrawal and imposed stiff economic sanctions against the aggressor.

Having failed in its blatant attempt to establish a puppet regime in Kuwait, Iraq displayed its true intentions with less concern for world opinion a few days later when it formally annexed the country, describing it as Iraq's nineteenth governorate. The mounting sense of revulsion at Iraq's actions led to the formation of a unique coalition of countries determined to oppose this flagrant aggression and to defend other Arabian countries under threat from the formidable Iraqi war machine. The story of how that coalition successfully held together and eventually ousted the Iraqis from Kuwait is already well known and is the subject of a number of books about the war. The present book focuses on a different aspect of this tragic conflict.

In this chapter we shall be looking more closely, not at the political manoeuvres, international implications or military operations of this latest Gulf War, but at the damage caused by Iraq's invasion of Kuwait. It is a story about human victims and defenceless wildlife. Our own species is unique in its deep concern to protect human life; in being the only creature on earth to display the behavioural trait of cruelty; and in its power to cause mass destruction of all forms of life. Nowhere have these opposing facets of our character been more vividly demonstrated than in beleaguered Kuwait under Iraq's vicious and merciless occupation. The pain, injury and horrifying torture inflicted on Kuwaiti civilians were such that many victims prayed for release in death.

Others will write at greater length of the suffering and bravery of Kuwait's people. Our story is primarily concerned with non-human victims of the Gulf War but there is little doubt that the species which suffered most was humankind. The full extent of that suffering will probably never be fully appreciated. War is always ugly but this conflict contained some of the worst acts of depravity on record. It is impossible for us to discuss the war's effect on our natural world without emphasizing this human aspect of the story.

First of all there was plunder and pillage. Having urged foreign governments to resist the temptation of lust or greed, the Iraqi government looted Kuwait on a scale which left most observers speechless. Among the first targets were the gold market, the Islamic Art Museum, banks and expensive showrooms for cars, electrical goods and furniture. Within days of the invasion Iraq was reported to have transferred between three and five billion dollars in gold, foreign currencies, art treasures and goods from Kuwait to Baghdad, significantly improving Iraq's financial reserves, estimated to have stood at six and a half billion dollars before the invasion. Such looting was carried out under official Iraqi government control and in the early days the Iraqi army tried to prohibit private looters: one Iraqi army officer was executed and hung up above his stolen goods in the centre of Kuwait City. But the discipline of trained Iraqi military personnel deteriorated under the influence of the raggle-taggle 'Popular Army' of volunteer recruits who descended on the city soon after the invasion. Over the following weeks and months virtually everything which was transportable and saleable was uprooted from Kuwait and sent to Iraq. Kuwaitis and expatriates, cut off from their bank accounts and in need of money to buy food, sold anything they possessed at a fraction of its true value to unscrupulous Iraqi dealers. Even the street lights were despatched to Iraq. Almost every shop and warehouse in the entire city was looted.

Crack Republican Guard troops leading the invasion were accompanied by well-briefed intelligence officers of the *mukhabarat* whose initial attentions were directed against members of the Iraqi opposition living in exile under Kuwaiti protection. Knowing precisely where to find these people, the greatly feared *mukhabarat* went straight to their houses in Bnaid al-Gar district. Heading their lists were communists and Shia opposition figures. Most reports of what was happening inside Kuwait during August and September emanated from Kuwaiti sources who were simply not believed by the international press. During the early days of the war, while we were trying to ascertain the fate of animals in Kuwait Zoo, we gleaned information from several Kuwaitis who had escaped from the country. Basing our report on their eyewitness accounts, we contacted most of the major national newspapers in the UK. One of their first questions was: 'What is your source?' When we replied that the information came from Kuwaitis who had managed to escape to Saudi Arabia, we were informed that they were not accepting such sources as reliable.

Widespread mistrust of information from Kuwaiti sources played directly into the Iraqis' hands, for they were able to arrest, terrorize, torture and abuse Kuwaitis with hardly a murmur of response from the world's press. In many cases these events took place under such secrecy that even the victims' own families were not aware of their fate. In other cases, however, Iraqi security forces resorted to measures they had already employed with Iraq: torturing detainees and finally returning them to their own doorstep, where they were either dumped as a corpse or were shot dead in front of the rest of the family. Within days of the invasion Kuwaitis had many heartbreaking stories to tell but the media tended to steer clear of such accounts, believing that they were most likely fabricated by people desperate to gain support from the international community for the ousting of Iraqi forces. Perhaps some reports were exaggerated or even untrue, but one of the aspects of liberated Kuwait which most shocked hardened war reporters was the extent of torture and murder inflicted by Iraqis on Kuwaiti civilians.

In the final stages of the build-up to a full-scale war, pressure was brought at the United Nations

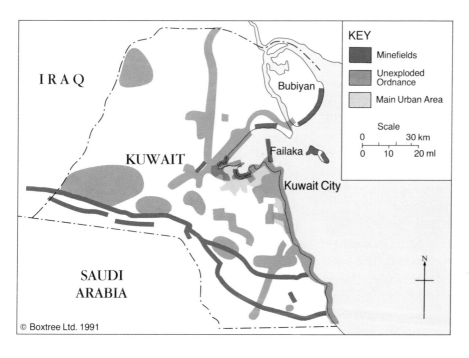

Mines and unexploded ordnance spread over a wide area still pose a serious threat to the people and animals of Kuwait.

for international condemnation of serious human rights violations by Iraq, including torture, detentions, summary executions and disappearances. Amnesty International published a report on December 19, 1990, the same day as the UN General Assembly meeting, confirming that thousands of Kuwaitis had been tortured, raped and killed since the invasion on August 2. Basing its analysis on carefully researched information, Amnesty highlighted thirty-eight cases of torture by Iraqis. But the Iraqi clamp-down in Kuwait, including terrorization of the entire population, made it extremely difficult to collect accurate information. Whereas Kuwaiti sources claimed, on December 17, that seven thousand Kuwaitis had been killed and twenty-five thousand arrested, the human rights group Middle East Watch estimated much lower figures of around a thousand killed and five thousand arrested up to that time.

A report issued by the US army on February 26, 1991 claimed that up to a quarter of the population of occupied Kuwait might have died, been injured or suffered from cholera or dysentery. It also cautioned that outbreaks of plague could recur as a result of an exploding population of rats which were feeding on rubbish which had not been removed since the invasion. Kuwaiti estimates of the number of their citizens killed by Iraqi forces were supported in a report dated February 7, issued in the USA and Denmark by Physicians for Human Rights. It stated that at least seven thousand people had died and seventeen thousand had been imprisoned and tortured in camps in Iraq and Kuwait. The report also chronicled three cases of premature babies dying after being removed from incubators.

Set against this terrible indictment of inhumanity, concern for wildlife and the environment may appear somewhat exaggerated. The war's assault on nature was, however, so massive that its implications affect us all. Unless we recognize that our own, and our children's, existence on planet Earth is directly dependent on our care and management of the biosphere, we shall suffer the consequences of our environmental abuse on a much greater scale even than that of the human death toll triggered by Iraq's invasion of Kuwait. Rare or endangered animals and plants are not simply important in their own right, but their well-being serves as a barometer for gauging the pressure we impose on our environment. The war not only demonstrated the severity of our behaviour to one another, but also our ability to destroy the world in which we live. Long after the liberation of Kuwait by the allied forces, the entire region, and land far beyond the Gulf, is suffering the consequences of this massive violation of nature.

Iraq's attacks on wildlife and the environment began soon after its forces entered Kuwait. Animals at Kuwait Zoo were among the first to suffer since most of the keepers fled and the Iraqi soldiers who used the zoo as a billet made no provision for care of the animals. Within days reports were received of large animals staggering under intense mid-summer heat, unable to gain access to their shaded quarters and no longer fed or watered. Some of the animals were transported in their cages to Baghdad Zoo, and others were shot, cooked and eaten, or left to suffer a lingering starvation and death.

Incredibly, some of the larger mammals, including a lion and a cheetah, were released from cages to roam freely into Kuwait City. In the early days after the invasion there were two reports of a young child being taken by a lion; a second escaped lion was shot. Unable to bear the thought of further unnecessary suffering, a young Kuwaiti told how he tried to enter the zoo to feed some of the animals with which he had built up a special relationship over many visits. Soldiers barred his attempt but he confirmed that both elephants and giraffes were being denied access to shade and were dying under the unremitting glare of the summer sun. Away from the zoo other animals were also being left to fend for themselves. Stabled horses, other domestic animals and countless

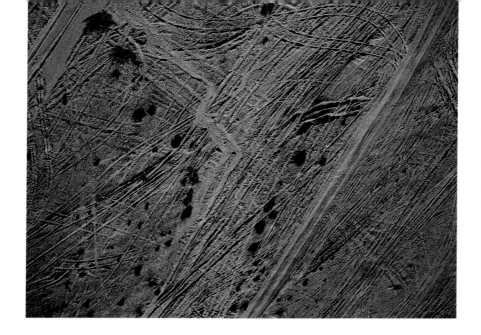

Thousands of military vehicles crossing the desert have disturbed plantlife and caused wandering dunes and more frequent sand-storms.

pets were left without food or water and died. Others were shot in front of their owners to spread fear through the local population.

The first visitors to the zoo after the liberation of Kuwait reported that two hippopotamuses were discovered lying on grass, starved almost to death, hardly breathing. Bodies of various animals lay rotting in their cages, including a leopard, baboons and a wolf. Inside the wolf compound the remains of a man's boots hinted at the nightmarish violence which had taken place here, as did the *guttra* head-dress lying on the floor of a tiger's cage. One giraffe was still on its feet, while three brown bears were showing signs of wilting.

John Walsh, Assistant Director-General of the World Society for the Protection of Animals (WSPA), was among the first Westerners to arrive at the zoo. He described how three zoo employees had remained to try to keep the animals alive but had been hampered by lack of food and by the Iraqi military hindering their efforts.

Conditions at the zoo were deplorable and the cages contained dead animals that I learned were shot by the soldiers during the early days of the occupation. Some animals were killed immediately, others were merely wounded and have not been treated. The elephant has a large swelling on the right shoulder where a bullet entered. The zoo workers explained that the animal is *'very tired' and I noticed that after we gave it water and hay, it immediately lay down amongst the filth, foul-smelling debris and mud in its pen. One of the bears has a leg wound and is in obvious pain. It prefers to remain lying down, making the most mournful sounds. Its cage is fouled with rotting bones, mud and filth. One rhesus monkey was reportedly shot by a three-star Iraqi general. It hangs its broken rear leg.* (John Walsh, WSPA)

Zoo workers reported to Walsh that military personnel taking animals to Baghdad Zoo had no idea what each animal was so they also took signs which were on the enclosures. The animals were transported by road in large trucks. Animals that they were unable to entice into transport boxes were shot, including a black leopard. Shocked by what he found at the zoo, John Walsh commented: 'It was evident in all the cages that the Iraqis had tormented the animals by throwing all sorts of objects at them. I emphasize that rotted corpses remain in all the cages, with some on various parts of the grounds, where it is evident that the dead bodies had been set on fire.'

A few animals, despite terrible suffering, did survive the ordeal and were nursed back to health after Kuwait was liberated. From the host of species originally housed at the zoo the list of survivors was depressingly brief. It included three 'Syrian' bears, five African lions, one camel, one giraffe, one Indian elephant, seven rhesus monkeys, two water buffalo, two hippos and a small number of wolves. Among the animals reportedly eaten by Iraqi soldiers were an eland, a llama, a nilgai and numerous waterfowl. They killed but did not eat a second eland, twenty-six 'wild pigs', three wolves, a lion, a black leopard, a nilgai and a donkey. The inventory of animals which disappeared in trucks reportedly destined for Baghdad Zoo, included two tigers, two camels, twelve parrots, five horses, seven kangaroos, five gazelle, seven peacocks, one donkey, two fallow deer, two gibbons, two nyala, five exotic sheep and a number of apes and monkeys.

Food and water continued to be scarce or simply unavailable for weeks after the liberation of Kuwait, making care and treatment of livestock extremely difficult. Walsh described horses with their tongues hanging out and he complained of a lack of Kuwaiti government cooperation in alleviating the situation. Gradually, however, things did improve and the chaos was cleared up.

Among Iraq's pillaging of Kuwait's assets, the destruction of the Kuwait Institute for Scientific Research (KISR) is particularly sad. Here was a centre of excellence where research was carried out in many different fields, from the medicinal properties of desert plants to the breeding of groupers and prawns in order to improve wild stocks or to establish mariculture programmes. The centre contained the results of thirty years of scientific research in Kuwait. Almost all of its records and experiments were destroyed by the invaders. Dr Saeed Akashah compared the senseless attack on the KISR's records to the burning of the library of Alexandria. He described how its buildings, which housed over a thousand scientists and as many supporting staff before the August invasion, had been reduced to shells. 'You cannot find even a pen or a pencil in the entire place,' he commented. The director of KISR's techno-economic department also mourned the loss, saying that while buildings could be repaired the scientific data might not be recoverable. 'The real

heartbreak is that data collected over thirty years has just been erased from human knowledge,' he said. One such project involved the improvement of Arab sheep by cross-breeding with European breeds. The Iraqis burned the files and consumed the products of eight generations of selective breeding.

Sanctions against Iraq having been deemed to be ineffective, the allies were eventually left with little choice but to mount a military operation to free Kuwait. Numerous mediation attempts were made but Saddam Hussein remained determined to hold on to Kuwait. One of the last attempts at persuading Iraq to withdraw before the commencement of Desert Storm was undertaken by the Secretary-General of the United Nations. Pérez de Cuellar's mission proved unsuccessful and was followed by an eleventh-hour, but equally unsuccessful, French initiative. Finally Pérez de Cuellar pleaded for common sense to prevail:

As . . . the world stands poised between peace and war, I most sincerely appeal to President Saddam Hussein to turn the course of events away from catastrophe and towards a new era of justice and harmony. . . . If this commitment is made, and clear and substantial steps taken to implement {the UN} resolutions, a just peace, with all of its benefits, will follow.

But it was not to be. Saddam Hussein had made up his mind that he would force his troops into 'the mother of all battles' against the allies.

With the passing of the January 15 deadline for Iraq's withdrawal from Kuwait, the die was cast. Shortly before midnight GMT on January 16, the air-war phase of Operation Desert Storm began. For the next five and a half weeks military targets in Iraq and Kuwait were bombarded relentlessly by the allied forces, who quickly gained complete air supremacy. As soon as Saddam Hussein realized that his airforce was unable to play any role in the campaign, he probably knew that victory had eluded him. Within days he set in motion plans to fulfil his promise to inflict such damage on Kuwait and its Gulf allies that they would suffer the consequences of the war whether he won or lost. The weapon he chose was oil.

Even before the start of Desert Storm it was known that Iraq had attached demolition charges to many of Kuwait's oil wells. Fears of what would happen if the charges were detonated were highlighted by King Hussein of Jordan at the World Climate Conference in Geneva in November 1990. King Hussein, who opposed the ground war to liberate Kuwait, warned that fires from burning oil wells could trigger a global ecological catastrophe ranging from a 'nuclear winter' in the tropics to super-acid rains and global warming. In early January the Green Party in the UK hosted a meeting to highlight the risks of allowing up to a hundred million barrels of oil to burn. Despite the political and media-oriented nature of this event, which received an introductory address from Abdullah Toukan, King Hussein's chief scientific adviser, a few scientists were present to place things in perspective. While they suggested that talk of a 'global catastrophe' was going a bit too far, they claimed that damage caused by the fires could be as dangerous to the human population of the region as the more direct effects of the war. The main paper of the meeting was delivered by John Cox, whose predictions proved later to be very close to the mark. He claimed that the burning wells would consume approximately three million barrels per day and that while this would have severe regional consequences it would not escalate global warming. 'In reality, the main dangers arise from the major by-products of uncontrolled combustion—carbon monoxide, sulphur dioxide, nitrogen oxides and, above all, smoke,' he stated. The meeting was also attended by Basil Butler, a managing director of BP and former chief engineer of Kuwait Petroleum Company. Butler warned the assembled press that once ignited the oil fires could take up to a year to extinguish.

Richard Turco, a prominent climatologist from the University of California at Los Angeles, was prominent among scientific spokesmen who believed that smoke from the fires could create a global climatic effect by reaching the upper atmosphere. He was reported in *New Scientist* as stating: 'Gulf oil fires burning for up to one month could release 3 million tonnes of black smoke into the upper atmosphere, shading up to 100 million square kilometres, more than a fifth of the planet's surface.' Turco agreed with other scientists who claimed that soot clouds would spread out across India and South-East Asia, but there were varying opinions as to whether the cloud would reach high enough to create the widespread climatic effects of his scenario. With prolonged burning of the oil wells, Turco was reported to have warned, a huge black cloud could build up in the upper atmosphere 25 km (16 miles) from the ground.

One effect of these dire environmental warnings was to place greater pressure on America and her allies to find a peaceful solution to the stalemate. It was just what Saddam Hussein had hoped would happen, for he had warned repeatedly that Kuwait's oilfields would be destroyed if he was forced to withdraw.

Gulf States were also afraid of the effects a war might have on marine life. Acutely aware of environmental damage during the Iran–Iraq war, they recalled the efforts made to ameliorate pollution caused by attacks on the Nowruz oilfield. How much greater would the impact be if Hussein ordered the release of oil from Kuwaiti facilities into the sea? Despite previous experience of war-generated oil pollution, very little was mentioned about this possibility in the build-up to war, primarily, one assumes, because the last thing anyone wanted to do was to put ideas in Saddam Hussein's mind. In the event, the concerted silence about the threat of oil pollution was unnecessary since the Iraqi president was fully aware of the potential oil had as an environmental weapon and he had every intention of exploiting that potential to the fullest extent.

EIGHT

THE
KILLING TIDES

FOLLOWING the start of the land war on January 16, 1991, early indications of impending environmental sabotage came from the Iranian news agency, IRNA, which reported that 'black-rain' fell for ten minutes on the province of Bushehr on Tuesday January 22. The 'black and greasy' rain emanated from burning oil installations in Kuwait and Iraq. But burning oil wells were about to take second billing to another environmental story: the world's largest oil-slick. At the same time that the first oil wells were set on fire, creating a thick pall of black smoke apparently aimed at creating difficulties for allied aerial bombardment, millions of gallons of crude oil gushed into the sea at Mina al-Ahmadi. For almost three days the oil spread silently across the Gulf's surface, partially obscured by smoke, unnoticed and unreported. By the time it was detected the slick was already 10 miles (16 km) long.

On Friday January 25 President George Bush formally accused Iraq of deliberately causing an environmental catastrophe by pumping millions of gallons of crude oil into the Gulf. White House spokesman Marlin Fitzwater added that this could be 'something that far exceeds any kind of tanker spill we have ever witnessed'. The basis for his concern lay in the belief that the slick was being continually enlarged from oil-storage tanks fed by oil wells; thus the flow could be maintained virtually indefinitely. Conjecture as to why Saddam Hussein might have authorized this measure included suggestions

Oil drenched sand up to a depth of 1 foot (30 cm)

that he wished to impede the amphibious landing anticipated by his military commanders, or that he intended to cause maximum damage to Saudi Arabian and other Gulf countries' desalination plants and sea-water-cooling intakes. Military sources denied that he would succeed in either aim but confirmed that the damage to the Gulf's marine life would be unprecedented. In reply to suggestions that the Iraqis intended to 'gum up the beaches and the landing areas to the point where we'd have trouble getting an amphibious landing craft in', the military claimed that they could easily 'plan around' such obstacles. To underline the futility of Saddam's attack on the environment President Bush stated: '. . . there is no military advantage to him in this, none at all'.

With the new Gulf slick already several times the size of the *Exxon Valdez* spill which devastated coastal marine life off Alaska, emergency measures to stem the flow were discussed. Environmentalists were quick to point out that this was a unique case of oil pollution, unlike anything the world had previously faced since it was apparently deliberate, malicious and raised serious problems for remedial action. On Sunday January 27, front pages of newspapers around the world carried pictures of cormorants dying in the thick, black oil sludge coating Saudi Arabian shores, south of Al-Khafji. News broadcasts showed graphic film of birds struggling from the sea only to die of heat loss, starvation and dehydration on tarred beaches. Amid a partial news blackout regarding military progress of the war itself, a posse of reporters grasped the story for its epic symbolism. Here were the innocent victims of war; here were the doomsday environmental consequences of which the world had been forewarned; here was death without reporting restrictions.

Notwithstanding the genuine problem presented by the growing oil-slick, the allies turned disadvantage to advantage. While it is highly unlikely that any of them ever wanted such an environmental catastrophe to occur, military public-relations personnel saw in it a useful vehi-

cle for pressing home several messages. First of all President Bush wasted no time in stressing that this evil act of aggression against nature followed Iraqi torture, oppression and the killing of Kuwaiti citizens. The message hit home exactly where he needed it most, among the environmentalist anti-war lobby, both in the United States and across the world. Many opponents of the war had been willing to overlook reports of the Iraqi regime's vicious treatment of Kuwaitis, and support long-term sanctions, believing that greater evil lay in the waging of war. It is ironic that their hearts were finally stirred by television images of the loss of innocent lives, albeit those of birds rather than people.

The second advantage which the allies gained from the oil-slick was that it helped to create a media diversion while they continued to press home attacks on Iraqi positions. Given that the Iraqi military were tuned in to Western radio and CNN (Cable News Network) television broadcasts which provided a major source of strategic information, the more the allies could engage the press corps's attention with non-military events, the freer it would leave them. Thirdly, the impressive and precise coalition airstrike mounted to close off the flow of oil from Al-Ahmadi by destroying the export crude live manifolds provided an opportunity to publicize, both to the allies and the Iraqis, the incredibly accurate nature of American bombing techniques, creating fear among the Iraqis and admiration among the allies. Fourthly, it provided an opportunity for military spokesmen to discuss the mechanics of mounting an amphibious assault on Kuwait in the light of the spillage. This helped to fuel the impression that the main push to enter Kuwait would come from the sea whereas that, apparently, had never been the intention.

On the assumption that the slick was deliberately caused by the Iraqis, working under orders from Saddam Hussein, three main reasons were proposed as to why he had done this: (1) to prevent or hinder an amphibious assault on Kuwait or

Toxins from oil enter the food chain in a variety of ways. These oil splattered crabs are feeding on fish killed by the oil slick in Kuwait's Sulaibikhat Bay; April 1991.

southern Iraq; (2) to cause damage to Saudi Arabian coastal facilities; and (3) to 'trick' the allies into launching a full-scale ground offensive before they were fully prepared. Despite allied claims that Saddam would gain no strategic advantage from the oil-slick, many experts disagreed. Experience of other heavy oil spillages had shown that water-cooled engines in shallow-draught assault vessels could be incapacitated. It was stressed that although the allies' inventory included hovercraft, they depended to a significant degree on large numbers of more traditional landing-craft for moving heavy equipment. The oil-contaminated waters would also render underwater operations more hazardous. Divers involved in underwater mine clearance could suffer blocked demand valves and their inflatable boats' outboard engines could seize up.

President Bush continued to reiterate his condemnation of the Iraqi actions: 'It's not going to help him at all. Absolutely not. He is clearly outraging the world,' he commented. A Canadian naval spokesman re-emphasized the scale of the problem: 'It's not just another oil-slick. It's in the middle of a bloody war zone. It's atrocious, it's outrageous. If it's intentional, it's unforgivable.'

The first televised slick shown strangling the Saudi shoreline, killing cormorants and grebes, was not, however, the same slick which President Bush and the military were commenting on. This smaller one had already started coating the Saudi shoreline before the deliberate spillage from the Al-Ahmadi terminal. It clung to the shore and was in fact flowing not from facilities in Kuwait, but from oil-storage tanks at Al-Khafji in Saudi Arabia which had been severely damaged by Iraqi artillery fire several days earlier. Already confusion was growing about the amount of oil leaked, where it was coming from, and which side had caused each new flow.

The US delegation attending the OECD Meeting of Environmental Ministers in Paris were issued with the following brief in a situation report dated January 29:

Iraq caused the Mina al-Ahmadi oil slick, which now contains from 8–10 million barrels of crude oil, by releasing oil from two sources. The first source was the 5 ships still located at the piers of the terminal. As General Schwarzkopf said, those ships had been low in the water, apparently fully loaded. They are now riding very high, an indication that their cargo, 4 million barrels of crude oil, has been emptied. The second source of the slick was the oil released from the tank farms on the mainland; this added another 4–5 million barrels of crude to the slick. The valves controlling the flow of oil are in Iraqi hands.

This slick has nothing to do with US military activities. There have been none in the area. In fact, the existence of the growing slick was not known to us until January 24th, probably 4 days after the valves had been opened by the Iraqis. We notified the Saudi Government as soon as we discovered what the Iraqis had done and immediately began consulting with experts from Saudi Arabia about how to handle this environmental disaster.

Extent: The slick flowing from the Mina Al-Ahmadi fields is actually a group of oil slicks. It is currently 10–15 kilometers {6–9 miles} offshore and spreading south to the 28th parallel. On January 27th it was 10 miles {16 km} wide and 35 miles {56 km} long. It has not yet touched the shoreline.

There is another slick which has touched the shore

and is responsible for killing birds and animals. This is the slick seen on television. It is much smaller and was created in the first two days of the war as a result of Iraqi shelling that hit the Khafji refinery in Kuwait. The Khafji refinery is in the same area as a desalination plant and a power plant.

Apart from the obvious geographical error of misplacing Al-Khafji in Kuwait rather than Saudi Arabia, the official briefing document fairly represented the official US Government version of the oil-pollution story, intended for public consumption. The categorical denial of any allied responsibility called for a certain degree of caution, bearing in mind the high security surrounding military operations and subsequent reports concerning allied bombing in the vicinity of the oil terminal. However, it was hardly the time to debate the question of responsibility since massive quantities of oil were pouring into the sea and clearly something needed to be done to staunch

Far left Rising oil lakes often flooded roads betwen oil wells. Oil splashing against car exhausts can cause the oil to ignite, making access hazardous.

Left Michael McKinnon spent five weeks filming the fires.

Below Meanwhile Peter Vine explored beneath the oil slick.

the flow and minimize the environmental impact. It was not long before the leading edge of the Al-Ahmadi slick merged with the rear edge of the one originating at Al-Khafji and from then on the two slicks were widely considered as one, although they had already begun to separate into many fragmented patches of drifting oil.

The operation to stem the flow of oil from Al-Ahmadi was conducted with impressive military precision but behind the scenes this military activity had not been without confusion or traumas. General Schwarzkopf revealed details to the press corps in Riyadh at his regular briefing session on Sunday January 27. Using sketches from aerial photographs he outlined the situation prior to their attack. One picture, depicting events on the afternoon of Thursday January 25, showed a large oil-slick being fed from an 'oiling buoy' east of the Sea Island terminal. The conclusion was that Iraqi forces had opened control taps, feeding oil from storage tanks directly into the sea. Schwarzkopf added: 'The best thing we could do right away would be to set the source of this oil spill on fire'. According to the General, luck then took a part since allied forces detected a small Iraqi vessel next to the Sea Island platform and opened fire, sinking the ship. The attack also ignited floating oil and set the platform ablaze. Throughout the following day flames from the burning platform were visible from many miles away. Aerial reconnaissance revealed that the oil had ceased to pour from the Sea Island platform. At 10.30 p.m. on Saturday January 26, F-111 fighter-bombers fired GBU-15 laser-guided bombs at two computerized failsafe manifold systems which, once hit, would close off the flow of oil into the sea. At the briefing on the following day General Schwarzkopf showed video film taken from the nose cones of the missiles as they sped towards the manifolds, to score direct hits. The strike was made 21 km (13 miles) from where the pipes connected to the Sea Island loading terminal and terminal facilities, the reported intention being to isolate the two large land-based tank-farms from the marine loading terminal. General Schwarzkopf stated that he was cautiously optimistic concerning their success.

Others took a more sanguine view. Derek Brown, technical advisor to the Gulf Area Companies Mutual Aid Organization, was reported to have commented: 'As an oil industry man, I don't see how it could have stopped the spill, because the tank-farm runs by gravity to the sea, and you can't stop gravity. You could have damaged some pipes and slowed the flow, but you can't stop it until the tanks are empty.' Others expressed the view that damage to these supply pipes would allow oil from the tank-farm to continue leaking but that most, if not all of it, would soak into the sand rather than flow down to the coast. Whichever view was correct, the flow of oil into the Gulf from the Al-Ahmadi Sea Island loading platform was reported to have slowed down shortly after the US raid. It may be that this simply coincided with the emptying of oil-tankers moored at the loading jetty, since we were to discover later that the main slick probably originated not from the tank-farms at Al-Ahmadi but from oil contained in these ships. Saddam Hussein claimed that the slicks were caused by American bombers which attacked oil-tankers at the terminal. General Schwarzkopf categorically denied that allied military operations had contributed to the slick, reiterating the claim that five tankers had dumped their cargoes into the sea.

After the war, a MEPA spokesman, speaking on March 28, was reported to have claimed that the Saudi authorities had received new evidence to indicate that most of the oil in the main slick came from five Iraqi tankers which were moored at Mina al-Ahmadi, each of which had a capacity of around one million barrels of crude oil. The tankers were deliberately pumped dry, the speaker claimed, adding, 'This is where most of the oil came from.' He said also that these were not the only tankers at the terminal: 'There were another four tankers at the terminal which were hit by allied bombing but in most cases this was precision bombing into the engine room which did not result in a large spill.' An eyewitness report which only became available in April claimed that the Iraqis had fitted special pipework to at least two oil-tankers at the pier, enabling them to discharge their tanks into the sea.

Whether oil came from storage tanks ashore or from tankers at the jetty, or both, there was no denying the enormous size of the spreading slick. The allies blamed Iraq; Iraq blamed the allies. Given Saddam Hussein's record, few citizens of the allied countries had any doubts about which account to believe. The spillage invoked several pithy descriptions of Saddam Hussein, including one by Prince Abdul Aziz bin Salman of the Saudi Ministry of Petroleum, who described him as 'the lord of death or the lord of disasters . . . and definitely the father of destruction'.

Setting aside the question of which side's military actions caused the Al-Ahmadi spill, there is no doubt that the oil-slick made its presence felt to the allied forces. One military operation which did not reach the press briefing rooms involved a top-secret underwater mission by British mini-submarines operating along the Kuwaiti coastline. Information on these operations is still classified and it is very difficult to obtain confirmation of the details, but several stories were circulating in the Gulf during the war.

Unlike aircraft whose positions were constantly monitored by a sophisticated air-control system, and ships which were tracked on radar, the six-man mini-submarines were much more difficult to monitor. The US air attack on the small Iraqi vessel close to the Sea Island loading platform, which sank the vessel and in the process set fire to the terminal, may have been something of an own goal. Reports circulating at the time claimed that the Iraqi vessel had been directly above one of the

A lucky survivor of the heavy mortalities suffered by fledgling Socotra cormorants.

secret underwater vehicles and that it sank on to the allied mini-sub. It was also claimed that twenty-two men from Britain's Special Boat Squadron, who landed at the terminal, were unable to return to their submarine because of a localized fresh slick caused by the US bombing raid which took place while they were in the vicinity. The oil was so thick that as the men tried to swim it proved impossible to keep their heads above the oil. The incident is said to have resulted in a heated exchange among the allies over the lack of coordination.

But the military consequences of oil pollution were to take a more unexpected turn. As part of the great focus of media attention on the Gulf's giant oil-slick a number of journalists and television teams descended on the almost deserted town of Al-Khafji on the Saudi Arabian side of the border with Kuwait. There they enjoyed free accommodation at the abandoned Beach Hotel from where they filed stories about the oil-slick and life close to the front line. Despite their proximity to the war zone it seemed to be a safe enough place and one of their main concerns was how to filter black soot, emanating from burning oil facilities in Kuwait, from rainwater collected for washing. The beach was thick with oil and dying birds were sufficiently plentiful to keep cameramen engaged. Virtually all the military action was taking place in the skies over Iraq and occupied Kuwait—out of sight of an increasingly frustrated press corps.

Several camera crews, after visiting the Al-Khafji coastline to report on the oil-slick, turned their attention to the abandoned town, filming deserted streets remarkable for a general absence of military personnel. Television news teams who had come to Al-Khafji for the oil story often included these images of the town as establisher shots for environmental reports. The information they provided is believed to have persuaded the Iraqi command structure that they could capture Al-Khafji without much opposition. On January 29, Iraqi tanks approached the town with gun barrels turned away, in classic surrender posture, but then swivelled them to aim at allied positions in the lightly defended town.

The operation formed part of a two-pronged attack by Iraqi forces into Saudi territory and was repulsed by allied forces, principally Saudi units. Despite the fact that the Iraqis were defeated, it proved a propaganda victory for Saddam Hussein and an embarrassment for the allies, whose losses were reported to be twelve US marines and nineteen Saudi troops. The Beach Hotel, which had been forcibly vacated by the press corps the previous week, was for a few days occupied by Iraqi soldiers. At one point, when a military spokesman was unable to confirm to the press corps that

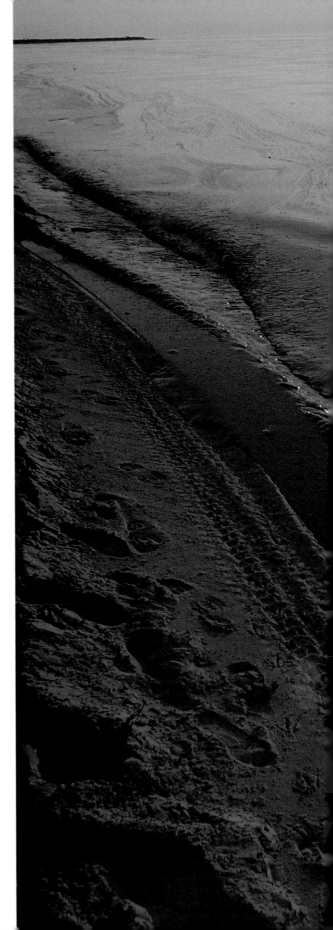

Al-Khafji had fallen, albeit temporarily, an Egyptian reporter picked up the telephone and dialled the Beach Hotel. He was answered by an Iraqi who informed him: 'We are with Saddam. See you in Jerusalem.' Removing the Iraqi forces from Al-Khafji was a difficult enough task carried out by Saudi forces with back-up from the allies. The intense land battle provided the press with a new story, more in keeping with our general perception of war than images of oil-slicks and dying cormorants.

Meanwhile the Gulf's waters were being afflicted by a new oil spill, adding to the already massive pollution from Al-Khafji and Al-Ahmadi. This new source began flowing from Iraq's main offshore oil-loading terminal at Mina Al-Bakr on Tuesday January 29. Once again the Iraqis were accused of deliberately pumping oil from the offshore terminal into the sea to create heavy oil-slicks, presumably to hinder an amphibious assault. Equally predictably, but possibly with somewhat more justification, the Iraqis blamed the slick on allied military action. The new slick streamed out around Bubiyan island and drifted towards Failaka island and across Kuwait Bay. Whether the slick was the result of Iraqi sabotage or of an allied air raid which targeted Al-Bakr remains unclear, but there was no denying the existence of the new source of oil pollution. Reports at the time spoke of the American bombing raid being made in an effort to stem the Iraqi-caused oil leak. Others conjectured that the raid may have caused the leak and a certain amount of disinformation followed.

By now it was clear that a considerable quantity of crude oil was floating in the northern Gulf, already killing marine life off Kuwait, Iraq and northern Saudi Arabia, and gradually drifting southwards, threatening coastal waters and shores

Oil slick sunset: a paradox of the images created by both the slick and fires was that they were often visually stunning, yet, when viewed at close quarters, were so devastating to the natural world.

of Saudi Arabia, Bahrain, Qatar, the UAE, Oman and Iran. Nobody was disputing that it was a big slick but the question was, just how big? Were the Americans exaggerating the size of the spill or were authorities in the Gulf States purposely playing down the extent? How much oil was really out there?

Estimates of the quantity of oil spilled into the Gulf continued to swing up and down during the spring and summer of 1991. While the earliest reports of ten or eleven million barrels were widely discounted, there remained considerable discrepancies between the various estimates, as shown by table 9.

Given the circumstances it is hardly surprising that considerable confusion arose over the extent of the pollution unleashed on the northern Gulf and surrounding countries. But this is one instance where the world press cannot be blamed for producing conflicting reports on the size of the oil spill or its latest position. Part of the problem lay with the difficulties encountered in identifying thin sheens of floating oil in a military zone unsafe for research vessels or surveillance aircraft. While satellites were of considerable use in tracking smoke from burning oil wells and storage tanks, there were major hitches with interpretation of satellite images of the sea's surface, apparently leading in some cases to extensive sea-grass or algal beds in shallow water being tagged as dark oil-slicks. Changes in sea conditions, and in water clarity, resulted in these phantom slicks appearing one day and disappearing the next. This did not help with the process of assessing the overall extent of the slick or with contingency planning by countries bearing the brunt of this marine ecological disaster.

By late March information on the slick was of a much higher calibre than it had been during the war. Daily flights over the sea with special monitoring equipment were producing regular updates on drifting sheens or thicker patches of oil and these flights were now able to enter Kuwaiti airspace without danger of attack. In addition,

intelligence reports were collected from Kuwaiti citizens and from other sources. One of these, referred to by MEPA, the Saudi Arabian environmental agency, on March 28, threw new light on the main source of oil in the slick which spread from Al-Ahmadi. Even at that late stage oil was still pouring into the sea from terminals at Mina al-Ahmadi and Mina al-Bakr and from a number of other damaged installations in northern waters. The official Saudi Press Agency quoted the MEPA report, which claimed that the slick from Mina al-Bakr was continuing to grow as more oil poured into the sea. It also confirmed that the Iraqi terminal was hit by allied bombing during the war and the resultant slick had since spread south as far as Bahrain and Qatar, where it formed a thin sheen.

Kingdom of Saudi Arabia
Ministry of Defence and Aviation
Meteorology & Environmental Protection Administration (MEPA)

Copy of report dated 26th March, 1991.

Overflight
Today's observation map is based on an overflight from a Coastguard jet equipped with SLAR. The Coast Guard SLAR flight covered the area from the coast out approximately 130 kilometers {80 miles} into the Gulf. The northern extent of the SLAR was Faylakah Island. The southern extent of the SLAR was the offshore region north of Qatar. Interference on the SLAR hindered portions of the flight, limiting the areas of observations. Navy C-12 and nearshore helicopter flights provided additional confirmation and independent details that are included in the maps.

Kuwait Waters:
Oil from the Al-Bakr Terminal and the Iraqi tanker, AMUYIYAH, grounded just to the east of the Al Bakr Terminal, was reported trailing about 60 kilometers {37 miles} to the south. A number of oil streamers and heavy sheen was seen along the Kuwait coast between the harbor and Mina Sa'ud.

TABLE 9: OFFICIAL ESTIMATES AND PRESS REPORTS ON SIZE OF GULF OIL-SLICK

Date	Source	Publication	Amount (Barrels)
January 25	Gen. Schwarzkopf	Press Briefing	11m
January 28	Pentagon Source	Press Briefing	6m
January 28	—	*Independent*	5–10m
January 29	Saudi Government	*Herald Tribune*	11m
January 30	Saudi Aramco		over 1m
February 1	—	*Guardian*	11m
February 2	Saudi Government	*New Scientist*	5–12m
February 7	Peter Aldhous	*Nature*	'probably over' 10m
February 8	Dr Abdulbar al-Gain	MEPA	7m
February 10	—	*Gulf News*	11m
February 12	—	*Gulf News*: Al-Khafji	0.5m
		Al-Ahmadi	11m
		Mina al-Bakr	undetermined
February 13	MEPA	MEPA	0.5–3.0m
February 13	Ken Wells	*Wall Street Journal*	11m
February 14	Walter Vreeland	Bahrain Meeting	7–11m
February 15	Walter Vreeland	*Gulf Daily News*	7–11m
February 19	—	*Gulf News**	
February 24	UNEP	NCWCD Newsletter	1–2m
February 27	ROPME meeting	*Guardian*	3–7m
March 1	IMO	—	1.5–2m
March 6	Saudi Aramco	*Arabian Sun*	over 1.5m
March 8	—	*Guardian*	'several millions'
March 9	—	*New Scientist*	'millions'
March 11	—	*Guardian*	3–7m
March 28	MEPA		over 4m
April 5	IMO	—	'more than 2m'
April 11	Samir Radwan	*Nature*	'about' 1.5m
June 20	UNESCO Paris	NOAA Spokesman	6–8m

* : admits confusion; queries deliberate attempt to underplay extent

Saudi Waters:
The heaviest concentrations of oil are still along the coast between Ra's al Ghar and Abu Ali island. Several sheens were reported about 80 kilometers {50 miles} east of Ra's al Khafji to Ra's al Tanajib. The largest of these sheens, reported off Ra's Saffaniya, covered an area of approximately 1,800 square kilometers {695 sq. miles}. Scattered sheens were reported between Abu Ali and Al Khubar.

Bahrain and Qatar Waters:
Oil was reported in the coastal waters off Al Khubar, between the eastern side of Bahrain and the western side of Qatar.

Two days later the MEPA 'Oil Spill Update' report stated:

Fresh oil continues to enter Saudi coastal waters from the north. . . . Most of the oil in Dawhat al-Musallamiyyah is under the surface of the water or near the coast. . . . Gurmah Island is the most affected island in the Gulf.

The U.S. Coast Guard reported that sheen has been washing up on the Bahraini coastline for five days. Small to medium size tar balls were seen mixed in with the vegetation of the western and northern shores of Bahrain.

Observers on the U.S. Coast Guard's SLAR flight reported seeing sheen and streamers of brownish-red and fresh black oil as much as one inch thick in Kuwait harbor. Oil is also coming from the northern shore of Faylaka Island and continues to flow from Al-Bakr and Sea Island terminals.

As we have seen, estimates of the total amount of oil released into the Gulf varied widely from half a million to over twelve million barrels. The public, having expressed its deep-felt horror at the death of large numbers of cormorants, breathed a collective sigh of relief when they were told that the slick might not be as large as previously estimated. Other sources cautioned

that a great deal of oil was still floating offshore and had not yet affected the coastline. Several organizations issued reports in which they estimated the quantity of oil released into the sea, but very few of them were able to support their statements with anything remotely approaching scientific evidence. Suggestions that deliberate misinformation was fed into the rumour machine during the height of the conflict cannot be discounted. And yet it was almost impossible to arrive at an accurate figure for the total amount of oil in the various slicks polluting the Gulf. Given the genuine uncertainty among technicians and scientists working with satellite and aerial images as to what did or did not constitute an oil-slick, one might forgive military and political spokesmen for contributing, quite possibly inadvertently, to the confusion.

The US Coastguard, cooperating with the Saudi authorities in their efforts to monitor and clean up the slick, were concerned primarily with oil impacting the Saudi Arabian coastline. During the course of the war it was extremely difficult to obtain information about 'other slicks' which were known to be drifting offshore. Since allied operations were mounted against coastal oil facilities and harbours in Iraq and Kuwait, as well as

Large numbers of greater and Socotra cormorants were present in the Gulf in the spring of 1991 when the first oil slick appeared and were among the first visible wildlife victims of the conflict.

The Sea Island terminal was sabotaged by the Iraqis in the first days of the air war, and quickly became the principal source of the greatest oil slick ever recorded.

against Iraqi ships, there can be little doubt that some of the oil pollution was 'collateral damage' associated with these war efforts. It was a central plank of the joint command's information control that such unfortunate and largely unavoidable side-effects of the conflict should not receive publicity which might lessen public support for Operation Desert Storm. This may partially explain why reporters were encouraged to report on the coastal slick but were not so fully informed about other slicks such as the one from Mina al-Bakr in Iraqi waters.

During early April, following several ceasefire weeks of SLAR (airborne radar) overflights, an estimate of 'at least four million barrels' was applied to the main area of oil-slicks which had been blown along the Saudi coastline. It was based on analysis of available data as well as intelligence reports of events at Al-Ahmadi. War operations damaged a considerable number of oil-storage facilities and ships, however, and there was little doubt that the final assessment of the pollution caused by the war would be much higher.

One reason for the great interest in the amount of crude oil released into the Gulf was that it had been widely described as the world's largest oil-slick. Suggestions that it might not deserve this title appear to have created disappointment in some quarters. Concern for the actual extent of damage caused to wildlife seems to have been clouded at times by the more sensational aspect of the story. As we flew over and walked the oil-soaked beaches of Saudi Arabia, watching many birds dying from the oil, we had little doubt that we were witnessing one of the world's worst cases of ecocide. Assuming the total amount of oil released into the Gulf to be 'only' four million barrels, the slick would still qualify as the worst ever, about sixteen times the size of the *Exxon Valdez* spill off Alaska in 1989 and considerably larger than the Ixtoc 1 spill of 1979, when 3.3 million barrels poured into the Gulf of Mexico.

One statistic which clearly contradicts the suggestion that the spill may have been much less than this, and possibly as 'little' as that from *Exxon Valdez*, which was reported to have released a 'mere' quarter of a million barrels, is provided by the official figures for oil recovered into Saudi Aramco facilities: already (at the time of writing) around four times the amount spilled in the Alaskan incident. By the end of April approximately a million barrels of oil had been recovered into Saudi Aramco's facilities. As the slick hit the coast it naturally accumulated in bays between Tanajib and Abu Ali where purpose-built sand bars helped to gather it in thick masses from which skimmers pulled it into pits on shore before it was pumped into trucks and carried away for processing. During March and April recovery rates were around 15–20,000 barrels per day and there was little sign of any shortage of oil to pump from the sea.

MEPA's official daily release dated April 13, almost twelve weeks after the oil-slick began to kill the Gulf's marine life, continued to report large quantities of oil and signs of a continuing impact.

A MEPA team that visited the area Friday estimated that as much as 100,000 barrels of emulsified oil (mousse) have been trapped in Dawhat al-Musharabiyyah.

A considerable amount of oil has entered Brice Bay, where recovery work continues. Light sheen and a few small brown lines were seen off the coast of Ras Tanurah. Dawhat ad-Dafi is the most oiled area in the Gulf. The northern half of the harbour above Khafji was moderately oiled. A dead dolphin was seen in a patch of oil south of Khafji; it was not known whether the animal died due to oiling.

Up to that time Saudi Aramco crews had recovered 715,045 barrels, with little sign of any reduction in daily figures.

Damage caused by the slick was ongoing and still under assessment as this book went to press. Countless birds, many turtles, sea snakes and other forms of marine life have been killed by the oil. On April 17 twenty-three dead dolphins were found in Salwah Bay. They had all died within the previous two to six weeks but the cause of their deaths could not be confirmed. By the third week of April, a total of thirty-six dolphins and three dugongs had been washed up dead on shores of Saudi Arabia and Bahrain over a six-week period. At least 460 km (290 miles) of Saudi Arabian coastline—the entire section north of Abu Ali—were severely impacted by the oil. Winds and high tides pushed oil far inshore, often 0.5–1 km (½–⅔ mile) from the normal high-tide mark and in one case as much as 5 km (3 miles) in from the coast. Natural vegetation of salt-tolerant plants on salt marshes and mangrove areas trapped huge quantities of oil.

The oil came ashore in the most critical region for these habitats, for surveys had indicated that 'approximately 90 percent of all the salt marshes and 70 percent of all the mangroves along the Saudi Gulf coast occur north of Abu Ali'. Within the 460-km (290 miles) section of oil-impacted Saudi coastline all mangrove habitats were hit by oil and less than 5 percent of salt marshes escaped the killing black tides. Scientists predicted the death of all the mangroves and the vast majority of

Migrating birds, like these black-winged stilts, suffered from the oil-drenched beaches and smoke-filled skies. Future surveys should indicate how seriously they were affected.

salt marshes north of Abu Ali and that recovery, where it does occur, will take at least ten years. Along the sandy shorelines a thick band of oil, 10–100 m (33–330 ft) in width, coated the beaches with oil, penetrating the sand to a depth of up to 30 cm (1 ft). In more exposed sections white sand was often deposited on top of oil, disguising the extent of pollution. Diving underneath the oil-slick off Ra's az Zaur in February, just before the short-lived land war began, we were impressed by the thickness of the floating oil, the fact that it totally cut out the light and that few organisms seemed to escape its poisonous sticky tentacles. It was a strange sensation, in less than 2.5 m (8 ft) of water, to find oneself swimming in pitch darkness in the middle of the day. To make matters worse the sky above was almost as black as the sea. In general, however, the impact of oil on marine life was less apparent underwater than between tide marks. Many fish died in certain localized areas such as around the heavily impacted Gurmah island, where one could pick up one to two dead fish per metre of beach. Here the impact was so severe that all types and sizes of fish were killed, from relatively deep-water bottom fish, through pelagic species, to those inhabiting the shallows.

In the aftermath of the war, as large quantities of oil continued to drift across the Gulf, and as aerial surveys enabled observers to assess the varied sources of these leakages, it became apparent that the Gulf War slick, estimated at around six million barrels, resulted from military activities by both sides, as well as sabotage by the Iraqis. Large numbers of plants and animals in the Gulf were affected by the oil, whose killing tides, despite an impressive coastal protection, oil-collection and clean-up programme, continued to smother Arabia's marine life.

There can be little doubt that the mega-slick in the Gulf is an environmental disaster of enormous proportions nor that the setting alight of most of Kuwait's oil wells is an even bigger catastrophe. In the months and years ahead we shall see just how lethal the combination of oil and smoke is for humankind and nature. Iraq's invasion of Kuwait provided an unexpected testing ground for the West's military muscle; now the area is proving equally challenging for environmental science and technology. Arabia's wildlife has already suffered from the impact of massive regional development; one cannot but hope that the great surge in public awareness of and concern for the Gulf's natural environment, stimulated by this ecological disaster, will not have come too late for the animals themselves.

NINE

FIGHTING THE FLOW

THE Gulf's waters flow in an anti-clockwise stream, entering from the Gulf of Oman and the Indian Ocean via the Strait of Hormuz, advancing in a north-westerly direction along the Iranian coast towards headwaters where the Shatt al-Arab waterway distorts the pattern, then picking up the nutrient-rich outflow and curling to the west along the shores of Kuwait and finally returning to the south-east, along the Saudi coastline, past Bahrain, skirting the tip of Qatar and being deflected by the coast of the UAE, back towards the entrance. The driving force for this circulation pattern is not wind but gradations in density of water caused by evaporation. But winds do play an important role in modifying the general drift of surface waters and it was not surprising that the Gulf States were praying for 'favourable winds' to push oil-slicks away from their shores. Currents flow with such predictability that computer models can quite accurately forecast the direction in which oil-slicks will drift in the Gulf and it was therefore clear to Saudi Arabia that both the Al-Khafji spill, and the huge quantity of oil released from Al-Ahmadi, would sooner or later coat its beaches with their killing tides. Fears of what might happen when this occurred stimulated immediate action by government and commercial enterprises whose facilities were threatened. They also triggered an impressive international response.

'Plans for protection of important facilities were prepared well in advance of the spill. These facilities are either now protected or in the

Burghan Oil-field, Kuwait, April 1991

process of being protected,' stated Dr Abdulbar Al-Gain, the head of MEPA, on January 28. In a bid to stave off fears that the oil-slick might affect the war effort or cause disruption within Saudi Arabia, Dr Al-Gain was eager to reassure the world at large that all was under control. 'There is no risk' to the main desalination plants at Al-Khafji and Al-Safaniya, he announced. Privately, however, officials were less confident that they would be able to keep all their Gulf-coast plants running. Kuwaiti officials, moved by a slightly different agenda, and anxiously observing the terrible destruction being wrought on their country, affirmed that the slick did threaten Kuwaiti desalination installations.

Apart from the inevitable impact on wildlife, the slick posed a serious hazard for vital facilities in Saudi Arabia and other Gulf States. 'Iraqi Oil Spill Could Be Potent Weapon As It Threatens Water Supplies, Refineries' shouted the headline in the *Wall Street Journal* on the same day as Dr Al-Gain offered reassurance. The article which followed put into words the worst fears of experts about the potential impact of oil pollution on the war effort and on the economies of Gulf nations. 'Even a temporary closure of two key Saudi refineries—at Jubail and Ras Tanurah along the Gulf coast—means the spill would affect the U.S. military more than officials have so far acknowledged,' claimed the newspaper's staff reporters, Barbara Rosewicz and Allanna Sullivan. Almost everyone who was interviewed at that time expected the oil to reach Jubail in a matter of days. It was already coating the shores of Safaniya to the north and urgent efforts were under way to protect vital sea-water intakes from contamination by floating crude oil. Initial worries were also greatly affected by estimates of the size of the problem faced by Saudi Arabia and her neighbours. The country's oil minister, Hisham Nazer, reported that the spill had grown to eleven million barrels, making it far bigger than anything the world had previously experienced.

From the very beginning of the crisis the government-owned company Saudi Aramco played a key role in operations to protect facilities. It was also clear that this organization was relatively well prepared for the task ahead. In a confident statement issued on January 30, Abdelaziz M. al-Hokail, a senior vice-president in the company, claimed that the oil-slick would have no effect on Saudi Arabian desalination facilities or Aramco's oil production: 'These critical facilities that use seawater for cooling purposes or as a desalination source have already been well protected and will, therefore, not be affected. As for offshore facilities, the oil will have no significant effect by its presence there.' He added, 'We feel quite confident at this time that we will be able to emerge from this incident without any effects on our oil production, processing or exporting capability. We also have confidence in our protective measures at other kinds of facilities.' But concern over the slick's impact on the environment was well founded: 'We fear the environmental effects could be serious, indeed. The Gulf is a relatively shallow body of water with limited circulation. Environmental damage, even if not catastrophic, could leave effects for years to come. Efforts to minimise this will have to be on a very large scale and probably an international undertaking.' Although they knew how to protect coastal installations, 'we need the expertise from the environmental and ecological area'. The statement went on to explain how the attack on the oil would be in three stages: firstly the emergency protection measures for critical facilities; secondly the containment of oil and its recovery into ships or trucks; thirdly the clean-up process.

'There is considerable military disinformation, not to say confusion, on all sides about the extent and source of the oil spills but it would appear that there has already been significant coastal damage,' wrote John Vidal in the *Guardian* on February 1, 1991. Given the strategic nature of the facilities at risk, the considerable problems being faced by the allies in protecting those facilities, and the possibility that some of the oil pollution had been caused by the allies' own military operations, it was not surprising that the free flow of information about the impact of the slick was halted. Some technical experts were less sure of the Arab States' abilities to avoid oil damage. Captain Don Jensen, a veteran of oil-spill clean-ups and former head of the *Exxon Valdez* clean-up operation in Alaska, who entered Saudi Arabia as director of the US team, emphasized that luck played a major part in such operations. 'Certain wind conditions could produce a very high risk that the spill will penetrate Saudi protective barriers and contaminate key water purification plants. It could affect drinking water,' he warned.

Oil refineries in eastern Saudi Arabia, Bahrain, Qatar, the UAE and Oman were working at full capacity to supply the extra fuel demand created by the war effort. With aerial sorties taking off around the clock, adequate supplies of jet fuel were absolutely essential. Much of this fuel was supplied by the Jubail and Ras Tanurah refineries, whose operations were under threat from the slick. In those early days oil company officials were indeed extremely worried that the oil would arrive before they were able to adequately protect the facilities. Some argued that such an event should have been foreseen by governments and oil companies and that the facilities should have already been fully protected. Various governments, for their part, put on a brave face and did their best to make adequate arrangements. For several days the oil advanced southwards at an alarming rate but then a fresh southerly blew up in the 'Sea of Changing Winds' and the slick slowed down. But although the extra time to prepare coastal defences was universally welcomed, it also created a new hazard, 'weathering' of the oil.

Intake valves at most of the facilities along the Saudi shoreline are situated a metre or so beneath the surface, helping to protect them from floating debris or oil. Unfortunately, however, as the oil drifted south it partially evaporated, losing its more volatile compounds and becoming thicker,

stickier and heavier. Much of the oil still floated but parts of it began to sink, forming suspended globules of oil in midwater, or tar balls drifting unseen beneath the surface. In these circumstances it is extremely difficult to protect intakes from these hidden oil particles which could upset control mechanisms.

Fears were growing that freshwater supplies could be affected by the slick. On February 2 Abdullah Dabbagh, director of research at King Fahd University of Petroleum and Minerals, was reported to have stated that he could not guarantee protection of the Al Jubail desalination plant, which supplies 80 percent of Riyadh's drinking water. He explained that oil could precipitate into the water column which feeds the plant. 'It's a very serious problem. We don't know if we will be able to handle it,' he was quoted as saying. He also commented on the difficulties they were facing through the military clamp-down on information: 'Much of the information normally available during an oil spill has been made unavailable to us, as a result of military action to defend the kingdom.' The allies were hoping that the southerly winds would continue, and they did.

As the scale of the slick was revealed, and the quantities of protection equipment required to protect their facilities were calculated, every government in the Gulf realized that they were inadequately prepared to fully protect themselves against such massive oil pollution. An international appeal for assistance was sent out. On February 3 the *Independent* reported: 'The Saudis admitted yesterday they do not have enough equipment to prevent vital water desalination plants from being polluted. . . . Shortages of water booms and oil skimmers are already crippling efforts to tackle the first slick, which is now about 100 miles [160 km] long and 40 miles [64 km] wide.' The problem was beginning to look more serious.

'The world's largest oil-slick has touched the shore at Safaniya in north-eastern Saudi Arabia and may threaten production in the world's largest offshore oilfield,' claimed the *Khaleej Times* on February 8. It quoted oil company personnel who reportedly stated: 'Aramco will not be able to process crude from the offshore field if oil entered the water-intake system at Safaniya. Fresh water is used to process the offshore oil. . . .' The potential threat to Saudi Arabia's crude-oil production, from this, the largest offshore oilfield in the world (and the fourth largest of any kind), struck a sensitive nerve among allied governments. Not only did the war effort require refined products such as jet fuel, it also needed adequate financing. Oil production and marketing were the heart of Saudi Arabia's economic strength. In addition, the international community was depending on Saudi Arabia and other friendly nations to stabilize oil supplies and prices by making good some of the shortfall which resulted from loss of Iraqi and Kuwaiti oil supplies. The last thing the allies wanted was damage to Saudi Arabia's oil-producing capabilities. The hidden agenda of this war was, after all, about oil. Now a surfeit of oil in the wrong place at the wrong time revealed the double-edged nature of oil as a weapon.

'Officials fear the slick could force the shut-down of numerous freshwater plants and oil refineries in Saudi Arabia,' reported the *Gulf Daily News* on February 9, the day after a temporary shut-down of the Safaniya plant. Despite predominantly southerly winds, a great deal of oil had drifted up along the Saudi shoreline and was already at Manifa Bay, a short distance north of Abu Ali island. Several years ago a solid causeway had been constructed, connecting the offshore island to the mainland and in the process creating a major obstacle to the longshore current. Biologists, who had been at the time somewhat critical of the coastal engineering, joined others in a collective sense of relief that the causeway and island formed a solid barrier and effective accumulation area, obstructing the slick's southerly movement and in the process helping to protect the strategically important facilities at Jubail and Ras Tanurah.

While the majority of international attention was focused on Saudi Arabia, other Gulf countries were also preparing themselves for the oil to arrive. Bahrain was particularly concerned since it had suffered severely during previous oil spills of much smaller proportions. It also found itself in a particularly vulnerable state, lacking sufficient equipment to deal with a problem on this scale. Tariq Almoayed, Bahrain's Minister of Information, gave a special press briefing on February 10 at which he expressed his government's deep concern for marine life. 'The darkness of this spill reminds people of the Dark Ages,' he said. Describing the slick as ten times the size of Bahrain, he appealed for international assistance, particularly in the form of skimmers and booms. Prompt responses followed from many countries, with large air-lifts of purchased or donated equipment being flown in to several Gulf States and numerous 'experts' arriving to assist in deployment of equipment. (See table 10.)

There are various reasons for the discrepancies between proffered assistance and that actually provided. These range from offers being made with unacceptable conditions to difficulties experienced by Gulf countries in absorbing materials and personnel from such a wide variety of sources and in assessing the future scale of the problems in the light of many conflicting reports.

By mid-February an efficient recovery programme was well under way. Moderate weather enabled Saudi Aramco to install extra booms and to gather oil at collection areas along the coast. They used skimmers and shore-based vacuum trucks to gather in the oil which was accumulating around sea-water intakes at Safaniya and Tanajib, substantially reducing the oil in these areas. In one week 30,000 barrels of oil were recovered, which seemed impressive enough at the time but was a mere drop in the ocean compared with the size of the whole slick. By this stage Saudi Aramco had seven recovery vessels and was about to receive two more. Special equipment for the recovery was flown in to Saudi Arabia on the world's largest

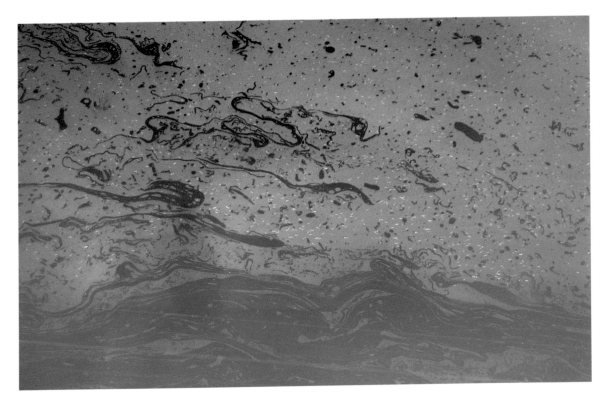

The port of Shuwaikh, Kuwait. Schools of small fish swim beneath oil spilling from sabotaged pipes within the port.

cargo aircraft, the USSR's Antonov 124.

Towards the end of February reports spoke of the situation at Safaniya and Tanajib being 'stable. . . . after a month long fight to prevent oil entering the intakes'. With recovery figures rising by the day it was becoming clear that the low estimates for the total amount of oil released into the Gulf were far too optimistic. Even the relatively small spill from Al-Khafji was being reassessed. A Saudi Aramco spokesman stated that the estimated total of 500,000 barrels for the Al-Khafji spill 'is probably on the low side'. Success with the recovery programme was leading officials to hope that the main accumulation of coastal oil could be prevented from rounding Abu Ali island by removing it from the sea before it was pushed further south. 'The hope is that the oil

now in the bays [Dawhat al-Musallamiyah and Dawhat ad-Dafi] can be swept up and kept from rounding the tip of Abu Ali and threatening ARAMCO facilities offshore of Jubail and to the south', commented the official ARAMCO newspaper, the *Arabian Sun*.

The task of protecting deep intakes from drifting oil globules floating in midwater or dragging along the seabed was tackled by the installation of 'bubble curtains', created by piping air under pressure through perforated pipes fixed along the seabed. The disturbance of the bubbles deflected oil particles away from the intakes. By the end of the month over 360 people, twenty-three vessels, twenty vacuum tankers and thirty-five skimmers were in use. A variety of booms were now deployed, ranging from sturdy offshore ones to more delicate fixtures suitable only for mooring inside protected inlet canals. Work was also continuing at both Safaniya and Tanajib on building sand berms to run the length of sea-wall intakes. The idea was that if oil did penetrate coastal defences

TABLE 10: INTERNATIONAL MARITIME ORGANIZATION CO-ORDINATION CENTRE: LIST OF GOVERNMENT EQUIPMENT OFFERED AND PROVIDED

Country	Offered	Provided
AUSTRALIA	600m coastal containment boom, 2 skimmers and 3 beach cleaning units and 2 troilboom giant model booms.	2 skimmers.
BELGIUM	6 vehicles and 5 lorries equipped with total 2,582m of harbour boom, 2 skimmers, 2 vacuum trucks, shore cleaning equipment.	
CANADA	20,000m coastal/harbour containment boom. 10 skimmers.	6,000m harbour boom, 5 skimmers, 2 mobile bird cleaning trailers to Bahrain.
DENMARK	2,000m open ocean and 1,800m coastal containments booms, 2 skimmers, 5 oil trawl units, 3 floating collection containers (100cu. m each), absorption material.	
FINLAND	600m open sea containment boom.	
GERMANY	Multi-purpose vessels with oil recovery systems; 400m open ocean, 1,000m coastal and 800m harbour booms, 5 skimmers and specialised shoreline clean-up equipment, 5 floating collection containers.	1,296m coastal and 1,800m harbour containment booms, 4 skimmers, 1 steam cleaning unit and shoreline clean-up equipment and 15 flexible storage tanks to Qatar.
GREECE	1,500m open ocean containment boom.	
JAPAN	30 portable skimmers, and 10 skimming boats for Saudi Arabia, Qatar and Bahrain.	21,000m harbour containment boom, and 6,000m ocean containment boom, 40 tons of oil absorbent to Saudi Arabia. 10 skimming boats to Saudi Arabia. 10,000m harbour containment boom, 5 tons oil absorbent to Qatar. 10,000m harbour containment boom and 5 tons oil absorbent to Bahrain.
NETHER-LANDS	800m open ocean containment boom and 10 skimmers	Equipment for the protection of Abu Ali Island, Saudi Arabia.
NEW ZEALAND	432m oil absorbent booms.	
NORWAY	2,000m open ocean containment boom, 1 skimmer and 2 oil mops to Saudi Arabia.	

Country	Offered	Provided
POLAND	2 vessels with oil recovery systems, 400m coastal and 1,200m of harbour containment booms.	
SPAIN	500m open ocean and 1,400m harbour containment boom, 2 skimmers, 1 supply vessel, 1 tug, and shoreline clean-up equipment.	
SWEDEN	1,600m open ocean and 4,000m harbour containment booms, 8 skimmers and 2 incinerators.	
UNITED KINGDOM	4 rope mops, 27 storage tanks, 3 beach vehicles, 4 steam cleaners.	1,400m offshore boom; 3,600m inshore boom; 1,000m absorbent boom, 4 skimmers, 4 storage tanks to Saudi Arabia and 6 skimmers to Bahrain.
UNITED STATES		Two AIREYE Falcon Jet Aircraft with oil slick detecting radar system to Saudi Arabia.
USSR	2 multi-purpose vessels with oil recovery systems, 1 small tanker, 3,100m open ocean containment booms.	

The following have also provided pollution experts to the Gulf area: Australia, Canada, France, Germany, Japan, Netherlands, Norway, United Kingdom, United States and the Commission of the European Communities (EEC).

Source: IMO Gulf Oil Spills Information Bulletin No. 5; March 13, 1991.

and enter the intake canals, the sand would absorb this oil. Workers at these northern plants were also aware of another ecological problem to the north. They commented that smoke from burning oil facilities in Kuwait was so thick that the automatic street lights turned on at eleven o'clock in the morning.

During the first week of March the Saudi oil response team was placed under a new coordination committee formed jointly by MEPA and ARAMCO. In the previous six weeks 40 km (25 miles) of oil booms had been installed and the success of the operation was confirmed by the fact that there had been 'no shutdown or slowdown in production due to the spill'.

By this stage workers were familiar with oil in all its forms, from light sheens, almost invisible on the surface of the sea, to heavy black tar, caking shores, building unwanted roads of hardened residues along sandy beaches. Unlike the 'heavy crude' which flowed from the Nowruz spill of 1983, the Kuwaiti oil was a 'light crude' containing a high percentage of volatile components which rapidly evaporated in the intense sunlight and spring breezes of the northern Gulf. Having lost these 'thinning agents' the oil thickened and continued to 'weather'. Fresh winds, blowing first from the north and then from the south before swinging back to the north again, created choppy seas, characteristic of spring seasonal conditions

in the Gulf. The turbulent effect of these waves on floating oil whisked large areas into a 'mousse', chocolate brown in colour and quite sticky in texture. Extensive rafts of mousse formed offshore and as the oil continued to lose more of its volatile ingredients it became heavier and heavier, causing the rafts to float lower and lower in the water until they eventually sank. Sections of these rafts then broke off and rose up to the surface, behaving at times more like drifting sheets of ice than our general conception of floating oil. As the mousse drifted it picked up small particles of sand, weed and flotsam. As it approached the shallows it thickened even more, forming giant tar balls which were washed on to beaches.

The immediate problems bedevilling offshore recovery were that a war was in progress, the seas were mined and there was a well-defined no-go area in the northern Gulf. In addition, very limited offshore recovery equipment was available in the area at the time of the spill. This aspect of the recovery programme never really got under way until after the initial ceasefire, by which time the northern Gulf had been awash with oil for five or six weeks. Although the allies were unable to do anything to clean up the slick during this period, other forces were operating. The American essayist and poet Ralph Emerson wrote, in 'Method of Nature', 'When Nature has work to be done, she creates a genius to do it.' In this case the 'genius' was microscopic life-forms: bacteria and algae, which literally devoured the oil.

Early claims that the Gulf's ecology would be destroyed for decades were possibly an overstatement. Provided stocks of various species survived as seed-beds for future recovery, nature itself would help to take care of the oil. Some bacteria relish oil. *Cladosporium*, for example, is so potentially prolific that aircraft take measures to prevent it fouling fuel tanks; *Desulfovibrio* occurs in oil wells, where it is so aggressive that the chemical effects of its digestive processes can etch through solid steel. As the bacteria break down the oil, they are in effect recycling it. In the light of previous experience in the Gulf it was believed that natural processes would ensure that most of the oil was degraded within three years. Research at Kuwait University's Department of Botany and Microbiology had already shown the dominant presence of the bacterial genus *Rhodococcus* in samples of soil in Kuwait. In a letter to the weekly journal *Nature*, published on April 11, Samir

Heavily coated rocks at Safaniya desalination plant.

Previous page Saudi Arabia depends upon vast desalination plants for much of its fresh-water. A range of devices protected these plants from oil pollution.

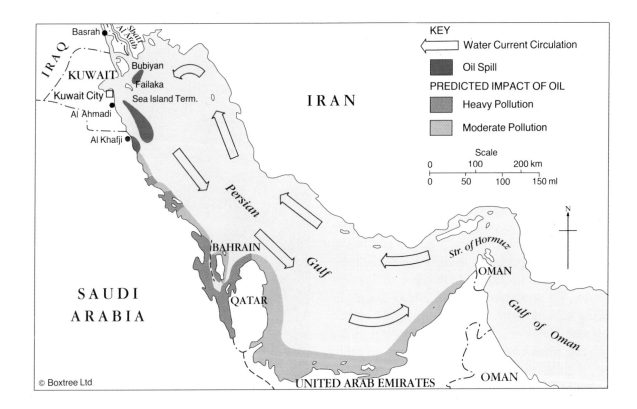

© Boxtree Ltd

Late January 1991 – predictions of heavy and moderate impact of the oil spillage in the Gulf waters.

Radwan of the Kuwait University team explained that Kuwaiti strains of *Rhodococcus* are well adapted to the extreme environmental conditions of Kuwait and the northern Gulf, and have 'proved much more active in oil degradation than strains isolated elsewhere'.

Experiments carried out on the *Exxon Valdez* spill in Alaska suggested that the addition of fertilizers can reduce the natural biodegradation period by as much as half by encouraging bacterial growth. In addition, microbial action reduced the toxicity of the oil by breaking down certain chemicals. A few commentators even argued that sulphates, produced by sulphur-loving bacteria, would promote plant life, stimulating the growth of sea grasses on which sea cows feed.

Apart from the natural process of microbial degradation there was the possibility of actively promoting this activity under scientific control. Trials held off the east coast of Britain during September 1990 showed just how effective this could be. Government scientists from Warren Spring Laboratory in Stevenage assessed a system known as 'Bioremediation' developed by the Texan company Alpha Environmental. The company's first major test had taken place in the summer of 1990 when the Norwegian tanker *Mega Borg* discharged four million gallons (one hundred thousand barrels) of crude oil into the Caribbean, 100 km (60 miles) off the coast of Texas. The 'enhanced natural clean-up' method was based on a unique collection of oil-loving microbes which had been harvested from various oil-slicks around the world by Professor Carl Oppenheimer of the University of Texas. Oppenheimer's mixed culture of bacteria, at a concentration of one trillion bacteria per gram ($\frac{1}{25}$ oz) dry weight of a nitrogen/phosphorus compound (added to provide nutrients), was diluted with sea water in a tank and then sprayed over the sea's surface. It proved to be a highly efficient method of stimulating microbial breakdown of the oil.

Bioremediation had definite possibilities as a clean-up method for the Gulf's oil spills, but there were problems in effectively treating the oil once it had spread across a large sea area. Alpha Environmental and its British associate, Alpha Biological Treatment Services, were reported to be poised to deliver a considerable quantity of the special bacterial 'cocktail' to the Gulf but Samir Radwan of Kuwait University warned that native *Rhodococcus* would be likely to compete with the introduced strains and could thus become antagonistic. He also pointed to an added danger in using enhancement techniques to speed up the bacterial decay of oil. When *Rhodococcus* feeds on oil, like many other oil-feeding bacteria it exudes large quantities of trehalose glycolipids as detergents. These are toxic to a wide variety of organisms and play a role in certain diseases. Since Gulf water provides drinking water after desalination, Radwan suggested that fertilization may create new hazards.

There was also the question of time. It was simply not feasible to wait for nature to do its job since the oil posed an immediate threat to many sea-water intakes as well as to the Gulf's vulnerable wildlife. In both cases it could hardly have come at a worse moment. The coastal facilities were vital for sustaining the military effort as well as providing essential support for the civilian community, while the natural world was gearing itself up for its annual spring party. Suggestions of leaving the clean-up to nature had little chance of falling on receptive ears in such circumstances. The main effort continued to focus on stage two of the three-part strategy outlined at the beginning

Offshore islands of the Arabian Gulf are vital breeding refuges for several species of tern including the lesser-crested tern.

of the crisis by Abdelaziz M. al-Hokail of Saudi Aramco: the containment and collection of crude oil.

The Secretary-General of the International Maritime Organization announced on March 15, 1991 the establishment of a special international Fund to 'combat the oil spill in the Persian Gulf'. He noted that IMO's role in such oil pollution situations had been envisaged by the recently adopted International Convention on Oil Pollution Preparedness, Response and Cooperation, 1990. The Fund's prime role was to 'mitigate its [the Gulf oil spill's] environmental impact and provide a framework which will enable Governments to support an international effort under the auspices of IMO'. By mid-May the Fund had received the following contributions: one million pounds from the UK government; one and a half million US dollars from the government of Japan; forty million Luxemburg francs' worth of clean-up equipment and services from the government of Luxemburg; and equipment as an in-kind contribution from the government of Germany. In addition pledges of contributions had been received from the governments of the Netherlands (one and a quarter million guilders) and Switzerland (250,000 Swiss francs). The Commission of the European Communities had also indicated that it would contribute one million ECU.

By March 27 nearly 600,000 barrels of oil and oil–water emulsion had been gathered and it was expected that the daily recovery rates would rise as a result of more equipment becoming available, notably extra skimming vessels donated by Japan. The plan was to have all floating oil collected by mid-May and to then focus activities on the clean-up onshore. The impact on wildlife was already making itself felt, with shallow coastal bays and inlets north of Abu Ali particularly hard hit. Serious damage was caused to salt marshes, mud-flats and isolated mangrove stands. Offshore the situation was not much better, with the islands of Jana and Karan, recently declared wildlife preserves, suffering the full impact of the slick,

which coated beaches where turtles were expected to arrive soon for nesting. One of the first concentrated clean-up efforts took place here, carried out by a team of volunteers from the UK Royal Air Force and Army and the US Marines. The military's welcome efforts at scraping oil and debris off sandy approaches to turtle nesting pits may have spared the Gulf's green turtles but fears remained that oil contamination in the sand would lead to heavy mortalities within buried eggs. The most heavily impacted island in the Gulf, Gurmah, had already suffered considerable damage to its mangroves and other coastal marine life. In the latter half of March, 350 m (380 yards) of absorbent booms were placed in intertidal channels to protect the remaining 20 percent of unpolluted mangroves on the island.

Plans were being laid for a major clean-up to commence with the signing on March 26 of a contract by Saudi Arabia and the Crowley Maritime Corporation. Crowley began work almost immediately, under the direction of MEPA. It was too soon, however, for any serious environmental protection work to have started in Kuwait, where a state of chaos continued to dominate.

Oil Spill Update from MEPA, KSA. April 6, 1991 Press Release from Nizar Tawfig, on-site coordinator, Oil Spill Response Center. Extracts:

Northwesterly winds blew heavy smoke from burning oil fields in Kuwait south of the Khobar area. The layer of smoke caused a 6-degree reduction in the maximum temperature since yesterday. Blowing dust is expected inland tomorrow because of the winds, but the smoke will blow back toward Kuwait.

Most of the oil in the Gulf is in the form of sheen and small and medium-size patches. Many of the small patches and lines of oil have been blown toward the shoreline by northerly winds.

The amount of oil has increased on the coast between

Khafji and Ras al-Misha'ab and on the coast between Saffaniyyah and Ras al-Misha-ab. A small amount of oil remains inside the Tanajib port and a large amount is in the back bay of Tanajib. . . . More oil has hit the east coast of Manifah and the north coast of Tanajib.

Crews in the Abu Ali area collected 6,470 barrels of oil today and those in Brice Bay recovered 2,400 barrels. Operations at a new site in Dawhat ad-Dafi will begin tomorrow. Workers on Gurmah Island are preparing for clean-up of oiled mangroves.

ARAMCO crews recovered 23,875 barrels of oil yesterday, for a total of 651,165 barrels as of Sunday.

Six of 10 skimmers donated by Japan and manufactured in the United Arab Emirates have arrived in Saudi Arabia; the other four are expected within two days. All 10 skimmers will be used in offshore operations.

New oil continued to arrive on the Saudi Arabian coast during April, as MEPA's daily briefings indicated:

Oil Spill Update from MEPA, KSA. April 10, 1991 Press Release from Nizar Tawfig, on-site coordinator, Oil Spill Response Center. Extracts:

The south coast of Dawhat ad-Dafi is still heavily affected by oil, and some small lines were coming from the north and affecting two small islands at the bay's entrance. The south entrance of Dawhat al-Musallamiyyah and the north and east coasts of Jana island are more oiled than before. Brice Bay, the east coast of Manifah, and the north and east coasts of Ras az Zawr also are more affected than previously. . . . An increased amount of oil including small patches was visible off the south coast of Tanajib. New lines and a patch of oil were seen in the Saffaniyyah oil field.

But the oil recovery programme was beginning to have a visible effect on the oil still floating in the sea. On April 10, ARAMCO crews added a further 14,410 barrels to their accumulated collection of recovered oil, giving a total from their operations of 683,141 barrels up to that time. On April 27 they added 11,520 barrels, taking their total to 816,645. Two weeks later, on May 10, the total recovered by ARAMCO stood at 922, 554 barrels of which approximately 100,000 barrels had been blended into the incoming crude stream to the Ras Tanura refinery. In addition to these operations other smaller recoveries were taking place, often at areas of special wildlife interest. One such team was that led by the Crowley Maritime Corporation which concentrated its early efforts in Brice Bay. They estimated the oil content of recovered fractions at 85 percent.

Thus by early May Saudi Aramco had recovered more oil from the Gulf than the total quantity of oil spilt in the *Torrey Canyon* oil-spill disaster off the south-west coast of Britain, and four times the amount spilt by the *Exxon Valdez*. Provided weather conditions remained stable, ARAMCO expected to considerably increase their recovery total, taking it well above the million-barrel mark. While 10–20 percent of the recovered oil was suitable for mixing with freshly pumped crude and adding into the refinery process, other oil was stored pending further processing. Throughout the spring and early summer it was a matter of growing concern that considerable quantities of oil continued to leak into the Gulf from at least five key sources. Estimates of the quantities involved varied from an unconfirmed estimate of as much as 125,000 barrels per day to a much more conservative figure of around 3000 barrels per day. Although it remained difficult to pin down the exact quantities involved, one oil worker claimed in late April that at least three major point sources in Kuwaiti waters were leaking at a rate of three thousand or more barrels per day and that additional oil was seeping from Iraqi oil-tankers presumably damaged by allied bombing raids.

The IMO Persian Gulf Pollution Disaster Fund was used to accelerate the clean-up process at

environmentally sensitive sites. The first such project was on Karan, where the task of removing oil from turtle beaches around the island was given to a Scottish company, Alba International Ltd. In places the tar mat which had congealed on the beaches was up to 36 cm (14 in) thick. A total of 14,200 cu. m (18,570 cu. yards) of tarmac was removed and buried in pits in the interior of the island. Clean sand from pits excavated to receive the tar was transported back to the shore and the beach contour re-established. The project was completed before the season's first turtles returned to the island to lay their eggs. Since 80 percent of the Gulf's green turtles use Karan, it was a vital project completed just in time.

The second IMO Fund project involved protection of one of the few remaining areas of unoiled salt marsh along the Saudi Arabian coast. The contract for installation of a protective boom around the marsh was awarded to Target Construction Company Ltd, based in Riyadh. The boom, which was provided by the Government of Luxemburg, was installed by May 7.

Gurmah island, which was very heavily impacted by oil, also received the attentions of an IMO Fund project. The Dutch company Tanker Cleaning Amsterdam b.v. was given the task of flushing free-floating oil from the island's impacted mangroves and natural drainage system. Mangroves play a very important role in Gurmah's ecosystem, covering the southern two-thirds of the island. Eighty percent of the trees were heavily impacted and TCA's task was to clear the oil from channels into the open sea, where it could be recovered by skimmers. Following the completion of that job the Royal Commission's contractors, O'Brien Oil Pollution Services, tackled the clean-up along the shores of Gurmah. Other IMO projects included one in Kuwait aimed at identifying and stopping oil leaks from oil terminals; a project at Musharrabah Bay to provide a protective boom around unoiled salt marshes and one at Musallamiyah Bay to establish a test site with a view to evaluating the most

Above The Iraqis sabotaged many oil installations with explosive charges. This damaged junction point in Shuwaikh port was still leaking oil into the sea several months after the liberation of Kuwait.

Previous page Burning wells dispersed oil into the atmosphere but those wells not on fire drenched the desert with a continuous spray. Plant recovery in these areas is likely to take a very long time.

appropriate clean-up techniques for salt marshes.

Survey flights by SLAR aircraft provided information on the sources of oil which continued to leak into the Gulf. An IMO report dated April 26 stated: 'The primary source of oil entering the Gulf has been identified as a drainage canal to a treatment plant at Al-Ahmadi refinery.' This leak was stemmed by placing a sand berm over the outlet. Damaged tankers had been removed from the site by Smit Tak. Sadly, spring tides refloated the oil, causing it to inundate one of the few

remaining unoiled salt marshes at Tanajib. The SLAR overflight on April 29 covered most of the important sites in the northern Gulf. It revealed that the Marjan oilfield was still leaking oil from one platform and that the Sea Island loading terminal was continuing to disgorge oil at an undetermined rate.

Even at this late date there were considerable quantities of oil at sea. IMO commented that a site survey at the end of April revealed that 75 percent of the northern shoreline was heavily impacted with oil and *sizeable quantities of oil continue to move to different locations within the bay structure, with the heaviest concentrations at Manifah Bay and Bilbul Bay.*

The loading terminal at Al Bakr also continued to leak large amounts of oil. A ship which was broken in half in the terminal area appeared to be the source of this leak. Only the bow and stern of the vessel were visible on the overflight, and oil could be seen trailing a few miles from the area.

So extensive was the damage to key sections of the offshore oil industry, and so dangerous were coastal waters because of the difficulties of mine clearance, that small leaks continued from a number of sources. While filming from helicopters we observed at close quarters the incredible extent of devastation wrought by Iraqi sabotage. Twisted and burnished pipes of offshore installations at the Sea Island terminal, once a key installation of Kuwait's oil export industry, appeared like the skeletal remains of an enormous beached whale. Fresh oil issued from beneath the broken structures and mixed in wind-rows with accumulations of ash that rained continuously on the sea. Studies have shown that global oil pollution results more from atmospheric sources than from spillage from marine installations or ships. In five days of aerial filming we saw no part of Kuwaiti waters without a sheen of oil. Toxic elements in such sheens have an incalculable impact on the microscopic plankton that forms the base of the food-chain.

TEN

OPERATION NINJA RESCUE

THE tragedy described in this book was not the world's first ecological catastrophe caused by oil pollution; nor will it be the last. One of the greatest problems of the Oil Age is that, despite the impressive social and economic progress made possible through the extraction and burning of fossil fuels, 'side-effects' have been have so serious that we have been forced to question the wisdom of present energy policies. Environmental effects of oil pollution are found throughout the world. During a voyage across the Atlantic in 1971 by Thor Heyerdahl of *Kontiki* fame, crew members were unable to use sea water on one occasion in mid-Atlantic to clean their teeth because it was so polluted by oil. The world's oceans are already burdened by millions of tons of tar, the product of leakages from ships, oil wells, coastal facilities and aerial pollution. This latter source is far more important than is generally realized. One study estimated that the total amount of oil deposited in the sea in 1969 was 14,000 million tonnes (13,780 million tons), of which no less than 9000 million tonnes (8860 million tons) reached there from wind and rain (Alcan, Montreal, 1972).

The world's first oil-tanker was the German *Gluckauf*, built in 1886. It would be totally dwarfed by today's supertankers, some of which exceed 300 m (1000 ft) in length and half a million tons (492,000 tons) in displacement weight. Supertankers have minimum cargoes of 100,000 tonnes (985,000 tons) and are one of the

Green turtles can hold their breath for over an hour

most potentially dangerous sources of oil pollution ever created. Several of these enormous ships have run aground and spilled their massive cargoes into the sea. One of the first to do so was the *Torrey Canyon*, carrying 117,000 tonnes (115,150 tons) of Kuwait crude oil (7.2 barrels per tonne), steaming at 17 knots when she struck Pollard Rock of the Seven Stones, 24 km (15 miles) west of Land's End, at the south-west tip of England. The accident caused the worst case of oil pollution the world had ever witnessed up to that time, when 842,000 barrels of oil devastated coastal marine life and killed at least fifteen thousand birds. Despite great international attention and growing concern over the risks inherent in transporting such large cargoes of oil around the globe, other similar disasters soon followed, involving such ships as the *Metula, Arrow, Pacific Glory, Ocean Eagle, Argo Merchant, Amoco Cadiz, Aegean Captain, Haven* and *Exxon Valdez*. The last of these caused widespread outcry in the United States and Canada since the ship released a quarter of a million barrels of crude oil in one of the most beautiful regions of the incredibly rich Alaskan coastline: Prince William Sound.

During the same period the great increase in offshore oil drilling led to a number of accidents which made the *Torrey Canyon* incident seem small by comparison. Among these the Nowruz oil spill in the Gulf and the blow-out of the Ixtoc 1 platform in the Gulf of Mexico are prominent. In both cases oil was released over a period of months, with the Ixtoc 1 holding the world record from 1979 to 1991 with a reported spillage of 3.3 million barrels. The new world-record-holder is the 1991 Gulf War spill in which over four million barrels were released in a single week, followed by additional quantities from a large number of smaller sources over the next few months (recent estimate is 6–8 million barrels).

Thanks to underwater filming, pioneered by Cousteau and Hans Hass and perfected in recent years by a growing number of film-makers, the general public has a much deeper appreciation of the sensitive nature of the marine world. Governments have responded to this increasing interest and awareness and during the Gulf War it was heartening to observe the deep sense of commitment to protect or save wildlife in people from all walks of life. Even more important than this concern, however, was the accumulated experience gained in techniques for rescuing animals from oil pollution, in the twenty-four years since the *Torrey Canyon* went aground. Early methods used to clean oiled beaches or to disperse slicks were often more toxic than the oil itself. In the analysis which followed the grounding of the *Torrey Canyon*, a report by the Marine Biological Association of the UK stated:

It is all the more necessary therefore in the light of our new-found knowledge of the nature and effects of detergents to examine (a) by comparison with other possible methods of oil clearance, the efficiency of the detergent method of disposal, and (b) the possibility of the modification of detergents to reduce their toxicity. (J. E. Smith (ed.), 'Torrey Canyon' Pollution and Marine Life, Cambridge University Press, 1968)

It is pleasing to report that both the above fields of investigation bore results over the following years.

A considerable body of information was available to scientists and technicians involved in the Gulf War oil spill. They knew that they were dealing primarily with oil from the Burgan and Wafra oilfields, and that densities of these oils differed very slightly from each other, the Burgan oil being slightly lighter at around 7.2 barrels per tonne while Wafra crude was closer to 7.1. Predictions of what would happen to the oil in sea water were based on previous studies carried out in Kuwaiti waters with these particular oils. The impact characteristics of the oil were thus divided into three phases: Phase 1, the first five days that the oil was in open water; Phase 2, the remaining period that the oil was in open water before landfall; and Phase 3, the period from when the oil first reached the shore.

Phase 1, during the first week of the spillage, was when the water column was most affected by water-soluble fractions of the oil and oil droplets. Large numbers of planktonic creatures are likely to have been killed at this time since the water-soluble fraction comprises mainly toxic hydrocarbons such as benzene and toluene. As the slick slid across the sea's surface these potentially lethal chemicals spread into the waters beneath, killing marine life. Studies had already shown that Kuwait crude oil establishes an equilibrium concentration of 20 parts per million in an oil/sea water mix of one part oil to nine parts sea water. The gigantic slick was such that this level of concentration was probably reached immediately beneath the oil. If so, at a depth of around 10 cm (4½ in) the concentration of hydrocarbons was around 2 parts per million, and half this concentration at 20 cm (9 in). Simultaneous to this contamination of the sea, volatile fractions of the oil were also evaporating. Acute levels of toxicity probably only occurred within the first metre of the water column but daily vertical migrations of many planktonic species, which swim towards the surface at night and return to greater depths during the day, is likely to have increased the death rate. Affected forms included eggs and larvae of many different species, including shrimps, oysters and fish.

At first the oil dispersed rapidly, easily pushed by waves and currents, but as it weathered and became thicker it spread more slowly. During Phase 2 soluble hydrocarbons continued to leach out of the floating slick, but at a much slower rate than in the first few days. A weathered 'skin' gradually formed, sealing the underlying oil–water emulsion from the atmosphere and partially protecting it from weathering. Toxicity levels in the water column beneath the slick were much less than during the initial period, reducing the impact on plankton, but the slick posed a serious hazard to larger forms such as birds and turtles.

As oil reached shallow coastal areas waves distributed particles throughout the water column, greatly increasing the oil–water interface and allowing more water-soluble hydrocarbons to dissolve, poisoning marine life in the shallows. Thickened oil finally coated the shores, blanketing the intertidal, physically smothering countless small creatures and sinking into the sand, continuing to poison this normally rich habitat for a considerable period. Over the following weeks and months tides and waves broke off sections of the intertidal oil mat, causing the intermittent release of more hydrocarbons, which had a much less dramatic effect on marine life than the earlier events. In fact by this stage the process of recovery was already under way, with algae coating the oil's surface and tiny gastropod molluscs grazing over the tar mats. Burrowing organisms gradually re-established themselves within the sand and restarted the process of turning over the sediment, often using oil particles as part of their burrows.

As the slick spread, its effects on wildlife were inevitable but hard to quantify. Many of the worst-hit areas in the northern Gulf were within the war zone where there was little that could be done to rescue animals or protect shallow marine habitats. Further south, however, there was hope that something could be achieved, even during the middle of the war. There was such a shortage of protective booms, and such a high priority was placed on defending vital sea-water intakes, that important shallow-water communities and key habitats were more or less left to their own devices during the first five weeks; and much of the habitat work took place after oil had already smeared mangroves, coated corals or clogged turtle beaches. Later on, absorbent booms were used to prevent further seepages of oil up mangrove channels and efforts were made to protect a few important sites such as the mangrove area of Tubli Bay in Bahrain. A great deal of energy, as we have seen, was directed at physically removing the oil from the sea and this had obvious environmental benefits as well as playing a key role in maintaining the functioning of economically and socially important facilities.

While all this was happening birds, turtles, dolphins and possibly dugongs were being killed by oil. The sight of a heavily oiled bird, floating so low in the sea that it struggles to keep its head above water, swimming rapidly to shore in order to avoid drowning, then waddling up the beach, feathers dripping with sticky black tar, huddling against the wind with nowhere to go and no chance of escape, poised to die of cold since feathers no longer performed their vital insulatory function, moved almost everyone who witnessed such scenes to a feeling of shame at the mayhem which humankind had unleashed on nature. Chasing after such beleaguered creatures, placing them in a numbered cardboard box, driving them as fast as possible towards the 'rescue centre' where they were revived with re-hydration treatments and delicately shampooed before being placed in nursery enclosures, was as much an act of atonement for our sins against nature as an attempt to save a particular animal from dying.

On beaches where hundreds of cormorants and grebes were either dead or dying, the capture and rescue of one or two still struggling individuals had little if any effect on these species' prospects of recovery from the torment of the Gulf War. The almost fanatical focus of attention and care on the 'rescued' individuals reflected more a sense of collective grief at the horrendous scale of the pollution than a belief that such efforts could ameliorate the ecological and environmental damage. Human beings were dying in their thousands, animals were being killed in their millions—all pawns in a gigantic chess game outside their understanding. Here was a dying cormorant. Here was a saddened human heart. Here was a person who desperately wanted to 'do something' to save life while others pursued their awful mission to end it. These were the elements which made the Jubail Wildlife Rescue Centre such a hub of activity throughout and after the main period of conflict.

The National Commission for Wildlife Conservation and Development (NCWCD) in Saudi Arabia has been a central player in the protection of Arabian wildlife during recent years. Apart from having a genuine concern about the effects of the oil spill on the Gulf's animals and plants, it found itself relatively powerless to make any real impact on the oil-slick's devastating attack on the environment. It was important, however, that the

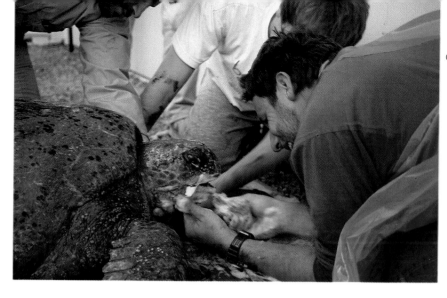

Opposite A clean-up of oil pollution on Karan Island enabled over a thousand green turtles to nest safely.

Left Oiled turtles are shampooed, tagged and released.

Commission should do something to help nature, and be seen to do so. This latter aim may sound slightly disingenuous but it is not, for a vital part of conservation work is education of the general public. The oil-slick caused widespread dismay at the plight of wildlife among local people in Saudi Arabia and other Gulf countries. It was one of the first times that such a general outpouring of environmental concern had been so openly expressed, reflecting an increased interest in, and awareness of, important conservation issues. This great surge in concern for wildlife needed to be harnessed by national wildlife organizations and directed towards long-term conservation goals. Establishment of the Jubail Wildlife Rescue Centre provided a means whereby both concern about the continuing environmental impact of the war, and a national commitment to protect nature, could find expression. 'Operation Ninja', as the volunteers codenamed their efforts, also saved lives.

The Jubail centre was established in facilities provided by the Royal Commission of Jubail and Yanbu, and staffed by the NCWCD, which also coordinated voluntary assistance from international organizations, Saudi Aramco employees, members of the armed forces and local volunteers.

Following their capture along Saudi Arabia's oiled beaches, invalided birds and other animals were brought to the centre by professional and volunteer collection teams. On arrival they were received at a reception desk where their details were entered into a book and they were allocated a 'patient card'. This was filled in with the basic details such as date, where found, and the identification of the animal, together with observations on its general condition. From there they entered a 'waiting area' and were sorted in terms of priorities. Many birds were in such a pathetic condition that there was little chance of saving them, but others showed more hope. Almost all the birds had taken in oil through breathing, skin absorption and, worse of all, preening. As a consequence they were suffering a combination of toxic effects. Almost invariably their ingestion of oil had inhibited their ability to derive fresh water from imbibed salt water and they had become dehydrated. In addition they were likely to have a host of other symptoms such as internal bleeding, inhibition of nutrient absorption from the digestive tract, organ damage (especially kidneys, liver and pancreas), malfunction of adrenal glands and immune system, together with a form of anaemia.

Apart from treatment for these toxic effects, oiled birds had to be protected from heat loss or overheating since their feathers were no longer an effective insulating mechanism. It was also likely that they had not been able to catch food since their first encounter with oil and were in danger of dying from starvation. If a doctor received a human patient displaying a comparable array of interconnected symptoms the prognosis would read: 'probably terminal'. The challenge facing rescue workers at the centre was to turn this into 'off the immediate danger list'.

The method of cleaning oiled birds has been developed over a period of twenty or more years, principally by the Royal Society for the Prevention of Cruelty to Animals (RSPCA) in the UK. Following the very low success rate achieved at the time of the *Torrey Canyon* oil spill, when less than one in ten of the oiled birds brought in from affected shores survived, a five-year research project was carried out at the University of Newcastle upon Tyne to establish the optimum methods for treatment. Research workers looked at every possible method of cleaning birds, including Fuller's Earth, white spirit, soap, dilute detergent and neat detergent. They finally fixed on three detergents, all of which by some quirk of fate, happened to be green. The RSPCA has since followed up with its own tests and has found that two products were particularly suitable. These could be easily purchased from grocery stores throughout the UK under the brand names Co-op Green and Fairy Liquid.

During the same period similar bird-cleaning trials were taking place in the United States, where researchers zeroed in on the detergent Dawn, which happens to be blue. Remarkably, both Fairy Liquid and Dawn are products of the Procter and Gamble group of companies and officials confirmed that the two brands are virtually identical in make-up. According to Tim Thomas of the RSPCA's wildlife section in the UK, recent trials in the USA 'proved beyond measurable doubt that Dawn left plumage in better condition than anything else that had been tried'. He is equally positive about Fairy Liquid. 'The great advantage of these products is that they work well, are relatively inexpensive, and readily available,' he commented. Dutch rescue workers swear by an industrial cleaning agent brand-named Teepol. This has also given good results, but it is less readily available and more expensive.

During our research for this book we talked with a spokesperson for Procter and Gamble Ltd

in Britain. Kate Minion is the company's environmental officer and has been actively involved with assisting the RSPCA and other organizations engaged in cleaning oiled sea creatures. She explained that the company had been donating supplies of Fairy Liquid to such organizations for over two years. Remarkably, the company has shunned publicity for its efforts, apparently agreeing with, and respecting, the wishes of wildlife groups that suffering animals should not become the subject of a commercial marketing programme.

Nevertheless the tremendous publicity associated with major events such as the *Exxon Valdez* spill in Alaska draws the media to all aspects of the story. In television broadcasts of wildlife rescue work after this spillage, Dawn was pictured in use on a number of occasions, much to the chagrin of its competitors. One major soap manufacturer pressed hard for its own product to be used, only to be rejected by wildlife experts who politely informed the company that their product had been tried and found to be less effective than Dawn. The same company is reported to have approached workers at the Jubail Wildlife Rescue Centre, again wanting them to use their product. Again they were informed that Fairy Liquid had been proven to be better. 'It can't be,' replied the executive, 'our product is almost the same thing.' The bid failed again but this time the company stated that it would run its own trials and come up with an entirely new product dedicated purely to cleaning oiled sea birds! It was certainly not hoping to make money from sales of such a product but was acutely aware of the tremendous publicity value of having one's detergent so vigorously championed by independent wildlife rescue workers under the focus of the world's media.

Another method of treating oiled sea birds which gained considerable publicity during the early days of the Gulf War oil spill was the use of 'woolly jumpers', much like socks, in which birds are cocooned. The method was not tried, however, since it was considered inadvisable to run experiments in the middle of a major environmental crisis. It was felt that the RSPCA's well-proven bird-cleaning method was the most appropriate for this occasion. According to Tim Thomas, a very similar method has been tested in the past and found to upset birds and interfere with their temperature regulation. However, he and his colleagues are keeping an open mind since their declared aim is to continually improve on treatment procedures for oiled birds.

Treatment of the Gulf War's oiled sea birds began long before they reached the Fairy Liquid. The first priority was to reduce stress. Placing them in the warm, darkened interior of cardboard boxes helped to achieve this. On arrival at the centre, they entered a quiet area, which further reduced stress. For the first few hours, birds brought into the centre, generally in the morning, were left in these warm, dark, quiet conditions, giving them a chance to recover somewhat from the trauma of their experience. On the afternoon of the same day their treatment began, aimed at building up their strength so that they would be fit enough to withstand the stressful cleaning process.

One of the first treatments was with an enzyme solution of an especially formulated product, lectade, designed to restore electrolytic balance, combating dehydration. Then the problem of starvation was tackled, gently at first, often with a liquid food called duphalite, containing essential enzymes, minerals and proteins. Gradually, over the coming days, fish were fed, by hand at first but later with the birds taking it themselves. As birds responded to this treatment, they increased in strength despite being still covered in oil. In view of the toxicity of the oil and the fact that it was almost impossible to prevent them from preening, it was vital to wash it off as soon as possible.

Oiled birds were given at least twenty-four hours and often two or three days to recoup their strength before washing. When a bird was ready for cleaning a booster of warm liquid food was administered before the bird was placed in a sink

of hot water and Fairy Liquid. While one worker held it in the bowl, taking care to keep its head away from the liquid, the other began gently agitating the water, moving the cleansing agent among the oily feathers. After a few minutes the water was almost as dirty as the bird had been. Following two or three water changes the body was more or less free from oil and it was time to clean the head. Finally the bird was thoroughly rinsed, gently blotted with a towel, and placed in a box in the drying area where blow heaters speeded drying.

Experienced operatives could clean a black-necked grebe in twenty minutes or a larger cormorant in just under two hours. However, many of the volunteers lacked this specialized experience and took up to twice these times for single birds. The washing process, although essential for the bird's recovery, was also probably the most stressful experience they endured at the centre. They were therefore left to recover in a warm, quiet rest area. After a short while feeding recommenced and when the birds were considered fit enough they were placed with others of their own kind, first in indoor holding pens, and later in outdoor pens with small pools or in a larger, sectioned and shaded swimming pool.

The RSPCA claims that this method, when used by its experienced staff, has a 60–75 percent success rate and that its workers at Jubail achieved a 64 percent success rate. But the main workforce at the centre was far from experienced. For many it was the first time they had set eyes on a grebe, let alone held one in their hands and gently nursed it back to life. The sheer number of birds requiring cleaning, and the time taken for each, meant that large numbers of helpers were required and close supervision was difficult. Staff from the NCWCD and from international organizations such as the RSPCA were constantly concerned with 'quality control on the assembly line'. Everyone involved in the project was anxious that they should do their best to help the birds survive. Anyone who had the privilege of visiting the

The small island of Kurayn is reputed to host the world's largest breeding colony of lesser-crested terns. It is also an important turtle nesting island.

Rescue Centre at the height of the crisis could hardly have failed to be impressed by the professionalism of the operation and the dedication of the many volunteers who worked there. Statistics from the centre reflect the extreme condition in which many of the oiled birds and other creatures were found. More experienced workers would probably have not even brought in many of the birds which volunteers collected, knowing that they were past saving.

By April 26 the numbers of successfully treated and released birds had increased significantly to: 192 Socotra cormorants, 118 greater cormorants, thirteen black-necked grebes, seven slender-billed gulls and two great crested grebes.

Use of such records to calculate 'success rate' can be misleading, however, since the RSPCA calculations are based on birds brought into its facilities which are eventually released. There was possibly less rigorous preselection by the Jubail Rescue Centre team members and hence the figures show a lower overall survival rate. It is also clear from the figures that there was a marked divergence in response to cleaning by cormorants and grebes. Of 328 greater cormorants brought into the centre, 44 percent were either fully recovered and released or still undergoing treatment. In the case of Socotra cormorants this 'success rate' was even higher, with 67 percent still alive at the beginning of April and ninety-two birds already released back into the wild. The figures for grebes, however, were desperately disappointing, with only 12 percent of the 224 black-necked grebes and 7 percent of the great crested grebes still alive.

In order to find out why grebes were not responding to treatment at the Jubail centre, an intensive pathological investigation was undertaken on behalf of the NCWCD by veterinary scientist, Dr Arnaud Greth. Following forty-two postmortems he concluded that the problem with grebes is that their preening of oiled feathers causes a ball of feathers, sand and oil to become lodged in the gizzard. He suggested that the time taken between collection and delivery to the centre was particularly critical in the case of grebes since their preening of oiled feathers needed to be minimized. On their arrival at the centre he proposed that they be treated with an emetic to encourage them to clear their gizzards of the tar-ball blockage likely to be present. His examinations of cormorants did not reveal similar blockages in the gizzard but did show bleeding and damage in the small intestine. For this reason Greth proposed use of antibiotics, kaolin and possibly charcoal during early treatment of cormorants at the centre. But the grebe treatment and survival problem was already quite well known to RSPCA workers, in whose experience the key issue was hygiene and other conditions in the nursery, as well as the need for more experienced washers. Typical problems caused by inadequate holding conditions, according to RSPCA workers, were cuts on the breast bone, stiffness in the leg and wing joints, dry feet and inadequate waterproofing on the feathers.

Such careful investigations and accumulated experience helped to improve the efficiency of the treatment process and will contribute to the future treatment of oiled birds, both in the Gulf and in other areas. Another factor which must be taken into account when considering the results obtained at Jubail is that it was a makeshift affair which underwent constant modification and improvement throughout the crisis. Given the fact that a war was taking place, that Scud missile alerts were a regular feature of life in the Eastern Province, and that many people had other things on their mind, it was hardly surprising that it took time to establish such items as a suitable supply of fish for feeding to sick birds. And yet the success of the project depended on such arrangements.

Construction of suitable pens was another problem, and this was tackled by volunteers from the armed forces, who spent their days building containers and pens for the constantly expanding list of patients. Everywhere one went, inside and around the centre, there were people busily playing their part in the great team effort. For a while it engaged the attention of the world press and television. Then the news people moved on to cover the real war and the volunteers at Jubail quietly soldiered on with their own battle in defence of wildlife. Few had any illusions about their role. Team leaders acknowledged that it was a mere drop in the ocean. That was not the point, they argued. They were saving lives.

One creature they saved had already been alive for a considerable time. On the afternoon of Thursday February 22, 1991, while the world was bracing itself for the start of a major land war in occupied Kuwait, we were filming at the Jubail centre when word came of an unusual arrival. Outside, filling the back of a Toyota pick-up truck, was a jet-black, totally oiled, mound which demanded close inspection before it revealed itself to be that most gentle and ancient of marine reptiles, a green turtle. It is hard to describe just how thickly smothered in tar the

unfortunate animal was. Operation Ninja rescuers, who had found it washed up on one of the heavily impacted, normally white sand, beaches of this section of Gulf coastline, had mistaken it for dead until a bubble of air burst through the coating of oil blocking its nostrils. On the off-chance that real life existed beneath its death cloak, they had gently carted its cumbersome bulk back to the centre.

No time was wasted as buckets of warm, soapy water and sponges were used to clean off the oil. Unlike birds, whose delicate feathers demand painstaking attention, the tough carapace and leather skin of turtles presents a much easier and quicker task. With the oil removed we were able to admire the delicate green tinge to its shell and the wizened face of this mature female. Along the front of her carapace notches had been carved by amorous males and the back of her vast shell had been scratched by partners during mating. When most of the oil had been removed, a staff member took cotton buds to clear her nostrils and eyes of the last droplets and by this stage the turtle herself was showing real signs of life, stretching out her neck as she occasionally gaped for air. Finally the magnificent creature was weighed and measured.

The rescued turtle, estimated from its size and weight to be around sixty years old, must have clambered down the deserted beach of one of the Gulf Islands, around the summer of 1931. In May of that same year four employees of the California-based Socal oil company arrived in Bahrain to establish a drilling rig at the foot of Jebel Dukhan ('hill of smoke') towards the centre of the island. In June of the following year oil first flowed from Bahrain's Well Number One, gushing up to the surface from a depth of 612 m (2008 ft). It was the first Arabian oil well and presaged a new era, both for humankind and wildlife, in the Persian Gulf and its surrounding lands. The rescued green turtle had lived through the entire period of Arabia's dramatic 'Oil Age'. Many of its species had already been killed by oil spills. The Gulf was becoming a difficult place for a turtle to live.

TABLE 11: JUBAIL WILDLIFE RESCUE CENTRE RECORDS OF ANIMALS RECEIVED UP TO
APRIL 1, 1991

Species	Total received	Living Dirty	Living Cleaned	In pool	Released	Dead
Greater cormorant	328	86	22	25	13	182
Socotra cormorant	364	71	37	47	92	117
Black-necked grebe	224	–	12	12	3	197
Great crested grebe	120	–	8	–	–	112
Slender-billed gull	12	3	–	–	4	5
Great black-headed gull	8	–	–	2	–	6
Herring gull	8	–	–	–	–	8
Caspian tern	2	–	–	–	–	2
Grey heron	2	–	–	–	–	2
Reef heron	3	–	–	–	2	1
Lesser sand plover	2	–	–	–	–	2
Curlew	1	–	–	–	1	–
Redshank	1	–	–	–	–	1
Pintail	1	–	–	–	1	–
Mallard	1	–	–	–	–	1
Shoveler	1	–	–	–	–	1
Red fox	1	–	–	–	–	1
Green turtle	2	–	–	–	2	–
Hawksbill turtle	3	–	–	–	2	1
TOTAL	1084	160	79	86	120	639

Source: National Commission for Wildlife Conservation and Development, Riyadh, Saudi Arabia

Inside Kuwait the human suffering had been so severe that it was difficult, and at times almost embarrassing, to be actively engaged in rescuing animals. In the early days it was left largely to 'romantic foreigners' to speak up for the greatly suffering creatures at Kuwait Zoo or in private hands. One prominent spokesman, and one of the first Westerners to enter the zoo after liberation was John Walsh, Assistant Director-General of the World Society for the Protection of Animals. Walsh sent urgent messages abroad, seeking help to save those animals which had not been shot, eaten or removed to Baghdad. Having coordinated a supply of animal feed and arranged for its delivery by Atlasair, British Airways and the Canadian Armed Forces, he turned his attention to urgent treatment of some injured animals which bore shot wounds. In the case of 'Beasley', the Syrian brown bear (named after Col. Michael Beasley of the US Army's 352nd Civil Affairs Unit, who took a special interest in the bear's welfare) this entailed an air-lift to Riyadh so that it could undergo surgery. 'Beasley clearly needed more help than we could give him in Kuwait if he is to survive,' said Walsh. 'He is suffering from loss of appetite, severe depression, and is in a great deal of pain from his injury.'

The zoo's one remaining elephant, Azizor, also carried evidence of Iraqi cruelty, with a bullet still lodged in its body. The wound was cleaned and surgery was ruled out. Another victim of mindless shooting was a macaque monkey whose leg had been shattered. Elsewhere in Kuwait many animals suffered during the occupation. Thirteen Arabian horses stabled at a racetrack near Kuwait City were nursed for a while by US veterinarians who reported that some of the horses had received gunshot wounds and were suffering from equine parasites and other health problems. 'The animals are truly silent victims of the war. They are dying by the thousands from oil contamination, oil-fire pollution, hunger, disease and injuries incurred during air and ground attacks. They are suffering as much as the human victims, yet they are unable to speak for themselves,' declared John Walsh, who believed he had an important role to play in 'speaking up for them, to ensure that animal welfare is taken into account during the rebuilding of this devastated country'.

It was estimated that twenty to thirty thousand birds were killed by the oil-slick between February and the end of April. As upwards of two million waders, belonging to seventy different species, migrated through the northern Gulf they collected a thin film of oil on their wing feathers whether or not they landed on oiled beaches. The burning oil wells and evaporation from the slick had injected so much oil into the air that this became virtually inevitable. Although many of these birds made it through the Gulf, the extra weight and decreased efficiency of their feathers took its toll, causing many to fail to complete their journey. Those that did arrive at their breeding grounds had suffered an unusually arduous journey and were relatively low in energy reserves, putting at risk their potential breeding success. By mid-May most migrants had continued on to their breeding territory. There were, however, still a considerable number of waders whose feet and lower legs carried accumulations of tar and who were limping as a result. It was difficult to believe that these birds could continue their migration. Out in the desert, between the burning wells, glistening lakes of black oil attracted wetland birds as they moved north. To the catalogue of pathetic avian victims of this conflict must now be added the corpses of swallows in search of imagined insects anticipated above these illusory wetlands. Countless migratory raptors, European rollers, bitterns and other wetland birds, blackened by the mist of oil droplets and smoke particles, made confused passage through corridors of smoke.

Kuwait and the northern Gulf may never fully recover from the ecological impact of the war. Despite extensive damage to the natural order, a by-product of the conflict may be a heightened awareness of the value and importance of wildlife to our world. It remains to be seen, in the constrained economic circumstances of reconstruction, whether the rehabilitation of wildlife habitats will be given the necessary support. The sense of achievement and jubilation evident in the faces of volunteers returning cleansed and rehabilitated turtles to the wild will hopefully encourage an extension of the emergency wildlife rescue efforts which were put in place to tackle this emergency.

ELEVEN

BURNING THE WELLS

NOBODY should have been surprised that Saddam Hussein ordered the ignition of Kuwait's oil wells. The writing had been on the wall for a very long time. He had demonstrated his grasp of the 'environmental weapon' on past occasions and shown little reluctance to use it. The Iraqi military were trained by the Soviets, who had studied in some depth the use of natural forces in war. General V. V. Myasnikov's 399-page unclassified textbook, published in 1989, explains how it is 'possible to use destructive forces occurring in nature for military purposes'. The author describes the possible use of 'flooding and pollution to disrupt navigation and disable irrigation and other hydrostructures and create obstructions in rivers, canals and other bodies of water'. Saddam declared soon after the invasion that if the allies interfered he would destroy Kuwait. Kuwaiti Resistance reported that Iraqi troops planted explosive charges on almost all Kuwaiti oil wells within weeks of their occupation. Military planners and political leaders were fully aware that the Iraqis were capable of keeping their promise to burn the oil fields. But everyone hoped it would not happen; or if it did it would not be as bad as some scientists had warned.

The consequences that might ensue if Saddam Hussein did carry out his threat were uppermost in the minds of military strategists. Their first question was whether burning oil wells accompanied by thick, black smoke would bring any military advantage to the Iraqis.

Oil well near Al-Ahmadi on fire

The public response was that it would not do so, but a somewhat more sanguine view was taken in private. The pall of black smoke may not have disguised any military offensive but it did help to camouflage a chaotic retreat. It seems unlikely, however, that the uncertain military value of creating the world's biggest smoke cloud influenced Saddam's thinking. A more plausible explanation is that the overt threat of setting the wells on fire was intended to deter a counter-attack against his occupying forces in Kuwait and, in the event that it failed to do so, execution of the threat would be aimed at inflicting the maximum suffering on Kuwait and her neighbours in the anti-Iraq camp.

Possible environmental consequences of the Iraqi promise to set oil wells ablaze were discussed by a large number of scientists. As part of his lobbying to discourage the use of force to expel the Iraqis from Kuwait King Hussein of Jordan was prominent among world figures who urged the West not to provoke Saddam Hussein to set the oilfields on fire. In a speech on November 7, 1990, he speculated 'if half Kuwait's oil reserves, about fifty billion barrels, were to go up in flames' the resulting disturbance to global climate would be extremely serious, further accelerating the greenhouse effect. Dr Abdullah Toukan, environmental adviser to King Hussein, stated at a conference on the potential effects of an allied invasion of Kuwait, 'The environmental cost of such a war is likely to outstrip all other costs, great though these will be. Burning oilfields are the most long-lasting, widespread and severe hazard to the environment.' Early in 1991 governments were being warned that the effects of a massive smoke cloud could spread as far as India. The British Overseas Development Administration commissioned an agricultural report to advise on the likely effects for farming of reduced sunlight, lower temperatures and interrupted rainfall. Whether or not the fires would cause a global catastrophe, it was becoming clear that the environment had become a bouncy propaganda

football in a game played by both sides in the Gulf conflict.

A special report by the UK Meteorological Office was issued in direct response to a British Government request for it to 'assess the environmental consequences of burning Kuwaiti oil wells'. The desk study took place in early January, and was published on January 14, shortly before the announcement of the start of Operation Desert Storm. The report states:

For the purposes of estimating environmental impacts, the Meteorological Office was advised to take the following worst case scenario: the quantity of oil burnt would be equivalent to one year of Kuwait's pre-invasion production of 80 million tonnes (Mt) {approximately 576 million barrels} per year spread out over one year. This would give rise to approximately 2 Mt of sulphur oxides, 0.5 Mt of nitrogen in the form of nitrogen oxides and 60 Mt of carbon as carbon dioxide gas. A further assumption is that 6% of the oil would be converted to black smoke, yielding 5 Mt.

According to Met. Office scientists the 'only possible long term effect' might be increased quantities of carbon dioxide influencing global warming, but they added that such an effect would be 'almost negligible'. However, they suggested that localized effects could be quite severe, with acidification created by very heavy deposition of sulphur and nitrogen compounds. They also suggested that citizens of regions affected by wind-blown smoke would experience similar conditions to those produced by the photochemical smog which had proved such a health hazard in some of the world's major cities. Additional conclusions were that there would be a considerable reduction in daylight and daytime temperatures.

Not everyone agreed with the 'localized effects theory', however. Fears that a major conflagration of Kuwaiti oil wells could stimulate a devastating famine on the Indian subcontinent were raised by a number of scientists. It was argued that a fall of a few degrees could disrupt monsoon rains and cause massive failures of the crops that are essential for the region's burgeoning population. Anne Ehrlich, of the Sierra Club of the United States, expressed such concerns when she stated in late January, 'If this goes on until spring and summer, it will be a direct threat to their food supply which is already marginal.' Others suggested that, whilst the monsoons could be affected, it may take slightly longer for the build-up of smoke to have such a serious effect. John Cox, a British chemical engineer, told a conference organized by the UK Green Party and the Campaign for Nuclear Disarmament (CND) in London, early in January, that: 'A year-long oil well conflagration within this sensitive microclimate region could influence the onset, duration and character of the monsoons. . . . Even a partial failure could cause more deaths than the total population of Iraq, Kuwait and Saudi Arabia combined.'

The question of how far the smoke might travel was addressed by the UK Meteorological Office report of January 14, which emphasized that distance travelled would be proportional to how high the smoke reached: 'Whether or not the smoke reached the upper atmosphere would depend critically on the absorption of sunlight by the smoke, which depends on its physical characteristics, and hence on details of the combustion.' Without precise information on the nature of the fires it was simply not possible to make more accurate assessments of what might happen. Nevertheless the report did take the view that effects of smoke and pollutants would be primarily local and regional. It suggested that shading of sunlight downwind of Kuwait would have a lowering effect on surface temperatures and may cause localized reductions in rainfall over parts of South-East Asia during the summer monsoon. But the authors cautioned that: 'The uncertainty of these estimates, and the great natural variability seasonally and locally in the monsoon, are emphasised.'

It was not long before the report's findings were put to the 'acid test'. During the last week of January oil-storage tanks at Al-Wafra and Shuaiba were set on fire. US and Saudi spokesmen claimed this had been done on purpose by the Iraqis to confuse the guidance systems of allied aircraft and to obscure the view of military satellites. The allies denied that the Iraqis would gain any military advantage from such a strategy, which the Pentagon labelled 'environmental terrorism'. In order to sustain the pall of smoke it seems that the Iraqis may have tested some of their explosive devices by setting a number of wells on fire. In early February coalition forces, targeting strategic targets in Iraq, set fire to facilities at the Zubair oilfield, causing smoke clouds which were still visible at the end of the month. In the week before the commencement of the land war oil fires were already pouring their thick, black smoke into the atmosphere, providing a foretaste of what was to come. Most of the smoke emanated from oil installations rather than oil wells. John Cox, using Meteosat satellite images to monitor the sources of pollution and their developing smoke clouds, claimed that one large plume was coming from Al-Khafji and a second from the Al-Wafra oilfield. In the latter case at least two small oil wells were burning, along with oil installations. The smoke, he claimed, was already spreading far from Kuwait: 'It penetrated the temperature inversion and caught the upper westerly winds. It has passed over Iran towards India.'

Despite denials by allied commanders, there is little doubt that thick clouds of black smoke did serve a military purpose, albeit short-lived and fairly ineffective. A British pilot flying from the Royal Naval frigate *Brave*, is reported to have commented, on February 24:

Usually we could see Kuwait City clearly from five miles out but not today. As we flew up to the coast, you could just make out the shape of the sun through the smoke but it gave off no light. You could smell the sulphur from the burning oil. Westerly winds made it worse, bringing the smoke off the coast and over the sea.

Shifting winds often blew dense smoke over Kuwait City, turning day into night.

The point was re-emphasized by Jonathon Porritt, former director of Friends of the Earth, who commented: 'It was clear right from the start this would be seen as a legitimate war effort on Saddam Hussein's part and the environmental damage is obviously going to be very serious indeed.' (Both quotations from Colin Randall, in the *Daily Telegraph*, February 25.)

In the latter months of 1990 a number of brave Kuwaitis who were aware of the explosive charges attached to their oil wells succeeded in bribing soldiers to disconnect some of the wiring. In addition resistance members were themselves trained in how to disable the firing systems attached to the charges. The hope was that a rapid departure caused by an unexpected allied attack would leave many of the wells intact. Unfortunately the Iraqi command came to hear of these efforts at sabotaging their own sabotage. Two days before the launch of the ground offensive the

Iraqis played for extra time, sending their Prime Minister, Tariq Aziz, to Moscow in a final attempt to negotiate a settlement. While the diplomatic mission was proceeding and the world's attention was focused on the outcome of talks, members of Saddam Hussein's Revolutionary Guard were making final preparations to ensure that charges already attached to the wells were effectively detonated as Saddam and his commanders had planned.

However secretive the Iraqis may have tried to be in their last desperate attempt to set Kuwait on fire, there was no disguising the evidence of their actions which was revealed to satellites passing overhead. The US remote-sensing satellite Meteosat relayed the first news of what they were up to at 10 a.m. on February 21, while Tariq Aziz was ensconced in talks with the Russians and the coalition forces were holding back from their imminent ground offensive. Images from the satellite, analysed by Vipin Gupta of Imperial College, London, showed clouds of black smoke emanating from the Al-Ahmadi refinery complex. Gupta explained that the pictures also showed: 'Other plumes of smoke, for instance from the eastern and western edges of the nearby Burgan oilfield, became much thicker at the same time, suggesting a coordinated action' (*New Scientist*, March 2, 1991).

The timing of these deliberately caused oilfield explosions is particularly revealing since they occurred before Saddam Hussein accepted the Soviet Union's first peace proposal. In the midst of subsequent last-minute negotiations, on February 22, huge volumes of smoke were shown to be rising from Kuwait's northern Rawdatayn oilfield. During the next few days the growing pall of smoke spread slowly, soon covering an area of 11,000 sq. km (4250 sq. miles) but remaining at its thickest over Kuwait's coastal region. Estimates of how many oil wells had been set on fire went up rapidly from less than a hundred, to over two hundred, then five hundred, then six hundred or so. Virtually all of the country's wells had been sabotaged in one way or another.

A recent census of grazing animals in Kuwait indicated over half a million sheep, 100,000 camels, 19,000 goats and 600 horses. Many died or suffered heavily as a result of the war.

Camels, like sheep, are affected by the smoke. Their coats are blackened by the dark soot particles absorbed from the air.

Differences between a burning refinery or storage tank and a burning oil well were vividly demonstrated during the first week of the major fires. The Al-Ahmadi tanks, set ablaze on the morning of February 21, had burned themselves out in three to four days, with no trace of smoke coming from them on February 25. Smoke from these intense conflagrations rose relatively high into the atmosphere and spread over an extended range. The oil-well fires, by contrast, could only burn at the rate at which oil from underground flowed to the surface. Their smoke was not propelled to such heights as that from the refinery fires and did not spread as quickly or as far as the higher-altitude pollution. Nevertheless the oil wells kept on burning, day after day, week after week, month after month. Their long-term impact was far more severe than that of the limited fires caused by sabotaging or bombing oil-storage tanks.

An assessment of the likely impact of burning oil wells was made by Richard Small of the Pacific-Sierra Research Corporation, who published his findings in the journal *Nature* on March 7. His analysis was based on a number of basic assumptions. He took the 1989 average daily production rate of 1,593,000 barrels, the average daily flow from each well being 4390 barrels. He stated that before the invasion 363 wells were in use but he presumed that shut-down wells were also blown which would, he said, reduce the flow per well and possibly not increase the overall flow since pressure in the reservoirs would be more rapidly reduced. He took what he regarded as a worst-case scenario under which a 25 percent increase in flow took place. Developing his calculation he used smoke-emission factors previously determined by laboratory experiments (ranging from 20 grams per kilogram of oil to 90 g/kg) together with the conclusion that roughly 69 percent of the emission is 'pure' carbon. He then calculated that the daily production of smoke from burning 1,593,000 barrels of oil per day, would be 16,000 tonnes (15,750 tons) per day. Thus, according to Small, almost half a million tonnes of smoke (492,000 tons) could be added to the atmosphere in a thirty-day period. He concluded his analysis by examining the likely height to which smoke would be injected into the atmosphere and concluded that this would be relatively low. Thus, while the smoke would probably not have a global effect, nor cause a failure of the monsoons, 'the amount of smoke produced would be large and cause a massive pollution event. It would impact the ecology of the Persian Gulf and fall out on a wide swath across southern Iran, Pakistan, and possibly northern India.'

The first scientific examination of what by now was known as the 'Gulf Oil Plume' was carried out using the UK Meteorological Office's C-130 Hercules research aircraft which returned to the UK on April 4 after seven flights into the oil plume, penetrating a wide range of altitudes and distances from Kuwait. The UK Met. Office also undertook helicopter flights to the heart of the burning area and noted that different wells gave off different forms of pollution, some belching out black smoke whereas others emitted white fumes of steam, or clean flames of methane.

At around 100 km (60 miles) from Kuwait City the maximum concentrations of smoke were located at an altitude of 2000 m (6560 ft): '1000 ppb of sulphur dioxide; 50 ppb of nitrogen oxides; nearly 30,000 particles of aerosol <0.1 to 10 microns in diameter> per cubic centimetre'. At this distance from the main source of pollution the top of the plume was typically at 3000–4000 m (9840–13,120 ft) with the base at around 1000–1500 m (3280–4920 ft). With smoke from the burning wells distributed over such an altitude range, wind conditions at the top of the plume could differ from those at its base, so that a 'windshear often carried the top of the plume away to the north-east, with the smoke below this usually blowing down the west Gulf coast'. Flying conditions within the plume were less than pleasant. 'Levels of sunlight were reduced to close to zero and night time lighting was required on the flight deck.' (Data and quotations from UK Meteorological Office Report dated April 4, 1991.)

Dr Geoffrey Jenkins, who coordinated the scientific programme, explained that their study was not directed at investigating whether the smoke would become a local health hazard but whether its major impact would be regional or global. By examining the plume's constituents and characteristics they were able to discount the global theory. It was clear that the smoke was remaining in the troposphere, and not penetrating the stratosphere where it would have a much longer atmospheric existence. Dr Jenkins explained:

The smoke only has a life of two or three days in the lower atmosphere, so we do not expect any major build-up of smoke over time. What is happening is that the smoke rises to around 40000 m {13,120 ft} or more, with the upper smoke carried from west to east, particles within it aggregate and as they become heavier start to drift back down to ground level. If they meet clouds they are incorporated with the moist particles and travel with them, eventually precipitating out as smoke polluted rain, hail or snow.

The major impact, Dr Jenkins added, would be from smoke and chemical pollution on the ground, within the Gulf region.

Photochemical production of ozone was noted at some distance from the main fires whereas closer to the source ozone levels were depressed due to nitric oxide 'mopping up' ozone. While the Met. Office study was concerned with more widespread implications of the pollution, an American 'Inter-Agency Team' was sent into Kuwait during March to assess the potential health hazards caused by smoke to the local population. Their report stated that: 'The fires may represent one of the most extraordinary manmade environmental disasters in recorded history'; and: 'More than 500 oil well, storage tank and refinery, and facility fires are currently raging in Kuwait and each day produce an enormous amount of smoke and other pollutants.' Emphasizing the potential for such fires to create major health hazards, the report stated: 'Chemicals such as sulfur dioxide and hydrogen sulfide as well as carbon monoxide and polycyclic aromatic hydrocarbons are often found along with particulate matter in oil fires'; and: 'Emissions from oil fires may have the potential of causing health effects of both an acute and chronic nature, although there is considerable uncertainty as to the extent of the threat.'

What surprised many scientists was that the American team failed to confirm the presence of 'such chemicals in any significant quantity'. Furthermore, 'Preliminary analysis of the substantial amounts of particulate matter did not reveal any

chemicals at levels of concern'. Summarizing the mission's findings, EPA Administrator William K. Reilly said, 'The preliminary data provide a snapshot of the air pollution situation in the Gulf region. No acute toxins were detected. I caution that our findings are quite preliminary and suggest that further monitoring and assessments are in order.' It seemed quite remarkable that, while concentrations of sulphur dioxide within the plume were as high as 1000 ppb, ground-level readings 'did not indicate levels of concern of sulfur dioxide or hydrogen sulfide, each of which might cause health problems and might be expected in oil fires of this magnitude'. The mission's spokesmen were at pains to emphasize that there was an urgent need for more detailed analysis and that their results should not be interpreted as a denial of health risks associated with the fires.

It was clear in the early days of the air war that official US reports were increasingly at pains to downplay the ecological and health hazards of the smoke pollution. One possible explanation for this was the degree to which allied actions might be held responsible for the pollution in this phase of the conflict. Just as an information clamp-down was imposed concerning analysis of the Gulf oil-slicks, in particular with regard to allied bombing of Iraqi tankers and the Mina Al-Bakr terminal, so precautions were taken to limit criticism of allied military activities which caused smoke pollution. Evidence of this widely acknowledged official media-management policy was published in *Scientific American* (May 1991) which quoted a memorandum issued by the US Department of Energy dated January 25: 'the extent of what we are authorised to say about environmental impacts of fires and oil spills in the Middle East follows: "Most independent studies and experts suggest that catastrophic predictions in some recent news reports are exaggerated. We are currently reviewing the matter but these predictions remain speculative and do not warrant any further comment at this time."'

Members of the US Inter-Agency team visited hospitals in Kuwait and confirmed that some people, especially those suffering from asthma, were at risk from the pollution. They advised that troops should not be given heavy physical work within smoke-polluted areas and should be provided with face-masks. 'The best we can tell at this point, at least, is people are breathing in soot. The particulates aren't carrying the chemicals of major concern for which we are testing,' Jim Makris, of the US Environmental Protection Agency, was quoted as saying in the *Wall Street Journal*.

'Seen up close for the first time last week, the ecological damage inflicted on the tiny country turns out to be worse than anyone dared imagine' (Philip Elmer-Dewitt, *Time*, March 18, 1991). Estimates of the quantity of oil being burned off or leaking each day were considerably more than the figure predicted in Richard Small's earlier analysis. The Kuwait Petroleum Corporation believed that as much as six million barrels per day could be going up in smoke and they stated that calculations based on previous flow-rates could be misleading since many of the wells were valved or 'choked' down so as to control their flow-rate, but that Iraqi sabotage had destroyed such control systems, allowing oil to flow at an unchecked rate.

The thick, black smoke was having a dramatic effect on wildlife. Observers in Kuwait reported large numbers of dead, soot-covered birds scattered across the desert downwind of burning oil wells. The first reported victims were slender-billed gulls and Caspian terns but the main spring migration was just getting under way and fears were mounting that there could be a serious impact on those species for which the Gulf represented a major pathway between their winter and summer feeding and breeding areas.

Physical effects of the smoke were apparent to everyone who entered Kuwait after its liberation. On some days the smoke cloud over Kuwait City obliterated all light. On many days light attenuation was such that photocell-controlled street lights automatically switched on. The air was

Left **Most collection and control facilities within the oil fields were destroyed along with the well-heads**

Previous page **By mid-summer many large oil lakes had formed. It is hard to imagine sensitive desert plant-life recolonising these regions.**

frequently painful to breathe and everyone feared the consequences to their health. Residents of the Al-Ahmadi area, immediately to the east of the major concentration of burning wells, not only lived with nearly perpetual gloom but were constantly afflicted by a fine mist containing droplets of unburned oil. As the weather gradually warmed, conditions became even more intolerable. A hint of what was yet to come was delivered in early April when a temperature inversion caused black smoke to suddenly sink to ground level, stinging people who were caught outside. Naji Saad, who lives and works at the oil town of Al-Ahmadi, complained that his face and hands felt as if they were on fire. Later on the same evening a second onslaught of acidic smog caused breathing problems for Naji's seven-year-old daughter, who was taken to hospital. The smoke had mixed with humid night air to form sulphuric acid. Dr Fatima Bulbara, of the Al-Ahmadi hospital, commented that it was possible that women were losing their hair as a result of the extreme pollution (Kathy Evans reporting in the *Guardian*, April 12, 1991).

With so many wells burning, and with at least two million barrels per day (some estimated up to six million) going up in smoke, the worst-case scenario was beginning to look either realistic or optimistic depending on one's prognosis for how long it would take to snuff out the flames and how high the plume might rise. Early effects were confined to Gulf and Middle Eastern countries, with black rain falling in Iran, Iraq, Syria, Jordan, Turkey, Kuwait and Saudi Arabia. Increasingly, however, new reports began filtering in of smoke reaching Asia. In early March Richard Turco, professor of environmental science at the University of California at Los Angeles, said that the dry spring weather would likely result in a stable pall rising over Kuwait and the Gulf countries with its upper surface being whipped off by high-speed winds towards Asia. Christopher Flavin, vice-president of the World Watch Institute based in Washington, warned that oily smoke spreading to India and Pakistan could damage crops and grazing lands as well as water supplies. He described the Gulf War as the 'most environmentally destructive conflict in the history of

warfare' and called for 'a workable environmental code for the conduct of war, including enforcement mechanisms for violators'.

By the end of March Swiss skiers reported that black snow was falling on remote Himalayan slopes of Kashmir, over 2400 km (1490 miles) from Kuwait and at a height of 4600 m (15,090 ft). The mixture of oil, soot and snow caused their skis to stick. On investigating further they discovered a buried layer of dark, oily snow, almost 5 cm (2 in) thick. The report did not surprise British Meteorological Office scientist John Gloster, who formed part of the study team investigating the Gulf oil plume. 'We've seen black rain in the Gulf and if the pollutants are carried to highland areas they fall as black snow. Certainly the plume can travel that distance' (reported by Steve Connor in the *Independent on Sunday*, March 31, 1991). Intriguingly some Indian scientists had previously toyed with the idea of sprinkling

Left Volatile gases collect above the oil lakes, unpredictably igniting and setting areas of desert ablaze.

Above Oil-flooded roads are very treacherous. At this site two *Financial Times* staff were killed when their car skidded into a pool of oil and caught fire.

Himalayan snow with black coal dust as a means of accelerating the rate of melting and consequent irrigation of areas hit by failure of monsoon rains. The plan was shelved due to objections from conservation groups.

'Black rain in Balochistan' read the headline in the *Karachi Business Record* of April 6, 1991. The report stated that the areas of Quetta, Loralai, Chaman, Kachchi, Dhaadar and Sibi had all received soot-laden rain. The Pakistan Meteorologi-

cal Office expected that large-scale pollution would increase as local temperatures rose. A report from Pakistan dated April 10 described how black rain had destroyed wheat crops in Noshero and Nawabshah districts. Heavy rain laden with soot which fell on April 9 damaged electrical and communications systems in the region. Crop growers reported that they had lost crops valued at 20 million rupees and claimed compensation from the Sindh Government (*The Frontier Post*, April 11, 1991).

As oily smoke continued to build over Kuwait and surrounding regions its effects on nature intensified. Agriculture in many areas of Arabia and the Middle East was already tapping dwindling water resources in order to irrigate increasingly acidic soils. There had been relatively few previous investigations of the possible impact of pollution on Arabian agriculture but one particularly relevant study was carried out in 1975 by Professor Nigel Bell, now head of the Centre for Environmental Technology at Imperial College of Science, Technology and Medicine in London (UCNW & Ministry of Agriculture and Water, Saudi Arabia Joint Agricultural Research and Development Project, Publication No. 85.

1977). Bell's work in Saudi Arabia was carried out at the invitation of the Saudi Arabian Ministry of Agriculture, which was concerned to establish whether there was a link between chlorosis of vegetation in the Al Hasa oasis and emission of pollutants from gas—oil separation plants in the Abqaiq oilfield.

Scientists working at the Hofuf Animal Production and Research Centre had noticed that crops grown at the centre were indicating signs of chlorosis and it was feared that this resulted from sulphur-dioxide pollution connected with the burning off of excess gases in the nearby oilfield. Chlorosis is a typical symptom of sulphur-dioxide poisoning in plants: leaves lose colour, dry up and are prematurely shed, leading to a fall in yield. As Nigel Bell was quick to explain, however, chlorosis is not solely associated with sulphur-dioxide poisoning. It may also occur through mineral toxicity in the soil or through water stress. Bell set out in his study to establish whether the suffering plants showed elevated concentrations of sulphur in their foliage tissues.

Results of this study, carried out over fifteen years ago, help to establish some baseline figures for sulphur-dioxide levels in the air over eastern Saudi Arabia. Mean levels during the April—May period at the Hofuf Centre were 0.062 micrograms, and the highest level recorded was 0.146 micrograms. The mean level was close to that found in rural Britain, which averaged 0.040 to 0.050 micrograms at that time, and these levels were not thought to pose a major problem for plants. Measurements were also taken in the desert, immediately downwind of smoke plumes from the oilfield and the highest concentration of sulphur dioxide recorded was 0.166 micrograms. Analysis of figures for the sun's radiation also proved interesting, showing an 8 percent fall between 1969 and 1975, corresponding with an increase in the number of gas—oil separation plants.

Bell commented:

Thus there is strong evidence that particulate pollutants, resulting from the burning of oil-well gases are reducing the net radiation at ground level at Hofuf. This situation could possibly lead to a depression in crop yield because of reduced photosynthesis, but this seems unlikely at Hofuf because the light intensity is usually so high that it is not a limiting factor.

Values for sulphur content in the foliage of green and chlorotic plants at Hofuf proved to be particularly interesting since they did not support the theory that observed plant chlorosis could be directly attributed to aerial pollution from the oilfields. Bell suggested that the root cause was more likely to be the result of lime-induced mineral deficiencies.

Like much of the agricultural region of eastern Arabia, the soil at Hofuf is rich in gypsum or calcium sulphate and it was felt that variation in sulphur content of plant tissues had more to do with this than with smoke pollution. Professor Bell commented that an impermeable layer near the surface of the soil tends to create mineral deficiencies because of excessive salt accumulation. Agricultural production was already affected by these factors, before the arrival of massive pollution from the burning oil wells in Kuwait. Bell had already shown that many Arabian plants were existing close to their tolerance levels in a steadily deteriorating environment. Thus the impact of oil-fire pollution was likely to be all the more devastating upon the region's agricultural production.

Millions of tons of smoke particles, falling back to earth in Kuwait and surrounding countries, continued to plaster the deserts with a thick layer of gradually hardening oil and soot. Huge areas in the vicinity of the fires were carpeted by asphalt, killing plant life and associated animals. Thousands of acres were turned into what some observers described as the world's largest car-park.

Male idmi gazelle. All five species of gazelle found in the Arabian Peninsula are endangered.

As fall-out from smoke further boosted soil acid levels over coastal areas of the Gulf, the Middle East and beyond, causing plant diseases and eventually reducing the population of some species, water bodies were contaminated by emissions from the burning wells, both on land and in the sea, adding further to the region's pollution problems. Spring became summer and ecological fall-out from the Gulf War intensified, causing widespread suffering and death among both wildlife

and humans. Just how lethal the effects of such heavily polluted air can be were amply demonstrated to Europeans by crippling city smogs of a few decades ago. Three particular incidents have entered the history books: the Meuse Valley smog in Belgium in 1930; the Donora smog in Pennsylvania in 1948, which killed eighteen people; and London in the winter of 1952. This latter smog resulted from a stationary anti-cyclone which prevented the normal diffusion of urban smoke

from coal fires and car exhausts. High concentrations of smoke and sulphur dioxide soon reached toxic levels, causing thousands of illnesses and at least four thousand deaths from heart and lung diseases initiated by the pollution. Daily concentrations of sulphur dioxide reached a staggering level of 4000 micrograms per cubic metre—over ten times the WHO safe limit for intake per hour!

But it was not simply these concentrations

Trees with extensive root systems like these *Acacia* at the edge of the Al-Ahmadi oil field displayed incredible tenacity, producing spring growth despite the rain of oil and smoke. Long term effects on vegetation have not been assessed.

which caused the London deaths. Atmospheric conditions favoured the formation of droplets of sulphuric acid, creating a potentially lethal aerosol. Several clues hinted at acid being the killer, including the effective use of ammonia bottles in hospital wards where the ammonia, diffused through wicks, helped to neutralize acid in the air. Another clue was the fact that cattle at the Smithfield Club's Show reacted differently, with the least cared for animals showing the fewest signs of suffering from the pollution. It was concluded that excrement left in the relatively dirty pens of these animals emitted ammonia which conveniently neutralized air inhaled by the cattle, whereas those animals whose pens were regularly cleaned out did not receive this benefit and suffered the consequences of breathing acid droplets.

Since these tragedies, considerable research has taken place, linking formation of acid aerosols with high mortalities. Sulphuric acid is formed from sulphur dioxide by a chemical reaction in which strong sunlight plays a vital role. In temperate countries it is especially associated with summer conditions, while in Kuwait and Arabia there is sufficient sunlight throughout the year to initiate the reaction. The photochemical conversion of sulphur dioxide occurs in the presence of other emissions from the burning wells, including nitrogen oxides and hydrocarbons. A particular danger posed by this acidic air is that sulphuric acid levels of 70 micrograms per cubic metre can trigger potentially lethal asthmatic attacks. (Death rates from asthma have increased by 50 percent in the past ten years in several industrialized countries.) Recent work carried out by Professor Jack Spengler of the Department of Environmental Health at the Harvard School of Public Health has highlighted the potential dangers of acidic conditions, particularly to children. Other workers have shown that acidic pollution plumes can travel considerable distances. One study by Bert Brunekreef of the University of Wageningen tracked a pollutant cloud over a

It has been estimated that more than 6 million mines were laid in Kuwait. Despite a massive clearance operation many explosives have been buried by sand or blown out of mine-fields.

distance of more than 1000 km (620 miles), right across Europe, from east to west. The Gulf War created a much larger plume of highly acidic air

which cast its toxic shadow over a vast area of
Arabia, the Middle East and Asia.

Jonathon Porritt, former director of Friends of
the Earth, severely criticized the first major BBC
television film on the environmental impact of the
Gulf war, in particular for its poor coverage of the
smoke story. The film, broadcast in the highly
acclaimed *Nature* series, appeared to be aimed at
demonstrating that environmental consequences
of the war had been sensationalized for 'political

reasons' and that neither the slicks nor the fires
presented particularly serious environmental
problems. Porritt charged that the programme's
'analysis was painfully simplistic' and that its
discussion of the oil-fire threat was 'so inaccurate
as to border on dishonesty' (*Daily Telegraph*). The
real problem, as Porritt stated, was that 'nobody
really knew what was going to happen because
nobody had ever simultaneously set fire to 600 oil
wells'.

TWELVE

OPERATION DESERT QUENCH

I have always imagined that an oil well which had taken fire must be a difficult thing to control, but I did not realise the virulence of these fires until I came across an account of a well of petroleum in Romania which has been in flames for no less than three years. The extinction of the blaze by means of a powder invented for the occasion marks the end of a campaign of fire fighting, in the course of which thirty-seven persons have lost their lives. The heat around the burning well was so intense that it was impossible to approach it, but numerous devices for its extinction were tried from a distance. These included the breaking up of the surrounding ground by bombs dropped from aeroplanes, and the dropping upon the column of fire of bombs filled with extinguishing gases. None, however, had any effect. The most spectacular attempt was that made by an American engineer, who succeeded in shooting an enormous bell of bronze over the mouth of the well, thereby cutting off the flow of oil. This seemed at first to have the desired effect, but after the fire had been suppressed for twenty minutes the bell was blown into the air with a terrific explosion, and the engineer was killed by the flying fragments. During the course of the three years' fire the wastage of petroleum must have been enormous; for the pillar of flame from the burning well rose to a height of over 750 feet. (*Irish Times*, February 27, 1931)

The above account was resurrected by the *Irish Times* newspaper

The Wild Well fire-fighting crew inspect a well-head

during the recent Gulf crisis. It was a particularly apt reminder of the great difficulty and danger associated with trying to douse burning oil wells. Of course, technology has moved on and new methods have been developed for extinguishing oil fires but it remains in essence a 'seat of the pants' operation, fraught with frustration and high risk.

Americans have held the lead in oil-fire fighting since the early 1940s when Texan oil man Myron Kinley developed the use of dynamite to extinguish burning wells. It was Kinley who taught Red Adair the tricks of the trade and Adair set up his own company in 1959, after Kinley retired. Despite the success of their techniques, new methods are continually under investigation and a special conference called to review the latest thinking in oil-fire-fighting techniques held in Washington during April 1991 brought to mind the wide range of methods tested in Rumania several years before the establishment of Arabia's first oil well. Since that time over a thousand oil wells had caught fire, requiring the attentions of specialized fire-fighters. But Kuwait's burning oil wells presented a unique set of problems. Never before had such a large number of oil installations been set on fire simultaneously and never before had the burning wells been surrounded by anti-personnel mines, rendering access extremely dangerous. Never before had the pollution from burning oil wells posed such a serious risk to surrounding lands, threatening to kill thousands of people. And never before had so much money been at stake in terms of permanent damage to oil resources and revenues lost from the cessation of an entire country's prime trade.

In these circumstances engineers argued that new technologies would have to be employed. Not only would they have to devise safe means to remove buried land-mines, but they also needed to perfect the art of capping wells swiftly. Whereas seasoned fire-fighters were talking in terms of two years or more, the Kuwait Government was looking for a seven-month programme

to put out all the fires. Many observers questioned, given the extremely difficult circumstances in which fire-fighters were working, whether such an ambitious target was realistic.

The Washington conference was organized by the Union of Concerned Scientists whose head, Nobel-prize-winning physicist Henry Kendall, stated in his opening address that conventional technologies were geared towards extinguishing a maximum of five fires at one time. Given that around five hundred wells were blazing, with ninety more spewing crude oil, he argued that the special circumstances demanded some newly devised unconventional methods. Step one, it was generally agreed, was to make each well site as safe as possible for workers to be able to operate without being blown up by land-mines, booby-traps or unexploded allied bombs. The conference was informed that this task had not been accomplished by the coalition's forces and it was simply not safe to depend on inaccurate Iraqi maps of minefields. In order to locate and remove land-mines, Stirling Colgate, a physicist from Los Alamos National Laboratory in New Mexico, proposed use of powerful compressed-air guns or sand-blasters. Large industrial compressors would blow air under great pressure through a pipe draped over a normal front-end loader and aimed at the ground surface of the advance vehicle, blowing away surface sand to a depth of 12 or 15 inches (31–39 cm), and also blowing away and possibly detonating any land-mines in that layer of soil. The dome would also be powerful enough to break up and blow away the concrete 'collars' surrounding the wells at a depth of 5–12 ft (1.5–3.6 m).

Colgate proposed that the special 'guns' would produce a blast of 140–280 cu. m (183–366 cu. yards) of air per minute at a pressure of 14 kg/sq. cm (78 lb/sq. in). Given that air and sand are both commodities in plentiful supply in the Kuwaiti desert, the proposal had great potential merit. Colgate suggested that turning the high-pressure air-gun into a sand-blaster would allow it to be

Snuffing out the fires is only one step towards the final goal of installing a new valve to control the flow of oil and gas.

used to break up concrete platforms and broken pipes on top of the oil wells, enabling fire-fighters to gain better access to clean sections of well-pipes, which could then be plugged. A further advantage of spraying vast quantities of sand around burning wells was that the sand would help to absorb radiant heat, helping to keep the surrounding area cool enough for workers and their equipment to operate. The brainstorming scientists, intrigued by Colgate's innovative pro-posal, brought up the added possibility that the giant compressor's exhaust could be included in the air blast, rendering that blast inert and there-fore potentially helpful in extinguishing the fire. It was noted that a system using the exhaust of a jet engine has been operated by the Soviets in fighting oil fires for several years. Oil company

personnel at the conference greeted Colgate's ideas with a considerable amount of interest. Jay Turley, director of Marathon Oil's worldwide drilling operations, was reported by the *Wall Street Journal* (April 5–6, 1991) as describing it as 'the best thing I've seen' at the conference.

Another plan for clearing the ground around the wells, proposed by William Wattenburg, a former nuclear weapons designer, and consultant to the Lawrence Livermore National Laboratory in California, involved the use of helicopters to drag giant chain-mail 'carpets' over the ground, both dislodging and detonating any mines present. The 'carpets' or sleds of chain-mail had already been developed by the Livermore laboratory and incorporated spikes or harrows which gouge through the surface of the ground for use by US military forces.

One of the great problems facing fire-fighters was leakages of oil from around burning wells, or wells whose fires had been put out but were not yet capped. Huge quantities of crude oil flowed

Many well-heads were encrusted with a carbon carapace which had to be scraped away before piping could be inspected. Surrounding oil lakes were filled with sand whilst seawater was used to cool the well-heads.

from broken well-heads, soaking into the surrounding desert, pouring into depressions to form lakes of oil. Sand barriers were constructed to contain the leaked oil and large pits were dug around the wells themselves. The quantities of oil were so great, however, that there was a grave danger of such temporary dams being breached and of oil leaking across the desert, flowing downhill, and possibly reaching the Gulf. Another

problem associated with this leakage was that the oil seeped back into the sand, contaminating groundwater resources. To the fire-fighters, however, these were peripheral considerations since leaked oil also threatened their own access to the burning wells, further complicating their already difficult task of dowsing the fires and capping well-heads.

Wattenburg, speaking at the April meeting in Washington, emphasized the urgency of capping wells, stressing that oil pouring from destroyed wells was making it increasingly difficult for fire-fighters to position their equipment. Dr Richard Garwin, a scientist working at the IBM Thomas J. Watson Research Center in the USA, proposed that a system of plastic-lined reservoirs and culverts should be constructed to channel oil away from the wells, possibly via long culverts, to coastal storage pits or existing facilities from where it could be pumped to waiting tankers.

Other proposals included digging tunnels to pipes feeding the burning wells; dumping a special mud down low-pressure wells in order to temporarily dowse the fire while control valves were turned off; and detonating explosives placed around the broken well-pipes in order to create an implosion, hopefully sealing the pipes and suffocating the fires. This latter suggestion had many collateral problems and was not recommended by the conference.

Ralph Brown, director of new business development of the Kuwait Oil Company (KOC) commented, 'The real value of the symposium was educating the people, directing them towards more realistic solutions. People came to understand that the real problem was to stop the flow and that extinguishing the fires was only part of the problem.'

While these debates were raging in the comfort and security of Western capitals, fire-fighters in Kuwait were getting on with the job of putting out the fires by the tried-and-tested means they knew best. The scene on the oilfields was dramatic. Huge pillars of flame and fumes emerged from hundreds of well-heads. Even from a distance the sound was ear-shattering, like an unhushed 707 jet at take off! 'The fire billows into a sky so black with oily smoke that Kuwait on most days looks like Kuwait on most nights,' wrote Tony Horwitz and Ken Wells, staff journalists on the *Wall Street Journal*. We had met Ken while he was in Bahrain, during February, to cover the oil-slick story. A veteran environmental reporter, he had also covered the *Exxon Valdez* oil spill and we were as interested to hear what he had to tell us as he was to learn about our knowledge of the Gulf's biology and likely impact of the spill. Our common interest in the environmental impact of the war kept us in touch with each other over the coming months as we shared our knowledge and first-hand experiences of the war's incredible devastation.

Many observers were impressed, not just by the massive fires and billowing smoke clouds which emanated from sabotaged wells, but also by the deafening roar of the flames.

Although many reporters and film crews were keen to get into Kuwait after its liberation, it was not easy to do so. After dealing with visa applications and managing to find transport into the country, one was then faced with the problem of living in a city whose basic services had been sabotaged. Even if one solved all these problems, there was the smoke. Frequently vehicles driven in the middle of the day on major highways would have to pull up because their drivers could not see beyond the bonnet. Within days of arriving in Kuwait people suffered from sinus symptoms, sore throats and chest pains. In most cases these

ailments disappeared as soon as they left the country and once more breathed reasonably clean air. Most were as keen to leave as they had been to arrive. Kuwait was no place to hang around unless there were compelling reasons to do so. The best of all reasons was to put an end to the crippling pollution: to snuff out the fires.

The big name in oil-well fire-fighting is Red Adair of Houston, Texas. The company, named after its legendary head, Paul 'Red' Adair, who carefully nurtures his image by, among other things, wearing red overalls and driving a red Cadillac, had people in Kuwait as soon as it was possible for them to be there. Their contract, signed with the Kuwaiti government-in-exile, committed them to fight the fires for one year at a daily rate of around $10,000 for each five- or six-man team working on the fires. Oil-fire-fighting

seems to have grown into a Texan monopoly, with three of the four initially contracted companies hailing from this pioneering oil state. Boots and Coots was formed by Asgar 'Boots' Hansen and Edward 'Coots' Matthews after Red Adair fired them for, according to Boots, 'insubordination'. In contrast to Red Adair's image of fire, Boots wears white overalls, a white helmet and drives a white BMW.

Another group involved in oilfield fire and well control operations was Safety Boss, from Canada. Joe Bowden's Wild Well Control Inc. is also a Texas-based company making a significant contribution to extinguishing the fires and capping the wells. When we asked Pat Campbell, Bowden's partner, to describe the level of cooperation between operatives and the degree of information exchange, he was quick to point out that

each well has very different characteristics. Pressures at the well-head vary greatly. Some wells are shallow; others reach down to 13,000 ft (3960 m).

At this time there were suggestions in the press that the four companies in place were proceeding at a leisurely pace. In fact discussions with them indicated that they were both fiercely competitive among themselves and evidently working to capacity, given the need for large-scale logistical support away from the well-heads. To our eye they appeared to have the dedication and the professionalism of a team of surgeons.

By the end of March these four companies, coordinated by the Sante Fe Corporation (who had been responsible for most of the original well drilling in Kuwait since 1963), had fielded around forty hard-core well-cappers in Kuwait. They faced severe operational difficulties, hampered by mines, unexploded allied cluster bombs, flooding oil, lack of water, shortages of equipment and suffocating smoke. Their task would have been made infinitely more difficult had it not been for the courageous efforts of a twenty-five-year-old female employee of KOC who, in the middle of the Iraqi occupation of Al-Ahmadi town, where the oil control centre had been turned into a military headquarters, and where torture and rape had become commonplace, managed to enter the KOC command and remove the only existing microfiche files depicting the precise locations and underground well details for the Ahmadi oil fields. Pat Campbell of Wild Well Control Inc., who alerted us to this effort, emphasized the value of this vital data source.

Each well presented its own particular problems, requiring careful analysis before an attempt was made to extinguish the fire and stem the unchecked oil flow. One of the main methods employed to cap the wells is generally a two-stage affair. First a water-sprayed bulldozer carrying an oil drum filled with dynamite, suspended on the end of a long boom in front of the vehicle, is manoeuvred into position. The burning well-

Previous page During the final capping men are drenched with oil as they lower the control head into position. *Above* An injection of 'mud' can sometimes counteract the upward pressure of oil.

head and surrounding glass-like crust are drenched with water to reduce temperatures and prevent operatives from being roasted alive. The bulldozer operator must contend with fierce heat

as he approaches the well and drags the volcano-shaped honeycomb of carbon resulting from the fire from the immediate surrounds of the well-head. The most common method for avoiding the intense heat is for the bulldozer to have a galvanized iron shed constructed on top, with a small peep hole for the driver. He deposits the drum of explosives slightly to one side of the well-head. As the charge is detonated it sucks oxygen from the surrounding air and, in theory at least, snuffs out the oil fire. We watched and filmed several such operations but in each case, despite a momentary disappearance of flames, once the explosion subsided, it took several attempts to extinguish the flames. A large pipe was placed above the spurting oil to allow inspection of the well-head. Observation and analysis of the well-head is the most important factor and only after this has been

Ruppell's sand fox is finely adapted to desert life. Although it is only one fifth the weight of a European red fox, it requires a foraging area at least six times as big as its larger relative.

thoroughly carried out can the fire be extinguished.

The failure rate underlined the great difficulty in putting out such fires. From very difficult sites oil pours from hidden fractures, forcing fire-fighters to drill diagonally towards the bottom of the target well. Mud is then pumped down the relief well which flows back up the target well, stemming the flow of oil.

By any standards it is extremely dangerous work. Fire-fighters are used to dealing with the problems of poisonous gas (hydrogen sulphide), or wells suddenly catching fire as they struggle to plug the flow, but they are not used to carrying out their work in the middle of minefields or undetonated cluster bombs dropped by American-led allied forces. As one old hand put it: 'You need eyeballs like a frog to come out alive.' But they were playing for high stakes. Fighting oil fires is not a business which can be marketed in the normal way; either a well blows, and urgent help is needed, or it doesn't. It is a fickle business which has been detrimentally affected by increasing safety standards and technological improvements, together with the oil slump and well closures. In 1980 Boots and Coots had their best year to date, bringing sixty-four wells under control. In 1990 that figure had fallen to twenty-seven and they were beginning to wonder where their next business might be coming from. Saddam Hussein's sabotage has brought

Right Cuttlefish are among the largest invertebrates found over the Gulf's sea grass beds.

Below Every year countless millions of birds, like these sand-martins, migrate to, from and through Arabia.

enough business to allow the company and its employees to live in comfort for a few more years. Whereas skilled operatives can earn around $100,000 in a good year the present crisis has brought the possibility of them making up to $500,000 in 1991 and even more in 1992.

But the stakes were much more higher for Kuwait. Officials there estimated that up to six million barrels per day were being lost through burning or leakages and that at most five percent of its total reserves could disappear before they had the situation under control. By itself, this was bad enough but it was not simply loss of reserves which was causing alarm. Beneath ground dramatic changes were taking place to the geological structure of the oilfields. Kuwait's reserves are unique for their shallowness and the fact that, before the oilfield sabotage, most of the fields flowed through natural water pressure. It was this that made their oil among the cheapest in the world to produce, at around $1 per barrel, compared to $1.50 in Saudi Arabia and around $6 in the USA. The effect of suddenly opening up over five hundred well-heads was likened to taking the cap off a soda bottle, letting off the fizz.

Under normal circumstances the flow of oil

from each well is very carefully controlled so as not to cause a major disturbance to the underground layers of oil and water. The Kuwait oilfields comprise a series of stacked layers of impervious shale and porous rock. Oil rests among the pores of sandstone or limestone, floating on top of an aquifer of water, held in place by a cup of shale. Oil-well pipes penetrate these layers and are carefully arranged so that perforated pipe sections pass through oil-bearing rocks while water-bearing strata are traversed by unmodified pipes. Intermingled with the oil is gas which keeps the reservoirs under pressure. Following the Iraqi sabotage there was no means of controlling flows and such quantities of oil and gas escaped that the pressure fell, geological formations were breached and water mixed with oil underground, contaminating both the oil itself and groundwater valuable for natural vegetation and agriculture. In the words of Allanna Sullivan, writing in the *Wall Street Journal* on April 26: 'Kuwait's oil fields are losing some of their providential fizz.'

In the last week of March the first oil well of the campaign was capped. It had been gushing fifteen thousand barrels a day on to the surrounding desert, causing massive local pollution, not to mention its contribution to a fall-off of pressure in the oilfield.

Difficulties with putting out oil-well fires caused mounting frustration in the Kuwaitis, culminating in an announcement on April 13 by oil minister Rashid al-Ameeri that non-American firms were to be brought in since the Americans were 'not working fast enough'. The intention was to cut by two-thirds the American estimate of two years to put out all the five hundred or so oil fires. The new seven-month target would also reduce projected losses which Kuwait would incur from lost production by 70 percent: from $43 billion to $12.5 billion.

With such high stakes to play for it was hardly surprising that the Kuwait Government decided to bring in more fire-fighters, nor that frustration grew at the slow pace of progress on the oilfields.

Projections of long-term damage to the Kuwaiti oil industry speak of a possible loss of five percent of pre-war reserves (*Opec Listener*) and future per-barrel production costs are predicted to reach at least three times what they were before the conflict. What is not known is the damage to the underground reservoirs as gas and oil have been released at uncontrolled pressures.

Kuwaitis may have the resources and social cohesion to rebuild their country but the pollution of land and sea will linger for many years. Of the many tasks facing them in the immediate aftermath of the war none was more urgent than clearing the city, desert and coastal region of weapons and unexploded ordnance and the huge numbers of mines. So extensive was the Iraqi sabotage that, at the end of May, we witnessed oil still leaking into the Gulf from at least five sources. At sea, mines were still being reported drifting in the Gulf and we observed previously buried land-mines being slowly rolled by the force of wind-driven sand across roads and through the desert, to areas beyond the minefields. Long trenches bordering the beaches were brim-full with crude oil, while others, stocked with crates of discarded explosives, were filling with drifting sand. Ordnance disposal officers expected mines and explosive heads to 'cook-off' in the coming summer. An average of six people per day were being killed by this discarded weaponry. Camels, sheep and goats, stumbling into trips wires, detonated mines such as the Italian Valmara version which jumps half a metre (20 in) into the air before exploding. Despite the massive clean-up efforts in which coalition ordnance teams were involved, Kuwait's desert and coastline will for years to come contain concealed dangers.

In the final analysis, when the cost of this terrible war is calculated, the reckoning should include a detailed account of its environmental impact. Whatever the scale of resources allocated to repair and heal the damage, it will never be possible to adequately compensate for the destruction caused to the region's wildlife.

LEGAL ASPECTS OF
ENVIRONMENTAL WARFARE

The Geneva Conventions and the Environment

Recent hostilities in the Gulf underlined in no uncertain terms the devastating impact modern warfare can have on the environment. The world watched in horror as fired Kuwaiti oil wells belched black smoke into the atmosphere and crude oil spilled uncontrollably into fragile Gulf waters. Cries of 'ecocide' accompanied by threats of war crimes tribunals underlined the gravity with which these activities were viewed. But such accusations beg the question: are there any specific legal rules which prohibit this kind of environmental destruction in time of war?

To find the answer one must look to the law of war, otherwise known as international humanitarian law. In this context most people are familiar with the four Geneva Conventions of 1949 formulated to protect the victims of war – namely the sick and wounded, the shipwrecked, prisoners of war and interned civilians in occupied territories – and which comprise a major portion of international humanitarian law. But the Geneva Conventions themselves do not deal with the actual conduct of hostilities, the traditional focus of the laws of war. In other words they do not contain provisions on methods or means of warfare nor do they incorporate guidelines on targeting. Until recently, the law governing these particular topics was to be found, in treaty form, in the 1899/1907 Hague Conventions, and in an amorphous body of unwritten rules, i.e. customary international law, which arises through the practice of states and which is binding on all parties to a conflict.

Throughout the many bloody wars of recent decades the International Committee of the Red Cross was acutely aware of changes in the methods and means of waging war brought about to a great degree by overwhelming technological developments which make a nonsense of reliance on conventions concluded at the turn of the century, not to mention the uncertainties inherent in customary international law. The Committee's ceaseless activity on behalf of war victims, bolstered by UN concern, culminated in the convening of a Diplomatic Conference in Geneva in 1974. Attended by the representatives of approximately 120 states, including many new post-colonial entities, and reinforced by the active but non-voting participation of national liberation movements, the Conference held protracted and lengthy negotiations over four separate sessions. Finally, in 1977, two protocols additional to the Geneva Conventions were adopted. These new instruments went a long way towards remedying the deficiencies in the law.

In particular, Additional Protocol I (but not Protocol II) contains two novel provisions based on the fundamental principle that 'the right of parties to the conflict to choose methods or means of warfare is not unlimited' but aimed specifically at the 'prevention of ecological warfare and the destruction of the environment through military operations'. This was not altogether unexpected since negotiations had taken place in a climate of rising environmental awareness as well as concern over the ecological disruption brought about by armed conflict, a concern fostered by the experience of Vietnam.

Additional Protocol I

Additional Protocol I covers the law governing the waging of international wars (including wars of national liberation) and Protocol II deals with non-international warfare, retaining a traditional but rather strained distinction between the two categories of conflict based on the principle of non-intervention in the internal affairs of states. In this appendix we are primarily concerned with the legal prescriptions contained in Protocol I since the Iraq–Kuwaiti conflict, although followed by a particularly brutal Iraqi civil war, was waged between states.

Protocol I has been ratified by 99 states (as of December 31, 1990) including the Soviet Union, China, Canada, seven of the EC states, many Arab states, but not by France, the United Kingdom, the United States and not by Iran, Iraq or Israel. States which are not parties to Additional Protocol I are only legally bound by those provisions which codify customary international law.

Iraq has not, to the best of our knowledge, explained its non-ratification of either of the additional protocols, but given its apparently cavalier approach to the Geneva Conventions and the Gas Protocol of 1925 to which it is a party, as evidenced by its use of chemical weapons in the Iran–Iraq war and its almost persistent commission of grave breaches of the Geneva Conventions, notably, in the Iraq–Kuwait conflict, the taking of hostages, treatment of protected persons and the wanton destruction of Kuwaiti property, one can only conclude that Iraq does not attach much significance to its legal obligations under the laws of war.

The main reason given by the Reaganite administration for non-ratification of Protocol I was the inclusion of national liberation wars under the regime governing international conflicts, which,

it maintained, imported political considerations into humanitarian law, but the United States was also fundamentally opposed to the relaxing of conditions of combatancy to include resistance fighters/guerrillas. In addition, even though it accepted many of the provisions in Protocol I which seek to alleviate the effects of war on civilians as codifying customary international law, and certainly strove to adhere to the letter if not the spirit of these rules in this latest conflict—Iraq did not undergo indiscriminate bombardment although the indirect effects on civilians of infrastructure targeting continues to give rise to concern—others, including the two articles dealing with environmental matters (Article 35.3 prohibiting methods and means of warfare which damage the environment *per se* and Article 55 which relates prohibited damage to the health or survival of the human population) were considered by the US to be both new law and militarily unacceptable. This is despite the fact that only damage (deliberate or unintentional) which is 'widespread, long-term *and* severe'—commonly held to be measured in decades—will infringe these provisions, and that short-term effects such as those caused by artillery bombardment are specifically excluded from its scope. It must be emphasized too that an infringement of Articles 35.3 and 55 is not considered a 'grave breach' and thereby a war crime entailing an obligation on all states parties to either try or extradite a suspect under their jurisdiction.

Although most commentators would agree with the US that the environmentally-orientated provisions of Protocol I are not, as yet, part of customary international law, and thereby not binding on non-ratifiers, it is also generally believed that they will be rapidly accepted as such.

Mention must also be made of Article 56 prohibiting the targeting of works and installations containing dangerous forces (namely, dams, dykes and nuclear generating stations) in certain very limited circumstances which was also viewed with much suspicion by the US. Although geared towards the protection of civilians, a breach of this provision would inevitably have a considerable impact on environmental matters. An infringement of Article 56 *is* defined as a war crime. However, oil installations were specifically rejected for inclusion under the special protection of this provision.

If we apply the standards of Additional Protocol I to this latest Gulf war what are the results? We know that oil was deliberately released and oil wells set on fire, partly in an attempt to hinder allied military activity, but predominantly in a campaign of revengeful devastation and destruction which was absolutely out of proportion to any military value gained. For the first time in warfare the threat of massive environmental damage played a significant role in the rhetorical posturings which preceded hostilities: for the final malicious and wanton enactment of that threat which has caused severe ecological upheaval but not the nuclear winter forecast by some experts, Iraq must bear the responsibility. We are also aware that the natural environment also suffered considerably from damage which was collateral to legitimate military operations – for example, the targeting of military objectives such as oil industry installations and possibly oil tankers – and that allied military operations contributed in this context. However, even though all the information is not to hand as yet, we can safely conclude that the ecological impact of military operations either deliberately or unintentionally inflicted will not reach the high threshold set out in Articles 35.3 and 55 of Additional Protocol I and, even if it did, such damage would not come under the listing of war crimes contained in this Protocol. Fortunately, that is not the full story: extensive destruction of enemy property by an Occupying Power which was not rendered *absolutely* necessary by military activities constitutes a grave breach and a war crime under the Fourth Geneva Convention. For political reasons, it appears that Iraq will be held accountable for this and other war crimes through reparations, and not through war crimes tribunals. But reparations will only be for economic damage and not for damage to the environment *per se*.

Environmental Modification Convention of 1977

Besides the rules contained in Additional Protocol I, there are a few other legal prescriptions which concern themselves to some degree or another with protection of the environment in time of war; for example, the extremely narrow prohibition on the use of incendiary weapons in Protocol III of the Inhumane Weapons Convention of 1980. But as the environmental impact of military operations unfolded, it was the 1977 En-mod Convention (Convention on the Prohibition of Military or any other Hostile Use of Environmental Modification Techniques), which prohibits the deliberate manipulation of natural forces as a technique of warfare or for other hostile uses outside of armed conflict, which was most frequently referred to by the media.

The En-mod Convention, like Additional Protocol I, was adopted in the wake of the Vietnam war where seeding of rain clouds and the extensive use of herbicides by the US were particularly controversial. It was specifically formulated to prohibit the artificial instigation of earthquakes; creation of seismic waves; an upset in the ecological balance of a region; changes in weather or climate patterns; changes in ocean currents; changes of the ozone layer or of the ionosphere—some of which are not yet within the realms of possibility. However, this is not an exhaustive listing and it is not entirely clear exactly what is prohibited by the Convention. In addition, the resultant damage must reach a certain threshold, in this case 'long-term, widespread *or* severe', albeit a threshold which is lower than that of Additional Protocol I. If Saddam Hussein had deliberately caused a hole in the ozone layer, which experts now agree is highly unlikely since the smoke, so far, has not penetrated past the troposphere, or meddled with the monsoon, there is no doubt that this kind of activity would be within the scope of the Convention. In any event, Iraq is not a party to the En-mod Convention, although both the US and Kuwait have ratified it. Neither is it clear whether the Convention could be considered to be part of customary international law. Interestingly, the threatened use of environmental modification techniques is not expressly forbidden by the Convention.

A Fifth Geneva Convention?

It is obvious from the above brief review that the few formal treaty provisions which attempt to alleviate the effects of war on the environment are deficient when it comes to the kind of environmental excesses experienced in the Iraq–Kuwait war, contrasting sharply with public opinion as to the moral gravity of such a degree of ecological disruption and developments generally in international environmental law since the negotiation of these treaties.

To remedy these defects Greenpeace, in conjunction with the London School of Economics and the Centre for Defence Studies, King's College at London University, organized a conference to brainstorm the drafting of a 'Fifth Geneva' Convention on the Protection of the Environment in Time of Armed Conflict which, it was suggested, would place the environment as a fifth category of victim alongside prisoners of war, the sick and wounded on land and at sea, and interned civilians. A comprehensive new regime was outlined by Rapporteur Dr Glen Plant which would draw together and reinforce already-existing environmental provisions in the laws of war and apply them to the environment in general in *all* situations of armed conflict; at the same time removing loopholes and exceptions on the basis of military necessity; and incorporating principles and norms of environmental law, including 'the principle that states are responsible for ensuring that activities within their jurisdiction or control do not cause damage to the environment of other states or of areas beyond the limits of national

jurisdiction'. The setting up of demilitarized zones containing 'ecosystems, species or genetic material of vital international importance' is also mooted, as is the setting up of a neutral Green Cross/Green Crescent, modelled on the Red Cross/Red Crescent, which would have access to the war zone during conflict to facilitate both the protection of the environment and perform a rapid response function.

Although this kind of focus on the legal issues underpinning environmental warfare is useful, especially aided by the wide background knowledge of responsible environmental groups, in the short term it is difficult to imagine that an international humanitarian law treaty dealing exclusively with environmental matters would receive widespread support from states when even the restricted environmental provisions of Additional Protocol I of 1977 have met with considerable opposition, albeit opposition which may be gradually eroding. Considerable danger could arise in having a treaty which is simply ignored. It is important also not to undermine the status of the Fourth Geneva Convention, which has gained universal acceptance, nor to undercut the hard-won protection for civilians incorporated in Additional Protocol I.

At the same time, something must be done to prevent a repetition of the events in the Gulf conflict. Renewed efforts must be made to improve both the interpretation, ratification and implementation of treaty law already formulated. In particular, efforts must be made to improve supervisory mechanisms stressing prevention rather than repression: although financial compensation can go a long way to alleviating the impact of ecological damage, the ravages to the environment are often impossible to quantify in monetary terms. The International Fact-finding Commission set up under Article 90 of Additional Protocol I to enquire into any facts alleged to be a grave breach or any other serious violation of the Conventions or the Protocol by those States who have accepted its competence, although limited in its mandate, may be of some use in this regard. At the same time the message needs to go out loud and clear that it is no longer acceptable to threaten or target the environment during the course of military operations.

Considerable propaganda value was derived from the 'environmental terrorism' wreaked on the Gulf region as the war was in progress. Those who benefited in this regard should not be allowed to backtrack from the positions they assumed when it was expedient to do so. But neither should environmental issues be used by others as a mechanism for pursuing a wider agenda. International humanitarian law has as its goal the humanizing of warfare not its abolition: to confuse the two could be of considerable detriment to the law of war and inevitably to the victims of war. However, in the final analysis, the only surefire protection for both humankind and the environment lies in the elimination of war as an option in the resolution of political disputes.

Paula Casey-Vine

REFERENCES

Roberts, A. and Guelff, R. *Documents on the Laws of War.* Oxford, 1982.

Levie, H. S. *Protection of War Victims: Protocol I to the 1949 Geneva Conventions*, Vol. 3. Oceana Publications, 1981.

Bothe, M., Partsch K., and Solf, W. *New Rules for Victims of Armed Conflict: Commentary on the Two 1977 Protocols Additional to the Geneva Conventions of 1949.* Martinus Nijhoff, 1982.

Aldrich, George H. 'Prospects for United States Ratification of Additional Protocol I to the 1949 Geneva Conventions'. *American Journal of International Law*, vol. 85, January 1991.

Kalshoven, F. *Constraints on the Waging of War.* International Committee of the Red Cross, 1987.

Detter De Lupis, I. *The Law of War.* Cambridge University Press, 1987.

Al-Awadhi, Badria A. *Legal Aspects of Maritime Pollution with Particular Reference to the Arabian Gulf.* Kuwait, 1985.

Swinarski, C. (ed.). *Studies and essays on international humanitarian law and Red Cross principles in honour of Jean Pictet.* Martinus Nijhoff, 1984.

Westing, A. H. (ed.). *Environmental Warfare, A Technical, Legal and Policy Appraisal.* SIPRI, Taylor & Francis, 1984.

'Customary Law and Additional Protocol I to the Geneva Conventions for Protection of War Victims: Future Direction in Light of the U.S. Decision Not to Ratify'. *Proceedings of the American Society of International Law*, 1987.

Plant, G. *Elements of a 'Fifth Geneva' Convention on the Protection of the Environment in Time of Armed Conflict*, June 1991.

FURTHER READING

Aladasani, M. *The West Kuwait Oil Fields*. Kuwait Government Printing Press.

Basson, P. W. et al. *Biotopes of the Western Arabian Gulf*. ARAMCO, Saudi Arabia.

Batanouny, K. H. *Ecology and flora of Qatar*. University of Qatar.

Buttiker, Professor W. (ed.). *Wildlife in Arabia*. Stacey International, London.

Buttiker, Professor W. and Krupp, Dr F. (eds.). *Fauna of Saudi Arabia* (Vols. 1–12). MEPA and NCWCD, Saudi Arabia.

Calvet, Y. and Salles, J.-F. *Failaka: Fouilles Françaises, 1984–1985*. Maison de l'Orient Méditerranéen, France, 1986.

Clarke, A. *Bahrain Oil and Development*. Immel Publishing Ltd, London, 1991.

Clayton, D. and Wells, K. *Discovering Kuwait's Wildlife*. Fahad Al-Marzouk, Kuwait.

Clayton, D. and Pilcher, C. (eds.). *Kuwait's Natural History*. Kuwait Petroleum Corporation.

Collenette, Sheila. *Flowers of Saudi Arabia*. Scorpion Publishing, London.

Cornes, M. and C. D. *Wild flowering plants of Bahrain*. Immel Publishing Ltd, London.

Dickson, H. R. P. *The Arab of the Desert*. Unwin Hyman Ltd, London.

Fisher, W. B. *The Middle East: A Physical, Social and Regional Geography*. Methuen & Co. Ltd, London.

Halwagy, R. et al. (eds.). *Marine Environment and Pollution. Proceedings of the First Arabian Gulf Conference on Environment and Pollution*. Kuwait University, Faculty of Science, 1986.

Heathcote, P. et al. *Oil Pollution of the Egyptian Red Sea and Gulf of Suez and its Effects on Birds.* A Report to BP International Ltd. May 1984.

Hill, M. and Webb, P. *An Introduction to the Wildlife of Bahrain.* Ministry of Information, Bahrain.

Hojlund, F. et al. *Failaka/Dilmun. The second millennium settlements. Vol. 2: The Bronze Age Pottery.* Jutland Archaeological Society Publications XVII:2.

Al Hout, Wasmir. *Insect Fauna of Kuwait.* University of Kuwait.

Jennings, Michael C. *Birds of the Arabian Gulf.* Allen and Unwin, London.

Jones, David A. *A Field Guide to the Seashores of Kuwait and the Arabian Gulf.* University of Kuwait.

Al Khalifa, Shaikha Haya Ali and Rice, Michael (eds.). *Bahrain through the Ages.* KPI, London.

Kuronuma, K. and Abe, Y. *Fishes of the Arabian Gulf.* Kuwait Institute for Scientific Research, State of Kuwait.

Lacey, R. *The Kingdom.* Hutchinson, London.

Mansfield, P. *Kuwait: Vanguard of the Gulf.* Hutchinson, London, 1990.

McCain, J. C. The intertidal fauna of the sand beaches in the Northern Area, Arabian Gulf, Saudi Arabia. *Fauna of Saudi Arabia* Vol. 6: 53–78.

McCain, J. C. The nearshore, soft-bottom benthic communities of the Northern Area, Arabian Gulf, Saudi Arabia. *Fauna of Saudi Arabia* Vol. 6: 79–101.

McCain, J. C. et al. Marine ecology of Saudi Arabia: A survey of coral reefs and reef fishes in the Northern Area, Arabian Gulf, Saudi Arabia. *Fauna of Saudi Arabia* Vol. 6: 102–26.

McKinnon, M. *Arabia: Sand, Sea, Sky.* BBC Books & Immel Publishing Ltd, London.

Mathiesen, H. E. *Ikaros: The Hellenistic Settlements. Vol. 1: The Terracotta Figurines.* Jutland Archaeological Society Publications XVI:1.

Mughal, M. R. *The Dilmun Burial Complex at Sar. The 1980–82 Excavations in Bahrain.* Directorate of Archaeology and Museums, Bahrain.

Nader, Dr Iyad, Abuzinada, Dr A. H. and Goriup, P. *Wildlife Conservation and Development in Saudi Arabia* (first symposium, Riyadh), NCWCD, Saudi Arabia.

Nayeem, M. A. *Prehistory and protohistory of the Arabian Peninsula.* Vol. 1. Saudi Arabia. Hyderabad Publishers, India.

Nightingale, T. and Overy, M. (eds.). *Wildlife in Bahrain.* Fourth Biennial Report of the Bahrain Natural History Society.

Rahim, M. A. *Biology of the Arabian Peninsula, a bibliographic study.* 1979. Saudi Biological Society, Saudi Arabia.

Randall, Dr John E. *Sharks of Arabia.* Immel Publishing Ltd, London.

Silsby, J. *Inland Birds of Saudi Arabia.* Immel Publishing Ltd, London.

Sivasubramaniam, K. and Ibrahim, M. A. *Common Fishes of Qatar.* Ministry of Information, Qatar.

Smith, J. E. (ed.). *'Torrey Canyon' Pollution and Marine Life.* Cambridge University Press.

Vine, P. *Red Sea Invertebrates.* Immel Publishing Ltd, London.

Vine, P. *Pearls in Arabian Waters: The Heritage of Bahrain.* Immel Publishing Ltd, London.

Vine, P. *New Guide to Bahrain.* Immel Publishing Ltd, London.

Vine, P. *Arab Gold: Heritage of the UAE.* Immel Publishing Ltd, London.

Walker, D. H. and Pittaway, A. R. *Insects of Eastern Arabia.* Macmillan.

Wells, S. M. (ed.). *Coral Reefs of the World.* Vol. 2. Indian Ocean, Red Sea and Gulf. UNEP/IUCN.

Winstone, H. V. F. and Freeth, Z. *Kuwait: Prospect and Reality.* George Allen & Unwin Ltd, London.

Woodward, B. *The Commanders.* Simon and Schuster Ltd, London.

Wray, T. (ed.) *Commercial fishes of Saudi Arabia.* Ministry of Agriculture and Water Resources, Saudi Arabia.

PICTURE ACKNOWLEDGEMENTS

The publishers and authors would like to thank the following sources for use of the photographs on the pages listed:

1 Anthony Bomford 3 Peter Vine 10 Michael McKinnon 14 Peter Vine 17 Peter Vine 18 Kuwait National Museum, Dar Al Athar Al Islamiya/Gulf International 19 Peter Vine 22–23 Michael McKinnon 24 Michael McKinnon 26 Darrogh Donald, SSPCA 30 Bruno Pambour, NCWCD 31 X Eichaker, NCWCD 33 Bruno Pambour, NCWCD 34–35 Bruno Pambour, NCWCD 38 A Vareille, NCWCD 39 Michael McKinnon 41 Michael McKinnon 42 Michael McKinnon 45 Michael McKinnon 46–47 Bruno Pambour, NCWCD 50 Bruno Pambour, NCWCD 51 Michael McKinnon 52 A Vareille, NCWCD 54 S Saustier, NCWCD 58 Bruno Pambour, NCWCD 62 Bruno Pambour, NCWCD (top) A Vareille, NCWCD 63 Michael McKinnon 66 Michael McKinnon 70–71 Michael McKinnon 73 A Vareille, NCWCD 74 Bruno Pambour, NCWCD 78 Michael McKinnon 79 Bruno Pambour, NCWCD 82 Michael McKinnon 86 Michael McKinnon 90 Michael McKinnon 95 Michael McKinnon 98 Michael McKinnon 101 Michael McKinnon 102 Michael McKinnon 103 John Bulmer (top) Anthony Bomford 105 Anthony Bomford 107 Michael McKinnon 110 Peter Vine 111 Michael McKinnon 113 Bruno Pambour, NCWCD 114 Michael McKinnon 119 Michael McKinnon 122–23 Michael McKinnon 124 Michael McKinnon 127 Michael McKinnon 130–31 Michael McKinnon 132–33 Michael McKinnon 134 Michael McKinnon 138 Bruno Pambour, NCWCD 139 Anthony Bomford 142 Michael McKinnon 146 Michael McKinnon 150 Michael McKinnon 151 Michael McKinnon (top) Peter Vine 152 Bruno Pambour, NCWCD 154 Michael McKinnon 157 Michael McKinnon 158 Michael McKinnon 161 A Vareille, NCWCD 162 Michael McKinnon 163 Michael McKinnon 164 Michael McKinnon 170 Michael McKinnon 171 Michael McKinnon 173 Michael McKinnon 174 Michael McKinnon 178 Bruno Pambour, NCWCD 179 Peter Vine (top) Bruno Pambour, NCWCD.

INDEX